D1594036

Multilingual Living

Also by Charlotte Burck

GENDER AND FAMILY THERAPY (*with Gwyn Daniel*)
GENDER, POWER AND RELATIONSHIPS (*co-edited with Bebe Speed*)

Multilingual Living

Explorations of Language and Subjectivity

Charlotte Burck

First published 2005 by
PALGRAVE MACMILLAN
Houndmills, Basingstoke, Hampshire RG21 6XS and
175 Fifth Avenue, New York, N.Y. 10010
Companies and representatives throughout the world

PALGRAVE MACMILLAN is the global academic imprint of the Palgrave Macmillan division of St. Martin's Press, LLC and of Palgrave Macmillan Ltd. Macmillan® is a registered trademark in the United States, United Kingdom and other countries. Palgrave is a registered trademark in the European Union and other countries.

ISBN 1–4039–3965–9 hardback

This book is printed on paper suitable for recycling and made from fully managed and sustained forest sources.

A catalogue record for this book is available from the British Library.

Library of Congress Cataloging-in-Publication Data
Burck, Charlotte, 1948–
    Multilingual living : explorations of language and subjectivity / Charlotte Burck.
        p.   cm.
    Includes bibliographical references and index.
    ISBN 1–4039–3965–9 (cloth)
    1. Multilingualism.   2. Multilingualism—Research.   I. Title.

P115.B87 2004
306.44′6—dc22

                                                          2004053757

10   9   8   7   6   5   4   3   2   1
14   13   12   11   10   09   08   07   06   05

Printed and bound in Great Britain by
Antony Rowe Ltd, Chippenham and Eastbourne

Contents

Acknowledgements   viii

Introduction   1
  Structure of the book   2

1 Researching Multilingualism and Multilingual Identities   9
  Children's language acquisition   10
  Language, thought and experience   12
  Supporting children's bilingualism and multilingualism   13
  Effects on children of speaking several languages   15
  First and subsequent languages   16
  Contextual factors and language use   18
  Migration, gender, generation and language   19
  Racialized identities, ethnicities, culture, class
    and language   21
  Narrative, discursive practices and identity   23
  Biculturalism and transculturalism   25
  Positioning in and between several languages   26
  Language signified as carrier of identity   27
  Bilingualism as an interactional resource   28
  Researching bilingual/multilingual speakers' views   30
  Summary and conclusion   30

2 The Research Framework   32
  Research questions   33
  Epistemology and research framework   34
  Conducting the research interviews   35
  Research participants   36
  Transcription   37
  A synthesized approach to analysis   41

3 Childhoods in Several Languages   46
  Growing up in multilingual colonial contexts   46
  Growing up in bilingual/trilingual contexts   54
  Growing up with a minoritized language   56

Fleeing from one's country of origin   66
Concluding discussion   73

4 **Adulthoods in Several Languages: Constructions
    of Self and of Language**   76
   Constructing oneself anew   76
   Inarticulacy   79
   Performance   80
   Coming to own a language   84
   A sense of doubleness   85
   Constructions of language   91
   Concluding discussion   99

5 **Language Identities and Power Relationships:
    Strategies of Hybridization**   101
   Racialization processes and language speaking   101
   Second-language communications and misunderstandings   105
   Strategies of hybridization   108
   Concluding discussion   121

6 **Language Use and Family Relationships**   122
   Language and power in family relationships   122
   Parenting and language use   131
   Using language to claim identity and alliances in families   148
   Complexities of speaking several languages within families   156

7 **Positioning the Researcher**   158
   Personal contexts and researcher hypotheses   159
   Co-constructing the research accounts   161
   Constructions of new meanings   163
   Similarities and differences in the research relationship   164
   Evaluative aspects of the research interview   165
   Self-reflexivity throughout the research process   166
   Recursive influences of the research and personal context   166

8 **Concluding Discussion**   169
   Living with multiplicity   171
   Constructions of self   173
   Doubleness as trope   175
   Performing linguistic identities and owning language   177
   Languages and family relationships   179

Contextual resources 181
Relationship to language and place 182
Advantages of speaking several languages 184
Implications for individuals, families and professionals 187
Concluding implications 192

Appendixes
1 *Protocol for Research Interview* 194
2 *Transcription Notations* 197

References 198

Index 213

Acknowledgements

This book owes a great deal to Ann Phoenix and Margaret Wetherell, whose intellectual rigour, interest, and generosity have profoundly informed my thinking during the research on which this book is based.

A number of friends have most generously supported me during the research and writing, especially Gwyn Daniel, Avi Shlaim, Sara Barratt, Judy Hildebrand, Christine Peters, Marilyn Leask, Nick Kettle, Elaine Bander, Gerrilyn Smith, B. Loader and Elsa Jones.

This book is dedicated to the research participants who have been so interested and willing to discuss these issues with me, and to my son, Ben Dalton, who offered support and sensitive consultation at key moments, and whom, regretfully, I did not bring up multilingually.

Introduction

Why should it be important to research and write of issues of living in several languages?

Over half of the world's population are thought to be either bilingual or multilingual (Grosjean 1982). Sometimes it is difficult to keep hold of this fact while looking through some of the British and North American linguistics literature where negative connotations about bilingualism were prevalent until thirty years ago, and which continue to exert a considerable degree of influence. Many writers, Pinker (1994) and Abley (2003) among others, are urgently drawing to our attention that we are in danger of losing 90 per cent of the estimated 5,500 languages in the world in the next hundred years. There is also growing evidence that loss of language involves not only loss of cultural knowledge and histories, but also loss of biodiversity, because of invaluable environmental knowledge embedded in language (Maffi 2000). This is fuelling efforts to find ways to maintain languages and to disrupt language loss.

Speaking several languages is valued very differently in different societies. In Britain, despite the fact that London is the most linguistically diverse city in the world (Baker and Mohieldeen 2000; TES 2003), there is more antipathy towards other languages than elsewhere in Europe (Zeldin 1997), and there is considerable pressure for those who speak other languages to assimilate by speaking English. This context poses enormous challenges to individuals and families who want to continue to live in several languages.

This book explores the ways in which bilingual and multilingual individuals living in Britain experience and use their languages, and their perceived effects. It is based on a research study which has aimed to contribute to our knowledge of bilingualism and multilingualism and whose focus has been to invite individuals to be reflective about their

1

own language use. It traces the ways in which individuals who live in several languages have come to think about themselves and their relationships. To analyse subjective experiences of language use it has been important to take account of issues at different levels – the individual, the family and the wider context – and to explore how these are interlinked. The book considers the meanings languages are given in the wider as well as local contexts and how these contribute to the construction of identities and inform social interactions. It presents an analysis of the effect speaking several languages has on family relationships. It examines the advantages of sustaining minoritized language speaking and the challenges of doing so in a context which does not support it.

By taking those who speak several languages as an exemplar, this book can also be said to explore issues and dilemmas of living with multiplicity more generally.

Structure of the book

A diverse literature from linguistics, as well as cultural/critical theory, the translation field, and discursive psychology, has been drawn on in order to ground the study. In Chapter 1, Researching Multilingualism and Multilingual Identities, this literature is mapped out, looking at the way in which language speaking has been researched, referring to pertinent studies about the differences individuals experience in their different languages, and discussing approaches which have taken an interactional focus and included speakers' perspectives. This allows the reader to get a sense of some of the debates and controversies in the research carried out of bilingualism and multilingualism, as well as of research findings which sparked the curiosity underpinning this study.

The conceptualization of multiple subjectivities by contemporary theorists (cf Brah 1996; Henriques et al. 1984) is reviewed here as it informs the analysis of these individuals' constructions of living with multiplicity. The ways in which languages are given meaning through social and political struggles, and language speaking intersects with the construction of racialized, ethnic, and cultural identities are considered. Translation literature also sheds some light on the effect of power relationships between languages. I reflect on the overlap of bilingualism and multilingualism with biculturalism and transculturalism, and their connections with histories of migration. Language speaking also acquires meanings within family relationships, the context in which language is first learned. Gender difference has mainly been neglected in work on bilingualism (Burton, Dyson, and Ardener 1994), but the concept of 'mother tongue' is widely used in the literature, and I critically examine it.

In Chapter 2, the research study itself is presented, the way it was formulated and explored. I articulate the research questions here: How do individuals construct their experiences of living life in several languages? What meanings are given to speaking more than one language and what relational issues arise from this?

The study is located in a research paradigm which considers language as constitutive and performative. This approach, informed by social constructionism, regards language and power as interlinked, with inequitable relationships socially constructed over time, through which symbolic and material resources are produced, distributed and validated (Norton 2000). The research examines interconnections between discourse and power in language speaking and straddles ideas of language performance, of psychological processes, and of interactional meaning making.

The argument is made for using insider accounts, interviews with 24 individuals who came to live in several languages in different circumstances, to allow an examination of the differences languages make to individuals, and of the ways in which individuals construct their identities and relationships. The sample is described here, and the way they were selected through word-of-mouth and snowballing techniques. The heterogeneity of the research participants enable an analysis of the intersections of language speaking and subjectivity, of language speaking and racialization, and of the construction and use of gendered meanings of language speaking, particularly in relation to child rearing. I discuss my analytic approach to the accounts, informed by discursive analytic concepts and narrative ideas.

In Chapter 3, Childhoods in Several Languages, I focus on accounts of childhoods lived in several languages in a variety of circumstances. I have organized these in relation to the different circumstances and contexts in which individuals learned and spoke their languages which demanded different tasks of individuals, and offered them different resources. Within these contexts, I use extracts from the interviews, to consider the ways in which individuals constructed their growing up and their different experiences in their different languages, their sense of self and their relationships. Several important themes emerged from these childhood accounts. Of central significance was how individuals lived with the discontinuity and disjuncture between their languages.

Those who grew up in colonial contexts had lived with stark unequal relationships between languages and very different positionings within language. This allows a tracing of the ways in which the differential status of languages impacted on the ways individuals experienced themselves and their relationships.

Those who had grown up in a family speaking a minority language faced a task of managing the distinctions of language and culture between their home and the outside world, and of being signified as different through their language. Individuals lived with a sense of their doubleness, connected to living in a doubled world, often kept very separate. This was, on the whole, constructed as a lonely struggle, with no context offering confirmation of the complexity of their experiences, and individuals often experienced tensions of polarizations between their languages and cultures. These accounts were often underpinned by a perceived demand for and a notion of an ideal of an unproblematic singularity.

For those who had to flee their country of origin, being rendered inarticulate in the new language and the need to find a positioning to counter experiences of powerlessness had been an immediate concern. These individuals had to make sense of the disruption and disjuncture in their experience in the context of traumatic loss. The way individuals defined themselves depended on the receiving context, and demonstrated gendered differences. The disqualification of their first language and culture in the new country had a profound impact on their sense of self, and the ways in which they attempted to claim identities as dominant language speakers. These experiences had an enduring impact on individuals' relationship to their languages as well as on the way they constructed their identity.

In the accounts of childhood the discursive work individuals carried out and the ways in which context was influential are identified. Individuals' different languages embedded different senses of self and were either separated by time and place, or kept separate. Research participants also identified encounters with contexts which had provided a shift in the way they had experienced themselves. These contexts can be considered as offering a 'third space' (Bhabha 1994), which provided individuals with a different kind of positioning in relation to their multiplicities. There was a variation in whether and how research participants had 'worked' their experiences of disjuncture and of their own diversities.

Chapter 4, Adulthoods in Several Languages, Constructions of Self and of Language, examines adulthoods lived in several languages, and explores some of the similarities and differences to childhood experiences. Some of those who had grown up with several languages had also moved into a new language in adulthood. Individuals who moved into a language later in their lives could explicitly notice some of the processes involved. It is through these accounts that we can explore the processes of the suture, in Hall's (1996, 1999) words, between subjectivity and language, the ways subjectivity and culture become interlinked. Those who moved languages and countries when they were older considered this a transition through which they had developed a different sense of themselves, and in which language played a central role. Entering a new language was experienced as a freedom from familial and cultural constraints for some. There were also constraints of being positioned, and of discrimination and racism.

Research participants made use of a notion of 'performance' in relation to the ways they entered a new language: that learning a new language entailed learning to perform themselves in the new language. However, neither learning a language nor a culture was straightforward. Individuals relied on stereotypical notions of speakers to inform the way in which they performed themselves – seeing language as monologic (Bakhtin 1986) and culture as homogeneous, as well as being constructed in stereotypical ways by others. Becoming a different kind of person in a new language also meant that individuals had to 'work' their different experiences in each language, manage discontinuities and disruptions of meaning, and contradictions.

Research participants who had moved languages and countries as adults, as those who did so as children, had to find ways to manage the disjuncture between their languages and cultures, across time and in a different place. Narratives of self in first languages became constructed as separate from developments in the new language. Some individuals conceived this as losing their bearings/meanings, and having to 'make themselves up' in a new linguistic context.

Individuals constructed quite different meanings within each of their linguistic/cultural contexts, and, significantly, this included making different meanings of themselves. In these accounts individuals made use of a number of different constructions of self, but particularly drew on a notion of 'doubleness' and I discuss some of the variations of this, such as the use of 'inner' and 'outer' selves, a 'core' first language self and a 'performed' second language self, a 'frozen' identity in a first language no longer spoken. There is some examination of what these constructions accomplished as well as what dilemmas they posed.

Individuals spoke of their languages informed by the meanings given to language speaking in the wider context, linked to power and status, as well as in relation to more personal and locally constructed differences. These meanings were interlinked with the ways in which they constructed themselves as speakers. First languages were most often constructed as 'owned' by the individual and attracted attributions of expressiveness and richness in the context of a second language. Second languages were mainly considered as more utilitarian and lending distance of various kinds. Languages differed substantially in the ways they encoded conceptions of personhood which in turn impacted on speakers' experiences of themselves in their different languages. The meanings of language speaking constructed in wider contexts also shifted with sociopolitical change and impacted on personal constructions.

Chapter 5, Language Identities and Power Relationships, Strategies of Hybridization, elaborates further how the meanings of language speaking are interlinked with the constructions of speakers. Here racialization processes and language speaking are considered – the place of language in racialization processes, and the effect of individuals' racialized identity positions on their experiences and construction of themselves as speakers. In colonial contexts, it was most explicit that necessity drove language learning, and those with least power spoke the most languages. English, the dominant colonial language, had offered each of the research participants' opportunities, but impacted differentially on their performance as speakers dependent on their 'race' and the way they were positioned. Drawing on postcolonial discourse, speaking English was viewed as having a central role in the processes of colonization. White research participants brought up monolingually in Afrikaans, struggled with the construction of their language as oppressive and with owning their privilege.

For speakers in Britain, their experiences were informed by subject positions available and offered dependent on their racialization. Those racialized as 'other', the Chinese, South Asian, Arabic, Israeli and Zimbabwean research participants, never had their English speaking taken for granted, and often had their claims to an English identity challenged. Although white research participants' minority language signified them as different, their identity claims were less challenged, although only a few presented themselves as aware of the privileges this involved.

The kinds of miscommunications which occur across language differences are examined here. Prosodic elements of language, such as tone of voice, conveyed different meanings from the speaker's intentions. Difficulties with humour in a second language created difficulties for individuals in their relationships and were often considered as personality trait rather than an effect of being a second language speaker. Aspects of being a second language speaker could be missed altogether or highlighted to disrupt communications, and affected ways in which individuals were regarded by others.

Despite the challenges involved for individuals engendered by their language differences, they all, bar one, constructed this multiplicity as advantageous. This was connected to the ways in which they had come to think about the differences of their languages and themselves in their languages, and how they had found ways to make use of these differences. A sense of their contingency on their languages was interlinked with the development of a self-reflexive positioning, an awareness of themselves in language and the differences their language made, through which they made use of these in their strategies of hybridization (Bakhtin 1981) – working contradictory perspectives, applying language in different spheres, choosing language to make salient their own and others' identities, and switching language for rhetorical purposes.

Language use and family relationships are considered in Chapter 6. The chapter first considers the issue of language and power in family relationships. Issues of how family relationships became unbalanced when children became more fluent than their parents are discussed – the ways in which fluency in the dominant language, English, confers power and competency. Differences of fluency are also tracked within marital/partner relationships to examine the ways it positioned individuals differently and how relationships did or didn't take this into account.

I go on to look at parenting and language use. Many individuals chose to parent, at least for some of the time, in their first language, even when not speaking this in their everyday lives. Women and men talked of the reasons for doing so very differently, and constructed their languages for parenting differently. Constructions of mothering and fathering came into play in these accounts, intersecting with constructions of language. Of particular note was the way in which the concept 'mother tongue' underpinned these accounts, and implicitly informed ways in which women and men made language choices, working against fathers speaking their first language with their babies from birth.

Individuals saw parenting in a first or subsequent language as having very different effects. Language choice had an effect on parental subjectivity and on parent–child relationships, with first/childhood languages mainly being constructed as conveying intimacy. Language choice also functioned as a claim of identity and a claim of alliance. It was also viewed as a way to enable children to claim successful dominant language identities. Issues of how families managed issues of inclusion and exclusion around language speaking were also significant to language use in families, as were children's own positioning. Children drew on ideas about English identity being monolingual – that speaking another language constructed one as different. Ways in which English became dominant in families speaking a minority language is noted.

Chapter 7, Positioning the Researcher, discusses the ways in which I have, as a multilingual individual myself, attempted to maintain self-reflexivity as a researcher. I discuss how I paid attention to the influence of personal and professional contexts at different stages in the research process – from formulating the research questions to the conducting of the research interviews, and ways in which the accounts were co-constructed. I declare some of my prior hypotheses and assumptions, and illustrate ways in which I have thought about the power relationships between the research participants and myself as the researcher. I include some of my own experiences and thoughts about my multilingualism, and the impact which carrying out the research has had on me both personally and professionally.

In Chapter 8, the Concluding Discussion, I highlight the advantages of sustaining languages at an individual and family level, which the study has confirmed and elaborated, alongside the challenges and the persistence required to do so. I affirm the importance of supporting and sustaining the speaking of minority languages in Britain.

I pull together theoretical ideas generated from the study of individuals' constructions of self and language in context. I look again at the use of the construct of doubleness in the accounts and its accomplishments, and consider Linde's (1993) argument that our popular coherence systems are not complex and rich enough. I elaborate on the discursive resources available to bilingual and multilingual individuals, their strategies of hybridization and their generative potential, and the celebration of multiplicities. I draw out the importance of reflecting on language use, and the implications for individuals and families as well as professionals, of the ways in which language and subjectivity are intimately interlinked. Alongside other writers who are perturbed by the rapid language loss throughout the world, I argue how important it is for all of us to find ways to sustain individuals' bilingualism and multilingualism in our dominantly monolingual context.

1
Researching Multilingualism and Multilingual Identities

In order to ground the study on which this book is based, this first chapter reviews some relevant literature on bilingualism and multilingualism from the fields of linguistics. Issues of language acquisition more generally are touched on, as well as some of the ongoing questions of the relationship between language, thought and experience. I map out changes in the ways in which linguistics research has been carried out, moving from a focus on individual competence to considering bilingualism as an interactional resource, and the more recent tradition in sociolinguistics of research which includes the views of speakers – an approach which I adopt in my own work. Findings about the effects of bilingualism and multilingualism, which have highlighted individuals' differential experiences in their languages, are discussed, and questions are raised about the implications that result. Ideas from identity studies, cultural and critical theory, and translation studies relevant to this work are then outlined.

Bilingualism is a term used in the linguistics field for the speaking of two languages, and its definition is hotly debated in relation to fluency criteria; indeed, Li Wei (2000) reported no fewer than 37 different categories of bilinguals. These definitional controversies are not particularly pertinent to this book because of their focus on individual language competency, while the individuals who are the concern here are those who had used or were currently using several, (indeed for some, more than two) languages in their everyday lives.

Up to the 1950s and 1960s many of the studies of bilingualism were criticized for their negative focus and their use of a deficit model. Romaine (1989) argued that modern linguistic theory, which originated in Western Europe and Anglophone countries, had contributed to pathologizing bilingualism because it had been based on monolingualism as the normative standard. Amati-Mehler et al. (1993) have suggested that there must be important psychological and sociological reasons to deny polylingualism and for the perpetuation of the myth of the Tower of Babel – the sense of a golden age when there was only one language and 'perfect' communication. If one considers colonial contexts and political ideology, dominant group members whose language became the prevailing one rarely needed to learn languages of other groups, so that bilingualism may have become associated with inequality and social disadvantage (Burton 1994), and more blatantly, dominant groups attempted to eradicate other languages and their speakers (Romaine 1995).

Despite challenges by sociolinguists regarding the pathologization of bilingualism, this negativity continues to have its effects on language use today, alongside assimilationist policies in many countries. Many multilingual speakers adopt monolingual values, viewing their own language use as deficient (Romaine 1995; Cromdal 2000). An idea still prevalent is that children who learn more than one language often do not learn any language well and should be considered 'semilinguals'.

Children's language acquisition

Before considering specific research on learning several languages, it is useful to review some ideas about language acquisition more generally. Chomsky (1976) proposed that infants' brains are specifically structured to acquire language – that they have a specialized biological programme, a deep structural grammar and a neural mechanism to do so. Chomsky's idea of a universal grammar has been variously challenged, and emphasis has currently been placed on the interactional development of language. Babies develop a relationship to language before they 'enter into language' themselves. Their intrauterine exposure to their mother's speech predisposes them to show a preference for it at birth (DeCasper and Fifer 1980 in Kuhl 1998). Babies participate with their carers from birth in reflexive sequences of communication; they are inducted into and participate in proto-conversations with their caretakers, taking turns (Cross 1977; Trevarthen 1977), imitating sounds, paying attention to others' speech movements (Kuhl 1998), and mutually influencing and being responsive to their carers (Stern 1985). I think it is helpful to follow Beebe and Lachman (2002) and Krause (2002) in considering language to include the full range of responsive human actions.

The process of language development as well as language use is diverse because contextually influenced (Burman 1994). Babies are invited into linguistic and cultural practices; they "enter the stream of verbal communication and through and in it reach awareness" (Vološinov 1986). By the time they can speak, language is already there in the shape of words "filled up with other people's meanings" (Vološinov 1986), and they become constituted as 'native speakers'. As Halliday (1975) put it, learning to speak is learning how to mean. Becoming a proficient speaker means knowing what to say to whom in what circumstances (Hymes 1972), being able to use and read contextualization cues (Gumperz 1992), demonstrating appropriateness structurally, rhetorically and discursively (Berman and Slobin 1994), with the ability to position oneself in the discourses that matter to action (Heilbrun 1988). It involves learning the many sets of discursive practices within a language, and the complex negotiations of self-presentation and of category membership of different social groupings (Miller 2000).

Acquiring language is conflated with acquiring relationships, because language is inherently intersubjective (Akhtar and Tomasello 1998; Anderson and Goolishian 1988). Learning language is learning to relate, and, as Bateson et al. (1956) highlighted, every communication is a statement about relationship as well as about content. Infant language learning in Western societies is still very much associated with mothers, despite attempts to alter and acknowledge other parenting arrangements. Psychoanalytic theory would suggest that this early relationship gives a particular significance to the first language (Tesone 1996: 879). This association is concretized through the term 'mother tongue' given to a first language, commonly used in both academic and fictional literature. My own concern is that this term 'naturalizes' a relationship to language and warrants deconstruction. I have therefore found it important not to use the term 'mother tongue' myself, using 'first language' instead, and to interrogate its usage and implications in the research accounts, particularly in relation to language choice for parenting.

There is some controversy about how language develops for polylingual children. McLaughlin (1978) has argued that the learning of several languages before the age of three should be considered as being acquired simultaneously. Researchers, such as Grosjean (1982), have traced a developmental sequence in which young children first conflate their languages and then move to differentiate these, while Genesee (1989/2000) argues that young infants use their languages differentially in contextually sensitive ways from a very early age. The process is very much influenced by the dominance of one language over the other, and whether languages are kept separate in different relationships and contexts. Certainly babies not only show a preference for their first language at birth (DeCasper and Fifer 1980 in Kuhl 1998; Mehler et al. 1998) but are also able to discriminate between other languages as young infants (Trehub 1973 in Genesee 1989/2000), and Geissler (1938) has argued that children could learn up to four languages without confusion (Romaine 1989).

Language, thought and experience

There remain very significant questions concerning the relation between thought and language, and between experience and language, which are vigorously contested in philosophy, psychology and related fields and lie far beyond the scope of this book. The following extremely brief review can only indicate the complexities of the conceptualizations of the relationship between language, thought and experience, and hint at past and current disagreements.

Burman (1994) noted that the liveliest area of debate in developmental psychology concerns research on language because of its connection to questions concerning theories of mind. Adherents to Chomsky's structural approach to language, such as Pinker (1994), propose that thought and language are independent, while those who follow Vygotsky take a more functional perspective, seeing thought developing as an internalization of dialogue. In this view, speaking is considered a socially and culturally situated activity, in which socialisation is a crucial aspect of language learning (Ochs 1996), and infants become agentive enculturated language-using persons by being treated as such (Burman 1994; Edwards 1997).

Within the field of linguistics much debate about language and thought became focused on the Whorf–Sapir hypothesis of the 1940s, which proposed a relation between the structural features of a language and specific modes of thought. Whorf had examined the different concepts of time in the English and the Hopi languages, postulating this to be connected to different grammatical structures. Many linguists who currently support the idea that different languages have different cultural concepts embedded in them, view differences in meanings as being shaped by cultural context rather than by grammatical structure. They posit a cultural relativity of interpretation rather than linguistic relativity as such (Gumperz and Levinson 1996). Differences found among interpretations *within* any one language are also seen to be dependent on socialisation into local knowledge and practices (Clark 1996), and as contested (Kress 2001). "Each word tastes of the context and contexts in which it has lived its socially charged life" (Bakhtin 1935/1981: 293).

There are also important and unresolved questions concerning the place of language in the conceptualization of 'experience' which is not put into language, with a range of positions taken. There are those who privilege that which is 'beyond language' (cf Frosh 2001 following Lacan) and those who privilege language as giving meaning to all experience whether brought into language or not.

My own view of language has been much influenced by social constructionist and discursive ideas – that is, I see language as constitutive and in recursive relationship with experience over time (Gergen 1985, 1994; Shotter 1993), and performative (Austin 1962/1980), comprised of discursive practices which produce meanings and values, as well as having material effects. This view has been informed by Wittgenstein's (1953) idea of 'language games' and their specific practices, that the meanings of words come from the context of their use, and by his notion that "the limits of my language mean the limits of my world" (Wittgenstein 1961/2001: 68). The context of the social-historical conditions under which particular linguistic practices become dominant and legitimate is also crucial (Bourdieu 1991). What is particularly significant for this book is how important it is to consider languages not only as constitutive of meaning, but also as contexts within which individuals position themselves and are positioned.

Supporting children's bilingualism and multilingualism

There is a body of work which has focused on how children can be helped to speak more than one language. Most striking in this is the observed impact of the sociocultural context on children's language use – whether families have resources and support or are pressurized by assimilationist policies (Smolicz 1979; Romaine 1989). Not so long ago, children were physically punished in schools in Britain, Australia, the United States and Scandinavia for speaking minoritized languages (Romaine 1995). It has been found to be very difficult for children to acquire and sustain active command of a minority language if that language does not receive support outside the family and particularly if it is stigmatized.

Ronjat (1913) introduced the 'one person–one language' recommendation for families, according to which each parent should conduct their relationship with their child in one language, preferably their first (Arnberg 1987; Romaine 1989), and this pattern is still recommended and preferred by many parents (Yamamoto 1995). In a context in which parents have different first languages, there is usually a shift to the dominant language, although mothers have a better chance of passing their language on to children than fathers do, most likely because in many cases they are still spending more time with their children (Lyon 1996), but another reason to examine the concept of 'mother tongue' and its effect on parenting decisions. Arnberg (1987) highlighted the importance of the dominant-language-speaking parent's attitude and support to their child's maintenance of their languages. Parents are also influenced by ideas that their children need to be fluent in the dominant language to be successful (Rindstedt 2000).

It has been found that teaching in a child's first language helps acquisition and learning in their second (Cummins 1984; Slavin and Cheung 2003), and that there is a direct relationship between a child's competence in their first language and their competence in their second (Skutnabb-Kangas and Toukomaa 1976). These findings have influenced educational policies to provide bilingual education in the United States and Sweden, although not in Britain where it was seen as segregationist and counter to equal opportunities policies (Rampton 1995). However, there is considerable controversy around what kind of educational programmes are most successful and their aims, whether of assimilation, transitional bilingualism, or sustaining bilingualism (Romaine 1995). Gendered differences and power inequities have also been found to be significant (Fisher 1974). Language policies do not remain static, and in 1998 the state of California decided to abolish their 'bilingual' language programmes in schools – these schemes had been instituted mainly for children from the Hispanic language communities, who constitute a substantial proportion of minoritized-language speakers in California. Clearly a number of factors contributed to this abolition, including passionate views that teaching in a minority language means that children will be less fluent in the dominant language (Rodriguez 1982), perceived threats that a minority language could displace the dominant one, and the ongoing negativity attached to bilingualism. Romaine (1995) has pointed out how easily bilingual programmes get blamed in complex contexts where many factors intersect. These studies point to the challenges of maintaining children's use of minoritized languages. The debate continues as a recent meta-review of research (Slavin and Cheung 2003) has found that bilingual education pro-grammes, particularly those teaching both languages at once, are more effective than English-only schemes.

Some researchers have examined processes of language loss. Rindstedt carried out research in Ecuador and found that, despite a strong belief in the need to speak Quichua being linked to Indian identity, young children had mainly switched to speaking Spanish because of its dominance in education and its use in sibling relationships (Rindstedt and Aronsson 2001). In the south west of the United States, where Spanish was considered as threatening to usurp English, it has been found that Spanish seldom lasts beyond the third generation (Pease-Alvarez 1993). Such studies, alongside other work on endangered languages (cf Abley 2003) demonstrate how easily individuals, families and communities can lose language.

Effects on children of speaking several languages

As noted earlier, until the last thirty years research into the effects of bilingualism had been concentrated on deficit, with findings that learning several languages was detrimental to children's ability to learn any one language well, and even that it was hazardous to mental health, with statements such as: "bilingualism can lead to a split personality and at worst to schizophrenia" (Adler 1977: 40) being widely accepted.

Challenging such focus on deficit, more recent studies have identified considerable benefits for children of speaking more than one language. However, social factors, and, in particular, whether there is social support for speaking more than one language, powerfully influence findings, and account for some of the contradictions found in research (Edwards 1994; Grosjean 1982; Romaine 1989, 1995; Smolicz 1979). Peal and Lambert's (1962) study of middle-class children with support for their language learning concluded that children's experience with two language systems seemed to give them mental flexibility, superiority in concept formation, and a more diversified set of mental abilities than their monolingual peers. This has been fleshed out by other research which found that bilingual children performed better in numerical ability, verbal and perceptual flexibility and general reasoning if they learned their languages before the age of four (Balkan 1970 in Romaine 1989). Bilingual children were found to reach a stage of semantic development two to three years earlier (Ianco-Worrall 1972); to show greater fluency in telling stories and using concepts (Doyle, Champagne and Segalowitz 1978); and to demonstrate greater creativity, more divergent thinking, higher levels of selective attention, and an earlier and greater awareness of the arbitrary nature of the assignment of words to things than their monolingual counterparts (Ben-Zeev 1977; Bialystok 1988, 1991, 1997; Carringer 1974; Grosjean 1982; Lambert 1977; Saunders 1982; Scott 1973; Swain and Cummins 1979).

Children with several languages learn that different distinctions are drawn within different languages and that some concepts are untranslatable. It has been proposed that exposure to two languages accelerates a child's ability to de-centre, to take other perspectives into account (Romaine 1995). And, indeed, in laboratory conditions bilingual children have been found to show an increased sensitivity to others' cues (Genesee et al. 1975), and to demonstrate a greater capacity to use feedback (Ben-Zeev 1977) than monolingual children.

These research studies indicate that learning more than one language, in the best of circumstances, has effects on children's flexibility of thinking, their ability to position themselves and hold multiple perspectives. Such findings imply important effects of speaking several languages on the ways individuals make meanings with others and on their relationships.

First and subsequent languages

Distinctions are drawn in the literature between individuals who have learned several languages simultaneously from infancy, termed 'polylingual' or 'compound bilinguals', and those who learn other languages when already established in language, called 'polyglot' or 'coordinate bilinguals', whose languages are considered to operate more separately (Amati-Mehler et al. 1993; Cromdal 2000; Ervin and Osgood 1954; Weinreich 1953). Polyglots have been found to make more distinctions between their languages than polylinguals because, it is argued, of being acquired at different periods (Amati-Mehler et al. 1993; Pérez Foster 1996, 1998).

There is ongoing controversy about whether the later acquisition of a second language is similar or different to that of a first language, and with its own critical period for acquisition (see Hakuta 1999 for a review of this literature). Many language researchers argued that we lose the ability we had as young children to acquire language as we grow older (Lenneberg 1967; Pinker 1994), but Grosjean (1982) proposed that the most pertinent factor in becoming fluent in a second language is perceived necessity. Lamendella (1978) and Hakuta et al. (2001) agreed with this position, having discovered no evidence for a critical period for secondary language acquisition as there is for primary language learning, although there is what has been called, a sensitive period. There does however seem to be general agreement that it is more difficult to acquire the accent of a 'native speaker' in later life.

Neurological findings of differences between first and subsequent languages are somewhat equivocal. The idea of particular areas of the brain being associated with particular functions (localization of function) has long been challenged and superseded by ideas concerning more complex interactions between various parts of the brain. Some studies have found different cortical networks involved in the speaking of languages learned at different ages (Binder et al. 1997; Hirsch 1997; Kim et al. 1997; Pinker 1994; Pouratian et al. 2000), with more right-brain involvement in bilingual speakers if they learnt their second language after the age of 11 (Grosjean 1982; de Zueleta 1984, 1990). Findings suggest that there are certain areas of the brain which deal with both languages and others which are involved with only one (Pinker 1994). New brain imaging techniques of functional magnetic resonance imaging (fMRI) and intraoperative optical imaging of intrinsic signals (iOIS) are enabling different kinds of research, but at present findings remain tentative (Binder et al. 1997; Pouratian et al. 2000). However, neurological differences have been linked to ways in which polylinguals and polyglots experience their languages differently.

Work with aphasics – those with disturbances of speech and language caused by brain damage – have also revealed pertinent information about language use. Studies of aphasics have found a range of different patterns of language recovery in those who speak more than one language (Chary 1986; Grosjean 1982; Paradis 1977). Some factors, such as the age at which the language was learned, were considered significant, suggesting that different neurological networks were involved. However, relationships, affective factors and context have also been found to be important; one aphasic man retrieved the language in which he had first fallen in love, months before the languages he was using currently in his life (Grosjean 1982). Such findings suggest complex multifactorial influences.

Of considerable note are research studies into adults who speak several languages which discovered that they describe different experiences in different languages. Ervin (1964) found that bilinguals told different stories in each of their languages when asked to relate what they see on Thematic Apperception Test cards. Studies by Di Pietro (1977), Ervin-Tripp (1968, 1973), Gallagher (1968), Haugen (1956) and Mkilifi (1978) demonstrated similar kinds of differences, with individuals presenting different values and affective content in their different languages. In another study (Javier 1996), individuals recalled events very differently in their different languages.

Even more startling, de Zulueta (1984, 1990) reported that bilingual psychiatric patients could suffer from hallucinations and thought disorder in one language and were still able to be coherent in another, and she linked this to neurological effects, differentiating between those languages learned earlier and later. Hughes (1981) discovered that patients with several languages who were diagnosed with major functional disorders reported hearing voices in only one of their languages, or heard critical and aggressive voices only in their second language and supportive positive voices in their first. Pérez Foster (1998) noted that different issues were presented in psychoanalytic psychotherapy, depending on which language was spoken.

These studies indicated that individuals develop very different meanings in each language, but the implications of such differences for individuals and their relationships have mainly not been pursued.

Contextual factors and language use

Linguists have often carried out research in bilingualism in laboratory situations on aspects of language processing, removed from everyday speaking situations, or in dissecting 'naturally' occurring language, with a focus on individual competence. Until relatively recently, many studies neglected issues of power and the effect of the social and political context on language use and individuals' positioning within language. Cromdal (2000) has made the point that much of this research was underpinned by an idea of language as a medium to communicate internal mental processes with others, where language was considered as a transparent conduit.

Critical linguistics' challenge to the idea of language as a system, which had become predominant following Saussure's work on structuralism and Chomsky's on the grammar of language, contributed to the turn to theorizing 'language use'. Critical linguists considered language as social, and meaning as contextual, constructed through power relationships and with 'stake' (Kress 2001). They researched bilingual language use in everyday social encounters, with a focus on interactional meaning making, cultural patterning of speech and the importance of context.

Such conceptualization of language as 'doing' power applies not only within one language, but also between languages. English is considered to be a 'strong language' throughout the world. Its status, built on its colonial past and promulgated through the dominance of the United States, means that it is intimately entangled with power relationships, and its use disseminated through globalization. It has had powerful influences on other languages in translation processes, rather than more equal two-way interactions (Asad 1986), although English always has and continues to borrow from other languages. It is reported that 88 per cent of scientific and technical literature is either published in English initially or translated into English almost immediately (Steiner 1998a).

The hierarchical and power relationship between languages, impacts on language use and meanings. Individuals are required to use the dominant language which at the same time constitutes them as assimilated subjects. Sociolinguistic studies researching adults' second language use at work have shown how hidden differences in participants' communicative resources disrupted discussion, generated negative social categorizations and resulted in the reproduction of racism (Rampton 1995), and different intonations used by second-language speakers are often 'misread' (Gumperz 1982).

Those who seek to oppress, exclude and humiliate often use language to do so because of its power to injure (Butler 1997). Attempting to destroy a language has been a common form of oppression. There is disagreement about the effect on individuals of losing their first language, although this can be linked to the meanings of this for the whole community. Adler (1977) thought attrition of language changed one's outlook, while Seliger (1989) proposed that one lost expressive, not conceptual, ability. The circumstances leading to language attrition have an important effect, and are often linked to the symbolic meaning given to language. In the context of genocide, Apfelbaum (1997) argued that the effect of not being able to speak one's first language, of 'not being at home' in one's own tongue, deprives individuals of self-assurance, sense of control and a link to one's heritage.

One form of 'de-authorizing' individuals is to change their names in a new language. Modood et al. (1994) have argued that the strategy of denying significant aspects of oneself, such as those signified by one's name, "is perhaps the tragedy of the immigrant experience in the West" (1994: 166). In turn, language can be used as an instrument of resistance; reclaiming or subverting language can also be employed for defiance and challenge.

Migration, gender, generation and language

For those individuals who have a history of migration, language issues may be conflated with migration processes. The circumstances – chosen or forced following traumatic experiences of torture and war, or for economic survival – under which families migrate have been found to have a powerful impact on their experiences, as have the political, cultural and economic power relations in which families become embedded in the new context. Individuals and families who have moved cultures and countries, those with identifications across contexts, most challenge traditional notions of cultural identity (Bhabha 1996; Bottomley 1992; Brah 1996; Chamberlain 1997; Turner 1991), and this often influences responses to them. "Migration, like revolution, is the making and the unmaking of the social, not something which happens within it" (Bull 2001: 24).

Class differences have been found to be highly significant to immigrant experiences. Upper middle-class families who move countries are generally able to retain their privilege and status and offer their children opportunities, while middle-class and working-class families face adversity and a reduction in opportunities, and suffer loss of status and class through language difficulties, racism and discrimination (Norton 2000; Suárez-Orozco and Suárez-Orozco 2001).

Migration itself is a transformational process, involving a change of physical environment, of sounds, and smells, the loss of the anchoring of memory to place, and the loss of relationship networks, and context. It involves contradictory processes of change, of opportunities and loss. Such processes are mediated through the construction of the narratives of migration, and notions of home and belonging (Chamberlain 1997; Falicov 1998; Papadopoulos and Hildebrand 1997).

But what is the place of language in these processes? Children and adults often engage with a new language differently (Grinberg and Grinberg 1989), and children often learn the dominant language faster than their parents (Burck 1997; Papadopoulos and Hildebrand 1997). Many adults find it harder to try out the new language in the environment (Grinberg and Grinberg 1989), and the methods used to learn are more formal than initial language learning processes. Individuals' attachment to their first language has been found to change on moving to another context, and, indeed, is often highlighted for the first time (Grinberg and Grinberg 1989).

Expectations are often placed on women who migrate with their families to be 'guardians of culture', to ensure that children continue to speak their first language, value and stay connected to cultural beliefs (Lau 1995). Women are theorized as symbols of the nation, of the collectivity (Anthias and Yuval-Davis 1992) and as such considered keepers of the language, where language is signified as carrying identity. Because women are signified as guardians of language, they are also blamed for 'language deaths' (Constantinidou 1994). Women may also be kept out of the new culture and language. When women learn the new language, they may position themselves in new ways to open up different opportunities, while their male partners struggle to maintain traditional roles which don't fit easily with the new context (Lau 1995). These different positionings in the new language and culture, in combination with ideas about women's relationships to their first language, can create differential gendered dilemmas.

Gendered differences may come into play when individuals and families move into a new language and culture, informed by different expectations. Developmental research points to important gendered differences in language acquisition and in children's relationship to language, although the meanings of these findings are disputed (Berko and Ely 2001). Interlinked with language acquisition will be complex beliefs about language learning. In Britain learning languages has been regarded as conventionally 'female', a recursive connection and construction, with very few male teachers teaching languages at schools and many fewer boys than girls learning them (Nuffield Languages Inquiry 2000). Research carried out with Arab adolescents in Canada highlighted gender differences with young women declaring integrative attitudes and young men instrumental ones to their learning of English (Abu-Ravia 1995), although what these students may have been demonstrating were ways in which they were 'doing gender' (Frosh et al. 2002).

Many of the dilemmas and processes involved in migration for individuals and families, which Falicov (2002) has described in terms of 'ambiguous loss', balancing physical absence and psychological presence, physical presence and psychological absence, will be reflected in issues around language speaking and use, interconnected with questions of identity and loyalty.

Racialized identities, ethnicities, culture, class and language

Interviews, which explore individuals' accounts of their experiences of their languages, also concern questions of subjectivity. Identity and the self are commonly conceptualized as private subjective phenomenon, but they are embedded in the social, in power relationships. The terms subjectivity, the self and identity are often used interchangeably, but it is useful to differentiate between them. In this book I employ a theorization of the 'self' as relational and discursive. I draw on a conceptualization of subjectivity as "dynamic and multiple, positioned in relation to particular discourses and practices and produced by these" (Henriques et al. 1984: 3). In developing narratives of self in interaction with others over time, individuals draw on culturally available resources, as they take up and resist various positions offered in relationship.

'Identity' has been posited as the term through which it is possible to untangle how discourse and agency interlink and are inscribed within unequal power relationships (Bhavnani and Phoenix 1994). It has also been formulated as something claimed, but never attained (Benjamin 1998) – longed for rather than 'owned' (Rose 1998) – in other words, a fiction (Hall 1987). Connell (1987) proposed the idea of an 'identity project', emphasizing the 'doing' of personality, the unification of diverse and often contradictory practices, through which disjunctions, fragments and incoherence are worked.

Over the past few decades important theoretical work has been carried out concerning the racialization of identities, and its intersections with gender, class, culture and ethnicity (Bhavnani and Phoenix 1994; Brah 1996; Brah et al. 1999; Hall 1987; Henriques et al. 1984), which has posited the usefulness of the notion of multiple subjectivities. Drawing distinctions between concepts of ethnicity, culture and 'race' is helpful, in order to examine their intersections with language speaking.

The concept of racialized identities emphasizes the processes involved, in the context of historical and everyday racisms and unequal power relationships, through which the social construct of 'race' is given meaning over time. Identities are constructed relationally through difference (Hall 1987); cultural and linguistic signifiers as well as biological and religious ones have been used to construct racialized boundaries and identities (Anthias and Yuval-Davis 1992). Work exploring racialization processes in different countries has highlighted how identities are racialized differentially and how they shift, dependent on context and over time (Silverman and Yuval-Davis 1999).

Ethnicity concerns identity at the level of the group in relationship with other groups, what Haarmann (1986) has called the experience of a community's self-identification in its ecological setting. Ethnicity is the process of boundary formation between groups shaped by socio-economic and political circumstances (Barth 1969), constructed in an ongoing way from within and outside the group through difference and dominant ideology (Krause 1998), but it is generally treated as if it is inherited, primordial and signifies a demarcated culture. Language can be used to mark boundaries, and where this is so, becomes considered a criterion of ethnicity. Accent has similarly been used as a marker of ethnicity (Wachtel 2000). Ethnic and linguistic boundaries are not fixed, but shift depending on context and time; so, for example, for returning Puerto Ricans, Spanish changed as a marker of belonging to the Puerto Rican community in the United States, to a designation as an outsider in Puerto Rico due to a loss of fluency (Clachar 1997).

Culture can be considered at a number of different levels: as a set of practices, theories, and material and institutional products (Ochs 1996); as that which is background, taken-for-granted assumptions such as of personhood, of relationships and of how life is lived and ought to be lived (Krause 2002); and as process, dynamic, evolving and contested, what Brah (1996: 234) has termed "the play of signifying practices; the idiom in which social meaning is constituted, appropriated, contested and transformed; the space where the entanglement of subjectivity, identity and politics is performed". The different ways in which individuals are positioned and position themselves within these signifying practices – that is, live their culture – is dependent on their racialization, ethnicity, gender, class, and sexual orientation among other factors. Speaking is a central signifying practice, and language, a context in and through which individuals are positioned. Language and culture are often inextricably linked. We can think of language as 'culture-soaked' – cultural concepts are embedded in language and its use, as well as language being signified as carrying cultural identity.

What becomes apparent in considering these definitions is that the processes of the construction of racialized identities, of ethnicities and of cultural identities overlap and intersect. Cultural difference has been used as a signifier in the racialization of identity, and as a marker of ethnicity, and vice versa. Language speaking has been designated as a signifier in the construction of racialized identities, ethnicities and cultural identities, while positioning within a language, is influenced by racialization, ethnicity and cultural identity. All of these constructions are given meaning through unequal power relationships. Interconnections between language use and class within one language have also been noted, with accent and different social languages constructed as markers of class.

What it means to be positioned in more than one language and culture varies considerably depending upon an individual's racialized identity, ethnicity, gender and class, as well as on the languages and cultures involved. This indicates some of the complexities involved in the place language speaking has in the construction of identities.

Narrative, discursive practices and identity

Narrative theory posits that the self is constructed, is storied through interaction with others (Bruner 1986), and that in this process language produces meaning and does not just reflect experience. Ricoeur (1984) believes that there is no other way for us to describe lived time other than through narrative, and that we emplot our lived experience. The construction, telling and reconstruction of the stories of our lived experience, marked by affect, *is* our memory, and is continually evolving. In this view, not all lived experience is storied and narratives of self are considered both as constructions and claims of identity (Linde 1993).

Each culture offers 'canonical narrative forms', stories of selves which provide templates for organizing lived experience. Kristeva (1986) and Irigaray (1985) argued that western narrative form created a demand for coherence through its structure, and required challenge as distorting and subverting experiences, which were fragmentary, multiple and contradictory. The forms and genres of narrative privileged in our cultures and the subject positions offered in relation to our gender, class, 'race', ethnicity and sexuality inform personal narrative construction, as do the resources available to sustain them. Narrative validity is dependent on audience, on affirmation of others with who we are in relationship, and on the resources available, dependent on what Polonoff (1987) has called believability, liveability and empirical adequacy. Research studies of unexpected events (Kleinman 1988; Kirkman 1996; Stern et al. 1999) have shown these to be disruptive of individual and family narratives, and highlighted the importance of expected storylines in individual's self accounts.

The relationships and context within which we create our narratives/ our memories, shape their selection and construction. Parents' and caretakers' developing stories about infants have effects prior to their own participation in the telling of these. Repeated storytelling in families has performative effects, constructing positionings and moral orders, as well as absences, in the family's narratives (Edwards and Middleton 1988). Individuals are positioned and position themselves through these practices and their subjectivity is constituted through the learning and use of certain discursive practices (Davies and Harré 1997). Children take up subject positions available in their parents' and others' talk addressed to them (Dunn 1995; Forrester 2001), and are positioned differently within their languages dependent upon their 'race', gender, ethnicity, and class.

Children in different language communities have been found to develop narratives of self differently. Some writers (Gee 1998; Holmes 1998; Kopijn 1998) link this to the different narrative structures available, others to the cultural differences in the conceptualization of the self (Budwig 1998; Morris 1994; Wierzbicka 1997), and yet others to the different ways of indexing oneself in different languages (Mülhausler and Harré 1990; Shotter 1989). Slobin (1996) proposed that children learn particular ways of 'thinking for speaking', by which he means picking those characteristics of objects and events that fit some conceptualization of the event and are readily encodable in language. His study of children's storytelling found that children using different languages focused attention on different aspects of events shown pictorially. Narratives in different cultures have different structures as well as content, and ways of telling and listening (Holmes 1998; Mistry 1997). Each culture has its particular ways of using language, telling stories, remembering information, and making inferences (Mistry 1997). Recounting a narrative is also a discursive strategy; narrative style is also self-presentation and a shift in style often accompanies a shift in social identity (Gee 1998).

This literature indicates that children and adults positioned in several languages construct different narratives of self in different linguistic contexts, related to differences of structure, conceptualizations of self, indexing, styles of presentation and available canonical narratives. However, there is also a privileging of coherence in narratives and the lure of 'canonical narrative forms' invite particular constructions of self. Individuals therefore can also be expected to experience demands for coherence and challenges in sustaining fissures or fragmentation.

Biculturalism and transculturalism

Individuals and families who speak more than one language are usually situated in more than one cultural context. Individuals positioned in two cultures have often been negatively connoted in similar ways to those who are bilingual, and come under intense pressure to acculturate, while at the same time experiencing exclusion. LaFromboise and her colleagues (1993) highlighted the dangers and stress associated with the processes of assimilation and acculturation, and noted that an individual's ability to alternate between two cultures, to develop 'bicultural competence', was found to be beneficial.

Apfelbaum (1997) asks how competing cultural histories impact on the construction of a person's identity, when attempts have been made to obliterate people physically and culturally. She noted that survivors often choose silence to try to protect their children from the knowledge of atrocities, but that silence itself can foster rifts from cultural histories and language with important effects on identities. In these contexts, language and culture may come to stand for each other – reclaiming language then can be considered as profoundly important in reclaiming heritage, as Hannah Arendt and Paul Celan have described in relation to German following the Holocaust (Apfelbaum 1997; Felman and Laub 1992).

Positioning in and between several languages

Translators are, by definition, individuals who operate between languages. There are obviously significant differences between translating as a writer and doing so as a speaker, where relational aspects are foregrounded and speech is embodied, but similar quandaries seem likely.

The translation literature warns of erasing differences between languages, and the effect of powerful languages on less dominant ones (Asad 1986). The ability to accept the 'foreignness' of other languages, as Walter Benjamin (1970) put it, is key to translation; for the translator to allow their own language to be powerfully affected by the other language. The process of translation can replicate power relationships or subvert them.

Derrida's (1978, 1985) position on translation is that it is both possible and impossible, and that translators are working at the limits of the differences between signified and signifier. Translators operate at the 'in-between', not only between languages and cultures, but also in the realm of the possibilities of representation. For this reason, Steiner (1998a) warned of the hazards of working in this in-between space. Translation makes acute and problematizes the relationship of language to experience and to the social world. But these hazards also entail the potential for creativity.

Many translators see the process of translation as an "elaborate act of improvisation" (Lockhart 1992), because of the many levels of difference between languages. And while Robert Frost said: "Poetry is what is lost in translation," Brodsky, who translated his own poetry from Russian to English, saw this as re-creation: "Poetry is what is gained in translation" (Jackson 2001). "That very exposure of limits and impossibilities also gives birth to new alternatives in a very grey area which is neither one language nor another, but a silent differing space not delimited by either one" (Gentzler 1993: 168). Venuti (1995) argued that translation could create possibilities for cultural resistance, innovation, and change. Simon (1996) concurred with this position, seeing potential in "bad/incomplete" translations which "open cracks in the usually solid facade of linguistic knowledge, suggesting larger and more troubling thoughts."

The hazards of being positioned between languages and the experience of the limits of language and representation therefore encompass possibilities for creativity. Bakhtin's (1935/1981) work, grounded in the examination of literary texts, acknowledged the complex positioning and tensions involved in inhabiting several social languages within one language. He addressed the struggle involved in the intersection of different social languages in order to make use of their dialogic potential, and to avoid monologic authoritarian language.

> It is the collision between differing points of view on the world that are embedded in these forms [...] such unconscious hybrids have been at the same time profoundly productive historically; they are pregnant with potential for new world views, with new 'internal forms' for perceiving the world in words. (Bakhtin 1935/1981: 360)

Bhabha (1994, 1996) made use of Bakhtin's notion of hybridity to emphasize the tensions in the complicated process of negotiation and re-evaluation between different cultural perspectives due to unequal power and polarisations, but also its subversive potential. Hybridity has also been viewed as problematic and dangerous, because of its challenge to binary oppositions (Gilroy 2000; Phoenix and Owen 1996).

Being bicultural and bilingual or multilingual involves not only a positioning in several cultures/languages, but also a positioning in relation to the differences between the cultures and languages, finding a way to relate different and sometimes contradictory cultural perspectives for oneself. Jessica Benjamin (1998) emphasized how crucial and fraught the recognition of difference in the encounter of two selves is, with the dangers of domination, idealization or disconnection, in a context in which 'difference' has been constructed as unequal, 'other' or obliterated. She argued that it is the ability of each individual to dis-identify without disconnection, which enables selves to be inclusive and multiple. Translating this into discursive terms, I understand this to mean that it is the ability to resist discursive positions offered in relationship, while staying in relationship, which is crucial. For bilingual and multilingual individuals this involves finding ways to interlink their different cultural and linguistic perspectives which subvert polarisations and the domination of one over the other.

Language signified as carrier of identity

Language carries symbolic meanings (Fishman 1996), and one central meaning given is its signification as the carrier of national and cultural identity. This is reflected in sayings in many different languages: Welsh –

Heb iaith, heb gendedl (No language, no nation); Bengali – Nanan deshe nanan bhasha bina shodeshi bhasha miteki asha (One can use the language of other countries, but one can only get fulfilment in the mother tongue); Hungarian Romani saying – Amari chib si amari zor (Our language is our strength); Hungarian – Nyelvében él a nemzet (The nation lives in its language); Sinhala – Bhashava jaathiye rudhirayaii (Language is the lifeblood of a people); Panjabi – boli hai Panjabi sadi rhoo jind jan sadi gidyan di khan sadi (Our language is Panjabi. It is our life and soul, it is a treasure of folksongs) (Alladina and Edwards 1991a, 1991b). The significance of language is accentuated when a country or community is threatened with extinction or has been territorially dispossessed.

Not surprisingly, then, language speaking can be used to enact both collective and individual identity and to make political claims. In this respect, identity can be considered a thing to be possessed and displayed for political purposes (Gilroy 2000), and other power relationships come into play. At a community level, the realization of loss of language, and everything it symbolizes, can lead to attempts to revitalize the language. But this is rarely a straightforward process (Abley 2003), as the dilemmas that arose in Wales about how to engage others in the everyday and living use of Welsh demonstrate. Some individuals experienced this as having Welsh forced on them by others, and there were complex intersections with class, with middle-class families sending their children to Welsh schools, while working-class families viewed English as the route to economic success (Stead 1997). Protests were also made against the introduction of Gaelic into the school curriculum in Ireland in the attempt to re-establish this language (Romaine 1995). The revitalization of Hebrew as the language for the State of Israel on the other hand, has been highly successful because its signification was coterminous with the building of the nation-state and meaningful for all in the context of the history of the Holocaust (Romaine 1995). Claims of identity are therefore important aspects of language choice and usage, and indeed have been the focus in a different approach to researching bilingualism.

Bilingualism as an interactional resource

Researchers turned to conversation analysis focusing on interactive process in order to study how the meaning of code switching is constructed in interaction (Li Wei 2002) taking into account power relations and participant-relevant local accomplishments (Auer 1995;

Cromdal 2000). 'Code switching', the alternating of languages within a conversation, had for many years been viewed negatively as evidence of not knowing either language well, linked to other negative ideas about bilingualism (Romaine 1989; Li Wei 2002), rather than as a sign of fluency which Poplack (1980) had pointed out was required for intra-sentential switching.

Studies of code switching highlighted its use as a rich discursive resource, for 'meta-languaging' purposes, a skill which children developed as early as two years and 8 months (Gumperz 1982; Romaine 1989). Code switching can be used to mark a type of discourse or genre (Maschler 1994), and to change 'footing' – the participation framework and/or performance format of talk (Goffman 1979). Switching between languages can change context or positioning (Auer 1988), or can be used for irony or to play. It can mark an interjection, reiterate something for emphasis, and qualify a message. Code switching can address a particular individual, draw distinctions between 'us' and 'them', and exclude or include others. Whole communities have developed norms of code switching which then come to define membership of that linguistic group (Maalouf 2000; Zentella 1997).

Sebba and Wootton's (1998) study of code switching by a group of black students in London between British Standard English, London English, and London Jamaican, demonstrated how they used switching to construct identities, a process negotiated by drawing on resources both inside and outside of the interactions themselves. They pointed out that boundaries of languages and communities were negotiated through the participants' situated and local practices. Cromdal's (2000) study of children's code switching between Swedish and English at a bilingual school in Sweden, demonstrated that bilingualism should be viewed as an emergent and interactionally managed feature of discourse. Similar to the ways in which individuals make an identity salient within one language, using strategies to claim and disown membership of social groups (Antaki et al. 1996; Widdicombe 1998a, 1998b), these studies demonstrated that language switching are resources for making identities salient.

Individuals are also able to draw on a new language to gain a 'voice'. Stroud (1998) showed how code switching could be used as a double-voicing technique which fostered an ambiguity about whose words were used and meant, and therefore protected from challenge. The use of a second language can offer possibilities of encoding meanings not permitted in a first language (Burton 1994). Tual (1986), for example, found that Iranian women were free to speak in front of men in their second language, which they could not do in their first.

This literature demonstrates that having several languages increased individuals' range of discursive resources, and can be used in complex ways to claim personal and political identities. In this language usage, the meanings of individuals' languages are of central significance.

Researching bilingual/multilingual speakers' views

Contemporary research within the sociolinguistics field has sought to include speakers' own views of their language use (Kanno 2000; McKay and Wong 1996; Miller 2000; Mills 2001; Norton 2000; Pavlenko 2002; Smith 1999; Velásquez 1995). This work has examined complexities of speakers' experiences in a number of different domains. Norton (2000) explored language learners' positioning in power relationships, and how this affected their opportunities to speak and claim legitimacy as a speaker. Mills (2001) and Smith (1999) researched the meanings given to different languages, and Pavlenko (2002) focused on different meanings in different languages, and their effects on individuals. A number of studies examined the interaction between language use and identity (Kanno 2000; McKay and Wong 1996; Miller 2000; Mills 2001). Despite recognition in sociolinguistics that self-report often reflects idealised rather than actual language use (Bucholtz 1995), these studies indicated the fruitfulness of interviews with speakers themselves to explore issues of power, meaning and identity.

Summary and conclusion

To summarize, research in the last thirty years has challenged the negativity associated with bilingualism and multilingualism, and demonstrated the importance of social, relational and contextual factors. Speaking several languages in supportive circumstances has been found to enable children to think in flexible ways and to hold multiple perspectives. Bilingualism and multilingualism has been demonstrated to provide a considerable interactional resource, through the use of code switching and flexibility in expressiveness. At the same time, the maintenance of minoritized language speaking is dependent on support and resources, which means it is particularly challenging to sustain in the context of the antipathy towards other languages in Britain.

Although many linguists had traditionally ignored contextual factors and meanings of language use, cultural theorists and critical sociolinguists have drawn attention to the importance of power and context. Language can come to signify national or cultural identity when a country or community has been threatened with dispossession or in a postcolonial period when a country is reconstituting itself. Language is used as a signifier in the construction of racialized identities and ethnicities, as well as cultural identities and class identities. Individuals and groups can make claims of identity and are defined through their language choice.

The literature on migration, gender and language highlighted the construction of women as central to the preservation of language and culture, and indicates that there are significant gendered differences in the experiences of living life in several languages.

Research studies in a number of different areas have found significant differences between individuals' languages, although the implications of these differences for individuals have, with some contemporary exceptions, received very little scholarly attention. Being positioned in two or more cultures and languages when there are unequal power relationships has the potential of replicating disqualification or creating something innovative. There are hazards of operating between different languages but there is also radical potential.

Speaking several languages therefore has significant implications for individuals' sense of subjectivity and their identity construction at several different levels, and we can examine these using individuals' own accounts of their experiences in and of their languages. An exploration of the meanings individuals give to their languages, and take from their languages is the focus of my research. This allows us to attempt to address the question of how subjective meanings are constructed from culture, and how individuals live the differences between their languages and cultures.

2
The Research Framework

In this chapter, I take up the implications of the literature reviewed in Chapter 1 and formulate the questions which are explored in the rest of the book. I locate the research project within a social constructionist framework, and discuss the theoretical concepts which underpin the research analysis. The descriptions of the research participants are included here, as well as the construction of the protocol for the research interviews.

Much of the traditional linguistic research into bilingualism and multilingualism had concentrated on individual on 'language competence' rather than 'language use' and had been permeated by monolingual norms. Despite challenges by researchers to the continued negativity associated with multilingualism, it has remained an undervalued and often-disqualified aspect of living. It has been important to carry out research into bilingualism and multilingualism in a way which is not permeated by monolingual norms as so many early research studies have been. The recent focus in research on 'language use' has proved productive, as have studies which have sought to include individual speakers' perspectives.

Research studies have indicated that speaking several languages in supportive circumstances gives individuals a greater flexibility of thought and provides them with more interactional resources than monolinguals. Yet such findings have received relatively little attention. Only recently has research sought to include speakers' own accounts, having previously considered it more appropriate to analyse their language use than ask individuals to reflect on it. Studies which have interviewed speakers themselves demonstrate their fruitfulness in examining the meanings of language speaking.

The literature suggests that conducting one's life in several languages has important effects on the construction of subjectivity and identity.

Studies have found a number of striking differences when individuals spoke different languages, but often did not pursue the implications of these findings. Narrative theory indicates that bilingual and multilingual individuals would construct different narratives of self in their different linguistic and cultural contexts. Hence interviewing individuals themselves concerning their diverse experiences in several languages offers us perspectives through which to explore and contribute to the theorization of 'multiple subjectivity'.

Questions of how individuals manage a positioning in several languages include the meanings language speaking is given in the wider context. These meanings are related to the power relationships and institutionalized practices within which individuals are embedded. Language speaking is used as a signifier in the construction of racialized identities, ethnicities and cultural identities, and in turn an individual's racialized identity, cultural identity and ethnicity impacts on their positioning within a language. Language choice and language switching are also used to claim personal and political identities. Individuals can replicate the unequal power relationships between their languages or find ways to resist these in various ways. The hazards of operating between languages identified by translators indicate there may be similar challenges for those who live in several languages.

The ways in which women are constructed as the guardians of culture and language point towards likely gendered differences of living in several languages, and yet, gender differences have rarely been examined in research on multilingualism. This suggests the importance of critically examining women and men's relationship to their languages. Questions of what effect speaking several languages has on family relationships are highly relevant.

Asking individuals themselves to reflect on their language use and its effects is timely and pertinent. The use of insider accounts of the issues involved in speaking several languages allows an analysis of the meanings of speaking languages constructed in family relationships and in the wider context. Insider accounts also encapsulate questions of subjectivity, and offer the opportunity of analysing the place of language speaking in individuals' constructions of self.

Research questions

The exploratory research questions were articulated to address areas from the literature which merit further attention as well as the absences. In order to encapsulate the different levels of meaning of language speaking and the diversity of individuals' experiences and circumstances, my questions were broadly formulated in order to elicit individuals' meaning making and to allow an analysis of their constructions of self:

> **How do individuals construct their experiences of living life in several languages?**
> **What meanings are given to speaking more than one language and what relational issues arise?**

To focus on the meanings individuals themselves construct, I conducted semi-structured research interviews. I have aimed to examine the differences their different languages made to individuals from their point of view. The territory that I set out to explore has included the circumstances in which individuals learned and spoke their languages, a mapping of where and how they used their languages, and their beliefs and perceptions of the effects of speaking several languages. (See Appendix A at the end of the book for the protocol for the interviews.)

Epistemology and research framework

This study views its research data within a social constructionist paradigm (Lincoln and Guba 1994). It draws on the proposal that our ways of knowing are negotiated through social interactions over time, and in relation to social structures, contexts and resources which support or suppress these (Shotter 1993).

There are particular challenges involved in researching individuals' descriptions of their experiences. The analysis of such accounts is concerned with questions regarding memory and what talk does and can accomplish. Social constructionist and discursive frameworks (Gergen 1985; Potter and Wetherell 1987; Wetherell et al. 2001) offer ways to theorize how experiences have been constructed. The research accounts are considered to be constructions, not transparent accounts of what individuals have 'really' experienced, but productions in the context of the social science research interview. Some of the interviews are also constructions of childhood and adolescence (James and Prout 1990). Following Bruner (1986) and the narrative theorists, I take the view that we continually construct and reconstruct our memories, from our present perspective, and in the light of our ideas about the future, in our interactions with others, and that not all our experience is storied. The genres of narrative privileged in our social contexts shape the construction of our memories (Hall 1987; Ricoeur 1985). In these processes of construction in our interactions with others, affect which is itself constructed through interaction (Harré 1986) is also significant (Beebe and Lachman 2002).

I know that individuals are profoundly influenced by their sense of the reality of their constructions. As a researcher this means that I need to attend to accounts at different levels – to find a way to make sense of why someone has constructed the account as they have, and to pay attention to the process of construction. These different levels are related to distinctions drawn in the literature between considering language as referential and as performative (Taylor 2001). I am also acutely aware that the ways in which individuals construct their experiences have consequences which matter, which is why others have argued for the importance of linking the material and the discursive (for example, Ussher 1996). This is where I consider my ethical accountability as a researcher lies, to take responsibility for my part in these co-constructions, both in the interviews and in the analysis. I discuss ways in which I have managed this aspect of the research in Chapter 7.

Conducting the research interviews

I chose to conduct semi-structured interviews with individuals, to enable me to cover different dimensions of living in several languages. This interviewing format meant that I, as the researcher, set the agenda and introduced the areas which I wanted to explore, although I followed participants' feedback in idiosyncratic ways to explore issues unique and significant to them, and to elicit and unpack multiple and contradictory perspectives. Like Squire (2000) and in view of participants' multiplicities, I was keen not to have individuals feel that they needed to present a story of self as a coherent autobiography. At the end of each interview I asked research participants about any absences or areas they thought I should inquire about, in order to try to open up issues that were outside my own imagination.

My research interviewing is informed by my work as a systemic psychotherapist. I am experienced at interviewing individuals using 'reflexive' and 'circular' questions, which enable inquiry and exploration of connections at different levels and in relation to different contexts (Tomm 1987, 1988). A 'circular question' is one formulated by the interviewer to follow feedback, using the answer given to the previous question to explore connections to it, and to expand contexts. 'Reflexive questions' are those which enable individuals to reflect on themselves in the context of different levels of meaning, as well as reflect on the relationships between levels of meaning. Following Cecchin (1987) and Tomm (1987, 1988) I consider questions as 'interventive' – research questions provoke individuals to make connections and to construct things in new ways.

This research project explored aspects of individuals' lives not much previously reflected on, and there were many moments during the interviews when individuals made new connections. This evident generation of new perspectives by individuals further highlighted the status of the interview material as constructed in the context of the research interview, and the need to consider the relationship between the research participants and myself, the researcher (Jorgenson 1991; Fine 1994; Wilkinson and Kitzinger 1996). My introduction of myself as the researcher and the rationale of the research question included positioning myself personally and politically, presenting myself as someone who had herself grown up speaking several languages, my awareness of how little attention had been paid in Britain to languages other than English, and my wish to redress this absence. As someone who spoke several languages, I was similar to the research participants, but otherwise there was considerable variability in my positioning as similar or different to those I interviewed, with regard to culture, class, 'race', ethnicity, gender, age, sexual orientation, and circumstances of learning languages. I knew some of the research participants in a different capacity and some were unknown to me. Attempting to maintain an awareness of the dilemmas of 'representing the other' in relation to difference (Fine 1994; Wilkinson and Kitzinger 1996) and of making assumptions around similarities has been an important challenge in this work, and I discuss this further in Chapter 7.

Research participants

It was remarkably easy to recruit individuals through word-of-mouth and a snowballing method. Individuals volunteered themselves, their family members and their friends as research participants, and long after I had stopped interviewing, individuals continued to approach me. This considerable interest has confirmed an idea that many individuals have not had opportunities previously to explore this aspect of their lives, and that it is significant to them. It is also possible that exploring issues of speaking several languages is an attractive invitation – to be able to talk about the self in an area which is not contentious and which, although negatively connoted, is not stigmatized. It is an area of discussion which is, on the whole, neglected and ignored in Britain.

My research participants were 24 individuals aged between 19 and 58, who lived in Britain at the time of the study. I also draw on one conjoint interview with a couple who had both been brought up bilingually in their families of origin, and who were bringing up their children bilingually. Half of the research participants had grown up speaking several languages and half had moved to live in a different language and culture either when adolescent or when older. This allowed consideration of differential experiences of childhoods and adulthoods lived in several languages. The individuals in the study had learned their languages in a range of different circumstances, to make possible a consideration of contextual influences on the meanings of language speaking. They were a heterogeneous group of individuals, from different cultures and languages, and with different racialized identity positions and ethnicities, to allow an examination of the ways in which language speaking intersected with processes of identity construction. Twelve were women and twelve were men, to enable gendered differences to be identified. Table A is a chart of the research participants, their gender, their languages, and the circumstances in which they acquired these. It shows whether they are/were in cross-language or same-language partnerships, and in what languages they had chosen to parent, if they had children. All research participants have been given pseudonyms.

What do these sampling decisions make possible? Although in this kind of research study there is no possibility of generalizing the analysis to a general population, we are able to examine the way in which individuals draw on resources of their language and culture in ways which have meaning beyond themselves. We can identify processes of meaning construction as well as the significance of the context of the resources drawn on, which will have wider resonance. The heterogeneity of the research group makes any identification of commonalities more striking.

Transcription

The research interview data used for the analysis were in the form of texts and the level at which the research interviews were transcribed was chosen for interpretative reasons (see Appendix B at the end of this volume for Transcription Notations). Pauses in talk were recorded because these often evidence moments in interviews when research

Table A Research Participants

Name	M/F	1st language	Culture &'race'	Languages in childhood	Forced/Voluntary migration	Parent in 1st/childhood language	Parent in English	Cross-lang partner
Angela	F	Sicilian Albanian Italian	Sicilian white	Sicilian Albanian Italian English in Britain		No	Yes	Yes
Bernard	M	French	French white	One	Voluntary as young adult	Yes	Yes	Yes
Cato	M	Hungarian	Hungarian white	Hungarian/ English	Forced Refugee as young child	No	Yes	Yes
Di-Yin	F	Shanghai dialect/ Mandarin/ rural dialect	Chinese	Shanghai dialect/ Mandarin/ rural dialect	Voluntary as young adult	Yes	Yes	Yes
Estelle	F	French	French white	One	Voluntary as young adult	Yes	Yes	Yes
Ffionn	F	Welsh	Welsh white	Welsh/ English	Voluntary as young adult	Yes	No	Yes
Gustav	M	Czech	Czech white	One	Exiled as young adult unable to return	No	Yes	Yes
Henka	F	Polish	Polish white	One	Voluntary as young adult	N/A	N/A	Yes
Ihsan	M	Farsi	Iranian	One	Voluntary as young adult unable to return	Yes	Yes	Yes

Justine	F	Dutch/English	Dutch/American/British white	Dutch/English in Britain		N/A	N/A	Yes
Konrad	M	Polish	Polish white	Polish/English in Britain		N/A	N/A	Yes
Lena	F	Serbo-Croat	Yugoslav white	Serbo-Croat Slovenian Macedonian	Escape from war as adult	Yes	No	No
Maria	F	Spanish	Argentinian white	One	Voluntary	Yes	Yes	Yes
Naadir	M	Arabic	Iraqi	One	Voluntary as young adult unable to return	Yes	Yes	No
Onno	M	Afrikaans	Afrikaner South African white	One	Voluntary as young adult	N/A	N/A	No
Petiri	M	Shona	Zimbabwean black	Shona, Nbele, English, Afrikaans	Escape from colonial army as young adult	Yes	Yes	Yes
Quinlan	F	Cantonese	Chinese	Cantonese, Dialect, English	Voluntary as young child	N/A	N/A	Yes
Renata	F	Hungarian	Hungarian white	Hungarian German	Forced refugee as young child & Voluntary as young adult	Yes	Yes	Yes

Table A (Continued)

Name	M/F	1st language	Culture & 'race'	Languages in childhood	Forced/Voluntary migration	Parent in 1st/childhood language	Parent in English	Cross-lang partner
Saskia	F	German	German white	One	Voluntary as young adult	Yes	Yes	Yes
Thérèse	F	Flemish	Belgian white	Flemish Dialect French	Voluntary as young adult	No	Yes	Yes
Ursula	F	Danish	Danish white	One	Voluntary as young adult	Yes	Yes	Yes
Venjamin	M	Arabic	Iraqi Jew	Arabic Hebrew	Voluntary as young child & adolescent	Yes	Yes	Yes
Wasan	M	Gujarati	Kenyan Asian	Gujarati Hindi English	Voluntary as young child	N/A	N/A	Yes
Xandra	F	Afrikaans	Afrikaner South Africa white	One	Voluntary as young adult	N/A	N/A	No

participants stop to think and are engaged in actively constructing an account for themselves. The transcription demonstrated only gross nonverbal aspects of communication, such as laughter, and excluded micro elements of communication. In presenting extracts of text in the following chapters, I have focused on material relevant to the points I am emphasizing, and have left out the diversions that characterize talk, which with a different research focus would have been fruitful to analyse.

A synthesized approach to analysis

I used a synthesized analytic approach to analyse the interview transcripts. A hybridity of methods has allowed me to consider different aspects of the research material and produce different levels of analysis. It has enabled me to analyse the material within a social constructionist paradigm as referential as well as performative.

Grounded theory approach

A grounded theory approach (Charnaz 1995; Glaser and Strauss 1967; Henwood and Pidgeon 1996) has been shown to have particular value for exploratory research questions in areas where there has been little prior theorization. The strength of a grounded theory approach lies in its ability to generate theory about processes, or at least, to develop conceptual analyses of social worlds. Other researchers have used grounded theory methods to explore insider accounts of social and psychological events and their associated phenomena (Bartlett and Payne 1997; Charnaz 1995; Pidgeon 1996), abstracting relevant concepts in a contextually sensitive way (Pidgeon 1996).

A grounded theory approach seemed particularly useful because I was a researcher exploring a question related to my personal experience, and the techniques of grounded theory methodology were developed to help researchers maintain self-reflexivity, and circumvent being overly organized by prior hypotheses. Like Charnaz (1995) and Henwood and Pidgeon (1996), who have developed grounded theory methods within a social constructionist paradigm, I consider that researchers always have hypotheses and theoretical interests which shape their choice of research topic, and influence the design of the interview format and the analysis. However, the very close reading of the data to generate coding in grounded theory approaches ensures that researchers build up their analysis slowly from considerable detail, which helps bypass assumptions and hypotheses somewhat, as these are often held at a more abstract level. The interplay, the iterative process, between data collection and analysis, through which an interview format can be modified to explore specific concepts further, and the use of theoretical sampling to choose research participants in a grounded theory approach, also suited the research study because it was little explored territory. The analysis of the research interviews allowed me to hone my questioning in particular areas.

Like Rennie et al. (1988) I coded 'meaning units' – sentences or several sentences which referred to a particular meaning – rather than every single line. I used the method of constant comparison to arrive at merged categories, selecting those most relevant to the research question, and to the questions of subjectivity, identity and relationships. The constant comparison of categories and the attention paid to variability in accounts are fruitful in creating new links.

A grounded theory approach was useful to identify and construct significant and unexpected categories and concepts, but some of these categories benefited from a different kind of analysis and deconstruction particularly in relation to questions of identity construction.

Narrative analysis

A theoretical interest in the construction of identities led to my use of analytic concepts from narrative theory (Bruner 1986; Ricoeur 1984) and narrative analysis (Riessman 1993) which allow an examination of the ways in which individuals present their accounts of themselves through a consideration of these as constructions and as claims of identity (Linde 1993).

As discussed in Chapter 1, narrative theorists posit that we *have* to describe lived time through narrative, that we emplot our lived experience (Ricoeur 1984), and that we construct narratives of self through interaction with others (Bruner 1986). In telling our stories of self, we describe our past experiences in the light of our current position and our imagined future which continually evolve (Freeman 1993). While compliance with culturally available narratives often goes unnoticed (Daniel and Thompson 1996), there are particular challenges for individuals who feel "locked out of a collective story which would give meaning to life" (Kirkman 1997). Narrative theories point to the demands for coherence on individuals, both externally and internally.

In this study it was most appropriate to consider the interviews as extended narrative accounts (Riessman 1993). The notion of canonical narrative forms and cultural genres (Ricoeur 1985) enabled an examination of how individuals' narratives were structured and which canonical stories they drew on, as well as considering the demand for coherence in the face of discontinuities of language and culture. Ideas about the ways in which personal narratives are temporally and spatially structured (Riessman 2001) and are constructed in relation to hypothetical and expected storylines (Kirkman 1997) offered a productive framework with which to consider the research narratives. It also drew my attention to the evaluative element of these narratives, the moral aspect of an account.

Discourse analytic research

To examine the way in which accounts were constructed, how identities were situated and accomplished in particular social interactions, constructed both through global discourses and through local and situated discursive practices, a discourse analytic approach was considered the most appropriate. Discourse analysis offers a way to scrutinize the 'orderly ways of talking' with which we account for and make sense of ourselves and our worlds (Shotter 1993). It could attend to the constructedness of accounts and identify contradictions and fragments, and individuals' positioning.

In order for individuals to co-construct their own and each other's narratives, they draw on the discursive resources of their languages, and position themselves and each other through their interactions. Here I take a discourse as a set of meanings, metaphors, representations, images, and stories (Burr 1995), as an institutionalized use of language (Davies and Harré 1997), which produces particular versions of events and the social world. "Language is the place where actual and possible forms of social organisation and their likely social and political consequences are defined and contested. Yet it is also the place where our sense of ourselves, our subjectivity, is constructed" (Weedon 1997: 21).

Ideas of discourses as global historical resources informed theorization concerning the interweaving of discourse, power and subjectivity (Foucault 1980). A Foucauldian approach focuses on the ways in which societal discourses are taken up in personal interactions, critically examines how discourse is shaped through power relationships and ideologies, and its effect on social identity, social relations and systems of knowledge and belief.

This is complemented by the notion of discursive practices to address questions of agency. The theorization of the ways individuals position themselves and are positioned in and through language in discursive psychological approaches (Davies and Harré 1997; Wetherell 1998) is particularly relevant for this research. In considering identity as

constituted and reconstituted through discourse use, this offers a theoretical lens with which to consider the ways in which individuals constructed their self narratives. Discursive practices are theorized as
offering 'subject positions', comprising of particular conceptual interpretative repertoires and locations. Individuals create subject positions
for themselves and others in their ongoing interactions, both in
unexamined taken-for-granted ways and explicitly (Davies and Harre
1997) – and each positioning has consequences and ideological dilemmas,
with 'troubled' and 'untroubled' subject positions offered and taken
up in interactions (Wetherell 1998). Considering the ways in which
speakers in interaction with each other are considered to invoke social
identities, negotiate their defining characteristics and claim identities or
have them claimed for them over time (Antaki et al. 1996) is also relevant
to the research accounts.

These discursive approaches provided a way to scrutinize the ways in
which individuals produced their self-accounts, the ongoing construction
and claiming of identity, to theorize links between the personal, social
and cultural, and to unpack connections between subjectivities and
language. The concept of 'performance' of identities has been particularly helpful – the idea that individuals 'do identity', that the taking
up of particular subject positions in the talk with others, is performative
and constitutive (Connell 1987). Such performances of identification
are constructed through relational practices, through distinctions drawn
of similarities and differences.

Bakhtin's theoretical ideas, developed about 'languages' within one
language in the context of the novel, which others have applied to questions of subjectivity and communication (Bhabha 1994; Maybin 1998,
1999, 2001a; de Peuter 1998; Shotter and Billig 1998) have also been
useful here. Bakhtin's (1981) concept of 'heteroglossia', an articulation
of how any utterance is positioned in relation to a number of different
and contradictory contexts, is particularly applicable to this research
study. It emphasizes the relations between shifts of meaning and shifts
of conditions and contexts, as well as the tensions of collisions between
different meaning systems. His idea of 'dialogism' concerning the
potential of the interaction of different meanings to produce a 'hybridization', the mixing of two different linguistic consciousnesses within
a single utterance, is very pertinent to the individuals in my study.
Loomba (1998) has argued that hybridity needs to be considered more
heterogeneously and as more specifically located than it has been to
date. I have therefore used this to examine ways in which individuals
make use of their language differences.

In summary, a synthetic methodological approach, of a grounded analysis to construct significant concepts, and a discursive approach, which draws on ideas of narrative construction, has allowed me to produce an analysis at different levels of a range of different aspects of living life in several languages.

3
Childhoods in Several Languages

In the following chapter, I examine constructions of childhoods lived in several languages. Half of the research group had lived their childhoods in several languages and I consider the impact of different circumstances and contexts on what is identified as significant for individuals as speakers, the meanings of language speaking and the ways in which individuals make meanings of themselves. I examine the accounts of childhoods in four different kinds of contexts: in colonial contexts, in other bilingual/multilingual contexts, in families who spoke minoritized languages, and among those who had to flee their countries of origin.

Growing up in multilingual colonial contexts

Four research participants had grown up in multilingual colonial contexts. Wasan, an Asian man, had lived in Kenya as a young child, Petiri, a black African Shona man, had grown up in what was then Rhodesia until his late adolescence, and Onno and Xandra, are white South Africans, both of whom had lived in South Africa until they were young adults. These countries had had clear hierarchies of languages, and these research participants and their languages were positioned differently. English, the language of the British colonizers, was dominant in all three countries, as was Afrikaans, in South Africa and Rhodesia/Zimbabwe, the legacy of Dutch colonialists. These research participants' constructions of themselves and their languages drew on ideas about colonial and postcolonial processes. Because of their different racialization and positioning, they constructed very different accounts of themselves as speakers and of their languages.

The place of language speaking in colonization processes

In Rhodesia/Zimbabwe, Petiri grew up speaking Shona as his first language, as well as Ndebele, several other African languages, English, and an Afrikaans dialect, in order to be able to communicate with a variety of different people with whom he came into contact. His education had taken place in English, and he presented its effect on him as part of colonizing processes:

> It had an impact in the sense that personally I began to feel that English was superior to Shona, therefore, there was some degree of cultural imperialism going there, I was aware of that, and also, the more fluent I became in English, the more I wanted to speak English to people I knew didn't speak it. [. . .] I would use more complicated words, which I knew they didn't understand, almost as a way of showing off. You know, I can speak English better than you. [. . .] It becomes very much like internalized racism where you actually become ashamed to speak Shona. Whereas with other people like the Kurds, they're very proud to defend their language, in my case you were glad to get rid of it, which is incredible. Including the way people spoke, they tried to get rid of their Shona accents, actually get rid of the African accent altogether and try and have, what is known, as an English accent, which is appalling.

Petiri drew on ideas of cultural imperialism, internalized racism and 'othering' here and his language is of note. He shifted from the use of "I", to "you", to "they" in this extract, perhaps as a way to distance himself somewhat from the "appalling" process in which he had participated and clearly been invested as an agent, and to demonstrate its pervasive effect. Petiri presented his learning of English as a performance of linguistic practices and attitudes, through which he was constituted and constituted himself as an English speaker, imitating the English colonizer. This is what Bhabha (1994) termed mimicry as colonizing process, although, as he argued, this is always ambivalently – "almost the same, but not quite" (p. 86), particularly because of racialization. A focus on gaining fluency, on the 'performance' of becoming a speaker of a new language makes it more likely that attitudes are enacted rather than challenged and reworked. In this account, language learning is central to the processes of racialization and colonization.

Alongside his 'performance' as English speaker, Petiri also began to perform himself differently as a Shona speaker:

> There was also some degree of pretending to be less fluent than
> I actually was. [...] I remember making a prat of myself (laughs).
> When I look back, I think, what was I doing that for, it was really so
> stupid.

The stance of disowning his first language/culture was taken from his
English-language perspective, with the effect that he participated in
disqualifying his own experience. Petiri positioned himself as 'I' in
this extract, shifting from an indictment of colonialism to personal
accountability – this 'performance' should have been resisted. This flux
between positionings of agency (hence responsibility) and of contextual
influences impossible to resist, may always play out as tension, but here
also functions to constitute himself as a self-reflective individual and as
someone who has moved on to a more helpful perspective.

Within an Asian community in Kenya where he lived as a boy Wasan
had mainly spoken Gujarati, attending Gujarati nurseries and schools.
His parents had arranged private tutoring for him in English from
a young age, and he also became familiar with the Swahili spoken by
Kenyan Africans. In common with others in Kenyan Asian communities,
his family had incorporated a number of Swahili words into their talk in
Gujarati, and this differentiated them from Gujarati speakers from
India. Wasan addressed the complexities in the experiences of racisms
in Kenya, when he spoke about challenging racist abuse at school in
Britain:

CB   I just wondered whether then um you can use language to
        kind of subvert racism or challenge it, whether then
        Gujarati can or whether it has that?

Wasan   I suppose it has certain elements, because then we could be
        abusive in Gujarati, and other people wouldn't know we
        were being abusive about them, because there are certain
        Gujarati or Swahili words which are probably just as racist,
        that some of the Asian children would use about white
        children, um so a carry over of that um (indistinct) which
        it's interesting in terms of Gujarati, Gujarati or Swahili
        words for black, (indistinct) being an abusive word used by
        Asian people about black people, (indistinct) kind of throwing
        it back.

The complex interactions between different racisms are illustrated here,
with Asian children having used words appropriated from Swahili with

racist connotations about black children, to be abusive about white children who were being racist towards them. The ability to use a 'secret' language as peers offered a certain protection and sense of power, but Wasan indicated a sense of irony and discomfort about this repetition/replication of racist terminology about blackness, purportedly for a different end. He, like Petiri, constructed himself as reflective about his own participation in such processes.

Onno and Xandra, as white South Africans, grew up speaking only Afrikaans, within communities in apartheid South Africa in which black Africans and white Europeans were expected to learn Afrikaans. Onno also constructed his narrative in relation to processes of colonization, but from a very different positioning. He presented his increasing awareness and discomfort during his growing up of the dominance of Afrikaans, his first language and his own challenge of apartheid when a student. It was when Onno moved to an English-speaking university in South Africa, that he experienced a major shift in his self-definition.

CB   Can you tell me a bit about what that was like. It sounds like you wanted to go for complete English, doing it all in English?

Onno   I think it was very hard, I think it was in some ways very traumatic, because I stood out. I came from one community where I was part of the dominant culture, and going to another where I was seen as part of the oppressing culture. And my language certainly was the one thing that most made me stand out. In other ways I could have been seen as anybody else there. I think it was because I was Afrikaans speaking that people certainly had a go at me for representing a culture even though I didn't feel myself necessarily (indistinct) views of that culture. I think it is very hard, very, very hard.

It was not Onno's whiteness as such, that became problematized in this different context; rather, his language identified him as the white oppressor. Afrikaans was viewed as the language of oppression, while English, despite its own colonial history, was a language with status, and one which offered opportunities in the wider world. Onno constructed the shift from seeing himself as a radical challenger to being defined as an oppressor as 'very traumatic'. Here slippage occurred, where grappling with the implications of his membership of a dominant group became conflated with occupying a 'traumatized' position of his own, and this is in striking contrast to Petiri's account. Being given a narrative as oppressor challenges personal constructions of moral and ethical personhood. Being defined by others as an oppressor had pushed Onno to define himself differently:

> I think it made it more difficult to see myself as an Afrikaner. I've never been able to do that.

Onno constructed himself through disidentification – as someone who had always positioned himself as 'outsider' in his community. He had totally immersed himself in English, as a way out of participating in the dominance of Afrikaans. He saw English as "opening doors" for him to learning and to broader worldviews, but also as leaving out aspects of himself.

> I think English is different for me, I think, English, I feel much more constrained I think in a way.

Onno's ideas about English had a powerful influence on his sense of himself as an English speaker, and he talked about being very organized by the status of English:

> I think maybe it's also going back to the way I grew up, that for me, English has always been better than Afrikaans in a way, or again I think it comes back to a political thing about Afrikaans being this oppressive language. [...] Afrikaans people, I think, is, would be talked about in the same way as Nazi people in Germany and I think, it leaves one with, a, I don't know, with shame in a way about who you are and where you come from.

Onno may have perceived speaking English as a way of disrupting his participation in the dominance of Afrikaans, but at the same time it constructed him as stigmatized. This is a similar process to the one Petiri experienced in which taking on the new language involves being defined, constructed as 'other' within it, although they were positioned very differently because of their racialization. Onno's different senses of himself in each of his languages encompassed tensions and contradictions. He experienced his Afrikaans-speaking self as richer and more expressive, but as a troubled and troubling identity. English offered opportunities but constrained him; and having been conceived as a way to distance himself from shame, it also constituted him as a guilty subject.

Xandra too had grown up monolingual, speaking Afrikaans throughout her university and professional training in South Africa. Her narrative was less explicitly interwoven with postcolonial discourse. In her 20s, Xandra had started to work in English in a culturally, racially and linguistically mixed work setting and she posited this as the point where she really first faced the inequalities in South Africa:

> I felt really ehm, uncertain of myself, ehm, unable to express, I found it very stressful, [...] struggling with thinking and using, trying to get by, and it was very stressful, [...] you know I felt I wanted to be seen as professional, ehm, I wanted to find, you know, find my own way of expressing myself, that I was defined by being Afrikaans and not being able to speak English very well. And, and just find, you know find that very limiting, yeah. [...] and I, I don't think I ever, ever felt really confident.

Xandra posited her relationship to English as a high status language and her struggle with her inarticulacy as impacting profoundly on her sense of self. This may have become entangled with, or even subsumed, the effort of taking on board the implications of her Afrikaans identity, her membership of an oppressive group, but like Onno, she had had to grapple with this and with the way Afrikaans was constructed by others:

> It represented also some really bad stuff, that Afrikaans in many ways was seen, was seen as evil, and the language of oppression and, you know, I remember, um, it still happens now when I think about it, the, the sadness for me that comes from that, and I think depending on the context, you know, I guess feeling saddened by it but also um, finding it, um, shameful in some way or, or um, embarrassing...

Afrikaans, her language for intimacy and emotional expressiveness, now carried contradictory and incompatible meanings, and, like Onno, she struggled with connotations of shame. Xandra too experienced English as a formal language, and herself as less emotionally expressive and humorous in it.

Living with multiplicity

Petiri had come to live in Britain, as a young adult, in order to avoid being drafted into the army to fight on the wrong (white Rhodesian government) side in the war of independence. It took him some years, and a repositioning through addressing racism at work, and at the prompting of his daughter, to begin to relearn the Shona language, which he now viewed as embedding the richness of a "culture that has been there for hundreds and thousands of years". Petiri also posited a relationship with a Shona colleague, who "presented as more African" than he, as significant in revaluing his language and culture, as it had highlighted their very different positionings.

Petiri had noticed that he currently presented himself differently in his two languages, and described this as follows in his interactions in Shona and with other Zimbabweans:

> There were certain things I wouldn't do because they would be seen as kind of pretentious so I become much more African, in terms of respect, the kind of deference [...] I'm more self-conscious. I know they can see through, they can see certain things which a Zimbabwean man wouldn't do, a Zimbabwean man wouldn't behave like that, so I tend to become more authentic, I think, an authentic Zimbabwean in the presence of a Zimbabwean, than in their absence. It's always there but I wasn't aware of it, until I observed myself, and thinking, I'm being different here. Even the whole thing about asserting myself, I wouldn't be as assertive because that's not the done thing. You have to be polite, and all those things, so yes, a huge impact.

Petiri drew on a concept of 'authenticity' here for his Shona identity, making a claim of an authentic, possibly even a core Shona identity, perhaps in relation to his past refutation of this. Interestingly 'self-consciousness', usually applied to an experience of performance, is here linked to authenticity. His use of "I know they can see through" may be referencing his past discomfort about his performance of English-ness. Petiri presented himself as someone who had come to view himself very differently over time with reference to colonisation.

Petiri had noted a shift in his attitudes and ideas in moving between his languages:

> Another thing is physical contact, you don't have physical contact with someone of the opposite sex. Whereas when I'm thinking in English I have no problems with physical contact, you know, that's fine. In a Zimbabwe context you wouldn't dream of it, it's not the done thing.

Petiri presented himself as being well aware of the way in which his sense of himself and his behaviour shifted dependent on his language and relationship context. He described himself both as "well rooted" and as "multiple", and noted the salience and helpfulness of the post-modern discourse of multiple subjectivity, the only research participant to make an explicit reference to this. Petiri described himself as using different aspects of himself to 'fit' with different contexts, posited as a survival strategy from childhood:

> I think the upbringing also prepared me for that, you know, things like when you're growing up in a politically divisive environment you know what conversations to have, when, and with whom, and you also learn that there are certain things which are not very wise to say. So I continue to do that, so again I can put on my Western hat and become like anyone else.

Petiri had developed a self-reflexive positioning, in which he used his multiplicity in explicit and at times in strategic ways.

Coming to live in Britain in her 20s, Xandra had been confronted even more starkly with being Afrikaans and with others' negative reactions to her identity. She described an African Caribbean woman telling her how difficult it was having to work with her. This incident had provoked Xandra into a re-examination of how others experienced her:

> I assume that this difference is something that I can be excited by, where often the other end of that is, is, is dangerous in some way, which, I mean a good example is, [...] that, I would say, "oh wow, somebody really different from me," and, she was thinking, "this is too dangerous, I'm not sure about this," and that I, that, that was not in my mind at all, so, so I really have to think more about differences, you know, that I can't just assume, they're that, what that means, and you know, that I should ask about that and I should be respectful.

Xandra presented herself as needing to develop a more self-reflexive stance in relation to her positioning as a white South African and her effect on others. She did not disidentify as Afrikaans, although she labelled the Afrikaans community as oppressive, and had to work to manage her identity as an oppressor, facing the "very painful side of being Afrikaans".

To summarize, these individuals drew differently on ideas about colonialism because of their different positionings. Petiri and Wasan both presented themselves as having participated in colonial processes, while Onno and Xandra struggled with their positioning as members of the colonizing oppressive group, with Onno disidentifying as an Afrikaner.

English was seen as a high status language by all of these individuals, but the meaning of becoming an English speaker varied considerably, because individuals were racialized differently. Petiri's performance as an English speaker mimicked English colonial attitudes, while Onno's stereotyped performance in English constrained him in a different way, as well as providing advantages. Petiri's journey to becoming a post-colonial subject, although a hazardous one, could be viewed as a heroic developmental account. He had relished the reclamation of his Shona identity and language, and the ability to position himself in various ways within English. Onno's account and his relationship to both his languages remained full of contradictions and tensions. Xandra focused more on internalized processes in her interview and her difficulties in encompassing the contradictory meanings of Afrikaans. A focus on her unequal relationship to English speakers may have left her own positioning as a member of a colonizing oppressive group under-explored, which she currently constructed herself as having to take more account of.

All of these individuals claimed a sense of multiplicity through language. Petiri and Wasan had to manage the unequal relationships between their first language and the dominant language as multilingual children. This impacted on their sense of themselves as speakers while they were growing up, but currently positioned themselves more easily in their multiplicity than Onno and Xandra, who had lived monolingually until they were young adults, and struggled with the ongoing contradictions and tensions in their identifications.

Growing up in bilingual/trilingual contexts

Several other research participants – Di-Yin, Ffionn and Thérèse – had grown up in contexts in which two or three languages were spoken (termed diglossic or triglossic), and in which everyone switched between languages. The meanings of different languages were constructed in relation to power relationships and the historical context.

Di-Yin grew up multilingually in China where it was common practice for individuals to switch between languages and dialects. Everyone learned Mandarin, the official spoken and written language of China. Di-Yin made few distinctions between her childhood languages and found it difficult to define one as her first, although she saw Mandarin as the most formal. At one point, when she had moved to Shanghai as a child, she had felt stigmatized because of her rural accent and had quickly adapted her accent.

Ffionn had grown up in Wales as a Welsh speaker in a bilingual community. The meaning of being a Welsh speaker for her had been constructed within the framework of the history of the struggle to maintain Welsh speaking and counter the dominance of English. A pride in Welsh speaking counteracted English constructions of Welsh-ness as inferior. For Ffionn, Welsh speaking had also acquired meanings of class, as it was the middle-class communities who most strongly supported Welsh education, while working-class communities had moved to sending their children to English schools. Meanings of language speaking were constructed locally within the community as well as in relation to historical traditions.

For Thérèse growing up in bilingual Belgium, the meanings of Flemish, her home and school language and of French, carried connotations of class and power differences, as well as of political struggles between the two language groups.

Thérèse   All the universities were in French and it was the high society language so in [P], the little, it was a little town, all the high society they spoke all French, the doctors and the lawyers, so there was also like a bit a resistance to speak Flemish, er speak French because of all the connections, political connections it had. My mother speaks French, and quite well.

CB   So it had other meanings, French, which had an impact on the way that you felt about it?

Thérèse   Yes, definitely when I go to Brussels, I would make a stand of not speaking French, because they are supposed to be bilingual, nobody's speaking Flemish. So I would resist, I would make a point not to speak French.

In these diglossic/triglossic contexts, children had participated with others in language speaking which embedded and enacted power relationships within their communities. The meanings of language speaking were constructed in relation to social and political struggles in which everyone participated. These accounts contrasted with those of children who had grown up speaking a minoritized language who presented accounts of managing the switch between languages on their own.

Growing up with a minoritized language

Angela, Konrad and Justine had been born in Britain; Quinlan and Wasan had moved to Britain and Venjamin to Israel when they were young children. They had all grown up in families speaking a minoritized language. This meant that they had had to manage the distinctions of language and culture between their private and public worlds.

Language as a marker of difference

Angela, a woman of Sicilian origin, grew up in a family embedded in an Italian community in Britain. She spoke four languages during her childhood because her parents spoke Albanian, Sicilian, and Italian. She had always considered herself different, because of language differences: Albanian in relation to Sicilian, Sicilian in relation to Italian, Italian in relation to English. She felt her sense of her difference had been confirmed when English parents had refused to allow their children to play with her. Angela recollected a longing to claim an English identity, a sense of belonging, which had not been successful. She constructed her childhood as lived in different languaged worlds:

> You became quite good at acting because you had to act in a different way in the English speaking community and then suddenly you're in the Sicilian community, to the point of dress, clothes, language, [...] the food, the food, yeah everything.

Angela saw herself as performing herself differently depending on the context. Her use of the pronoun 'you' rather than 'I' here, may be her positioning herself as an adult reflecting on her childhood self, or indicate having taken an observer position to herself as a child, linked to the idea of performance. Her sense of performance was interlinked with her construction of herself:

> And you live in no man's land, especially language-wise. You're neither one or the other. And it's quite, it's quite, and in childhood, it's quite an isolating factor in your life. Um. You have this dual personality. Only when you get older do you appreciate it, and you look back.

Angela constructed herself as doubled here, having a 'dual personality'. Although Angela switched between four languages as a child, she used a dual construction here, perhaps because this is a common conceptualization of the self, or because, in the context of English, the distinctions between Italian, Sicilian and Albanian were rendered irrelevant, making English–Other the most potent polarization. Angela did not refer to a primary language or cultural identity. Her identities were positioned in relation to each other. In such circumstances perhaps only an identity as an 'outsider', as different, could be experienced as 'authentic'.

For Venjamin, who had moved to live in Israel with his family at the age of 5, the status of his first language was extremely problematic. Although most people in Israel spoke several languages, Arabic was very negatively connoted and he saw this as profoundly affecting his growing up:

> I absorbed the norms of society which were that anything to do with the Arab world was inferior and to be ashamed of, so I was ashamed of the fact that I came from Iraq. I was ashamed of the fact that we spoke Arabic at home, and I had a huge inferiority complex about being an Oriental Jew, and um, I was also embarrassed about knowing Arabic, so I would never ever speak Arabic outside home and was embarrassed when my friends heard me speak Arabic to my parents....I could not say to them, "Please don't speak to me in Arabic in front of my friends." So I just felt embarrassed and ashamed.

Like Angela, Venjamin lived in a 'doubled' world, speaking his first language at home and Hebrew elsewhere, and he avoided speaking his stigmatized language in the public domain. He felt caught between loyalty to his parents and his wish to claim an identity as a dominant-language speaker. The way Venjamin's first language was constructed in the society impacted profoundly on his sense of himself and his identity. The meanings given to the language became the highest context marker for the construction of identity, overriding the commonality of a Jewish Israeli identity.

Quinlan, a young woman of Chinese origin, had moved to Britain at the age of five, and she also described herself as located in two very different cultures and languages, different worlds:

> Home was Cantonese and school was English. I used to think they were very, very separate.

Quinlan reported that she had not wanted to speak Cantonese outside of home, or in front of her friends when she was younger:

I really didn't like it. It wasn't as though I was ashamed of it, that wasn't it, but it was like different, and children don't like to be different.

As it had for Angela, speaking a minority language had acted as a marker of difference, and Quinlan tried to avoid this in the public domain. Quinlan's reference to children not liking to be different constructs this as a common positioning, and also works to avoid a connotation of feeling ashamed of her first language, unlike Venjamin's construction. Quinlan's languages and worlds, which were very different, were kept separate.

Konrad had been brought up in a Polish-speaking family in Britain and also had experienced himself as 'different':

I think I wanted to be like everybody else, but it [being Polish], I saw it as defining me as superior, ya, you know, superior equalling a way of surviving or, I also was different in that I always played with the girls and not the boys, but that's my sexuality, so there was that whole, it's difficult to disengage that from my Polish-ness, from, I think it all built up to actually, you know, it's left me with problems today feeling different.

As a child, Konrad had constructed his difference as superior, possibly in response to others' disqualification of him, but he recollected tensions between his wish to be the same as other children, and his claim to difference as special-ness. Konrad is a gay man and had challenged gendered rules at school, which also designated him as different. His differences of language/culture and of sexual orientation became conflated as markers for him, although it is unclear whether this was in relation to others' responses. A visit to Poland at the age of 15 had further confirmed for Konrad his sense of his difference, "I don't feel Polish at all in Poland", and left him feeling unable to find/claim a sense of belonging anywhere.

Konrad too had conceptualized his childhood as living in two different worlds of home and outside:

But I know that the world at home, the world behind the walls, you know, the inside of the house, was a world which was realer than the world outside. [...] And although it was an emotional world cause of the sort of family we were and my mother, it was more comfortable than being outside. And I was aware of having, I realise now that it was agoraphobia. I didn't like going, my mother used to send me to buy sugar or something. I used to stand by the front door and say to myself and I was quite little. "It's alright, you're just going out to buy sugar. Open the door and go out and buy sugar." And I had no way of telling my parents that that's what I felt, because by then I felt that it was something, you know, that they just wouldn't understand, and it was something wrong with me, and I had to pretend.

Konrad had not placed the difference between home and the public domain in the frame of differences of language and culture. He had viewed this difficulty of going out as personal failing, which he now labelled as agoraphobia. In response to a question about the place of his languages in relation to these experiences, Konrad developed the following explanation:

I was just trying to make a sort of language connection to that. [...] I mean by the end, I suppose the problem for me could have been, was I this English person, or was I this Polish person? [...] That's what I'm sort of forming in my mind at the moment. But that's why there was a part of me that I thought was totally separate from my parents. So it was like a part of me wasn't owned by me. [...] And I think this was, this was, I've never thought about this, but this whole issue was something to do with this English person and this Polish. [...] at the same time, I didn't want to be that boy they thought I was. So I think I had trouble in creating an identity that was, so I split my identities I suppose. [...] And I had to be the sort of English gentleman type and then the Polish person I was, was much more emotional and mixed up and puzzled really. The English part of me could be much more, 'this is who I am and this is how I behave', although that wasn't me. [...] That's really interesting. That's really useful for me.

A construction of a doubled identity, Polish and English, is drawn on here with Konrad's second language identity in English constructed as a performance, "that wasn't me", based on a stereotypical notion – 'an English gentleman type' (a very similar construction to the one adopted by Onno). Konrad also makes reference to "a part of me that was totally separate from my parents" – having a life in a different language from one's parents as a child created a marker of a separation, experienced internally as well as externally. Sante uses a similar construction in his autobiography: "At home he may be alone with his parents, but while they have an awesome power over his infant core, his growing English self is something they don't know and can't touch." (1998: 242). It is somewhat ambiguous what Konrad means by "a part of me that wasn't owned by me", but this may be referencing his 'performance' in English, and a distance which was conferred by his second language. What is also of significance here is that this exploration of the effects of living in two languages seems to have the effect of unsettling the ideas which he had previously constructed of personal difficulty.

Wasan had come with his family to live in Britain as a young child, and described considerable differences between home and outside home, both in his childhood and currently:

> I think it is the difference in the content, more depending on, the sort of conversations I would have at home are often quite different to outside conversations. So I think I would feel different in that way. [...] it's more of a sense of maybe having a different sense of identity in the different languages.

Wasan constructed himself as having a different identity in each of his languages, linked to different contexts. He conceptualized his Gujarati identity as constituted within his family in terms of his roles and responsibilities:

> Where I might connect more in Gujarati um would be through stories, (indistinct) a lot of the stories are very much about what you should be like, and as a son, what you should be like, and as the eldest son, so there are lots of, kind of, stories I remember as a child in Gujarati, all about duty to your parents and that kind of thing, so I think the emotional stuff in terms of looking after family and parents, then I think it would be more in Gujarati.

Wasan's construction of a 'doubled' world was one with substantial differences encoded in his languages. His account of himself in Gujarati encompassed very different values and attitudes from the ones he spoke about in English. These differences in his sense of himself in his different languages were reinforced through differences in clothes, food and behaviour in his different contexts.

Justine had grown up with a Dutch mother and American father, speaking Dutch and English at home in Britain. Because her family switched between these two languages, one of which was the dominant language, she did not construct the task of switching between languages and cultures as one which she managed on her own. However, speaking two languages at home did draw a distinction:

> Maybe it has also made for me a bigger difference for me between family life and other life.

This was, however, not such a major distinction as it was for those who felt that they moved between languages and cultures on their own. When asked how she defined herself, Justine replied:

> Euro-North American. When I fill in things, if they ask for, well now I have to get a bit sensible about it, and you have to think, when they ask for nationality, is it going to be compromising if I put down all three. Sometimes it's just easier to say right, when you're filling out your grant form, right I'm English, 'cause that will just cause, so it depends on context, much less problems.

Justine saw herself as having multiple identities, not easily officially validated, but lived easily enough within her family, and in her culturally, racially and linguistically diverse friendship group. She viewed growing up in London, with all its diversities, as key to the way in which she experienced her own multiplicities. Justine did not think her language speaking identified her as different, nor did she perceive any negative responses:

> I don't think I've ever had anything that's specifically to do with speaking another language but that's also because it's really not at all that obvious that I speak another language in England. I mean I'm white. You can't really tell. People occasionally say that I have a not quite English accent.

Justine saw her whiteness as protecting her from exclusionary responses by others; she is more easily and often assumed to be a 'native' than many of her racially diverse friendship group, and although her accent was occasionally queried, her other linguistic identity mainly remained invisible. This was in sharp contrast to the case of Quinlan, who, as a Chinese person, had experienced a continual questioning of her language speaking and her identity, because of how she was racialised on the basis of appearance.

Encountering a transforming context

Angela, who had described herself as struggling with issues of language and identity throughout her growing up, talked of a very different experience when she began to learn French.

> But I loved French, [. . .] I suddenly found a language, which was not English, not Italian. I didn't have to be one or the other, and it was my no-man's-land language, and I loved it.

French had provided Angela with a context that dissolved the polarizations she experienced between her languaged identities, and had provided some resolution to her discomfort with herself. We could say that speaking French had offered her an untroubled subject position, unlike the ones she experienced in her other languages. She saw this as highly significant in her choice of partner.

> Angela   And again, on reflection, there was a Frenchman who came along. Again, it was the no-man's-land syndrome, um, who and he took me on holiday to France and met his parents within the first three months, and I really felt I'd come home. [. . .] I really felt I'd come home, because they loved the fact that I was Italian, Sicilian. I wasn't English. And you know what the English and French are like. And the fact I wasn't, I knew I wasn't, I didn't feel Italian, and I felt I was in no man's land, and I had come home. And I felt totally at ease, with the language, the custom, the character. I could see through them. And, they had a mixture [. . .] Yes, because they had a mixture of the Italian exuberance and the British reserve, as well. They were a real, um they were a real dichotomy, ya.
>
> CB   So was it like two different sides of yourself also coming together?
>
> Angela   Meeting, yes, and I loved it. I really felt I'd come home.

Angela's husband's French family had valued her as an Italian, and she saw them as encompassing both Italian and British characteristics, which enabled her unproblematically to be multiply identified. This transformation of her sense of self, from polarized to validated as multiple, was experienced as profound, articulated through the trope of 'coming home' – coming home to herself.

Quinlan viewed growing up, becoming more mature, as the key to experiencing herself differently. She defined herself as being "half way in between" Chinese British and British Chinese. She posited her relationships with bilingual and bicultural friends as significant to her experience of herself.

> It has to really be somebody who has similar circumstances to me, maybe not necessarily English and Cantonese, but just someone who is bilingual or maybe more, who can sort of understand what, where I'm coming from (laugh), because some people just have no comprehension of what it's like to be able to speak two languages and understand two languages. [...] So yeah, people who can speak two languages. [...] we just talk about everything and then you feel like you're more yourself.

A multiracial multilingual friendship group provided a validating context, affirming her multiplicity and offering encompassing subject positions, and allowed her to express her different aspects of herself. Quinlan defined herself as multiple.

> When you come to think about it, you have to switch from being both, to being, to separating them all the time, depending on who you're with, what situation you're in.

Quinlan's sense of self shifted dependent on which context she was in, and she seemed very at ease with this multiplicity.

For Venjamin, moving to Britain as an adolescent had provided him with a different sense of himself:

> I think that I completely overcame this sense of shame about my culture and society as a result of living in England, so I um managed to achieve some detachment from this problem which was huge when I was a young child living in Israel. Here no one knew what Iraq was, or what Israel was, or what the differences were, and no one was aware of the snobbery of the Israelis, um, so I grew up here as a foreigner.

Britain provided Venjamin with a context, which rendered the tensions around his identity irrelevant and, through this, provided a sense of resolution. As the French language had for Angela, this offered what Bhabha (1994) would call a 'third space', a context that provided a reframing and a disruption of the polarization in his identifications. Although Venjamin experienced exoticization because of his racialized identity and ethnicity in Britain, this had much less impact.

When I asked how Venjamin currently defined himself, he said he considered himself to be "a rootless cosmopolitan" who felt completely 'at home' in Britain. Venjamin constructed himself as multiple, his use of the term "rootless cosmopolitan" both ironic and serious. What I did not realize at the time (and I assume he did) was that this phrase has been used, over the ages, to derogate Jews (Iyer 2000). As with many of the other research participants' Venjamin's conceptualization of 'home' challenged traditional notions of home as rootedness, and fits with Brah's (1996) conceptualization of a 'diaspora space', where transcultural identities are constructed.

In contrast to the others, Konrad's conception of himself as different and of his difference as problematic had endured over time and he was the only research participant who could see no advantages to living in two languages:

> I actually think that for me it's been a disadvantage cause it's split me in half. [...] Maybe if I was English with English parents, it wouldn't have built up to being such a problem.

Konrad considered his speaking several languages as troubling, and in his account this is positioned in relation to an ideal of an unproblematic monolingual monocultural subject. Konrad's experience highlights some of the challenges and difficulties of being bilingual when one's own differences engendered by one's languages remain unreconciled.

Konrad identified art as important to him in his life, and I attempted to explore its connection to his languages.

> That's beyond language and I really, it was terribly important to me. And that's when I felt really myself.

It seemed that doing art had provided Konrad with a different context, 'beyond language', not connected to either of his languages, and which could thereby be considered as offering him a less troubled positioning. Konrad's reference here to feeling 'really myself' when making art indicates a possible sense of unease in both his languages. His sense of being split may have been compounded because he experienced tensions within both his language identifications. Konrad told me that he had never had his sense of his multiplicity validated and I asked whether he had ideas of what might provide this:

> The only ideas I ever have are that I wish that when I was an adolescent or in my late teens I'd emigrated, I often, to somewhere like, totally foreign, where I would be a foreigner.

Konrad's proposal that becoming a foreigner could have been helpful indicated that it was not his sense of 'difference' which was the issue. His proposed solution is a context strikingly similar to that which Britain had provided for Venjamin – a place, a space which could render the sense of tensions and polarisation of identifications irrelevant.

To summarize, these adults who had been brought up in families speaking a minoritized language conceptualized this as having lived in a doubled world, separated by language difference. Individuals had to find ways to manage the distinctions of language and culture between home and the outside world and this was constructed as a task, on the whole, faced on their own. Speaking a minority language had been experienced as a marker of difference, and mainly been viewed as problematic and to be avoided in public. Claiming a dominant language identity as a child had rarely been experienced as successfully achieved. Individuals' racialization had impacted significantly on the meanings of their language speaking and their sense of themselves. However, those white individuals who had been troubled by how their language and culture defined them as different as children did not refer to their whiteness or the privileges it would have conferred.

Individuals had access to different resources with which to manage their transitions between their different languaged domains. Justine had discursive repertoires available in her family and community in London as she was growing up, with which to construct herself as multiple and to consider that her whiteness carried privileges, not so accessible some decades earlier to Konrad and Angela. Quinlan viewed her bilingual friendship group as providing resources which validated her multiplicity, as well as postulating her increasing maturity as important to the way she thought about herself. Angela had encountered a context, the French language, that had provided her with resources which offered her a different sense of herself. Venjamin too had experienced his move to Britain as resolving the tensions in his identifications. However, Konrad remained troubled both by his sense of outsiderness and his sense of being split, having never encountered resources which offered him a sense of validation.

Fleeing from one's country of origin

Two of the research participants, Cato and Renata, were forced to leave their countries of origin when they were young children with their families and moved to a new country. (Although Venjamin, who I discussed in the previous section, and his family had left Iraq alongside 100,000 Iraqi Jews in response to the backlash against Jews following the establishment of the state of Israel, he did not see this as having been made a refugee or even as a forced migration. This may be connected to the very different meaning given to arrival in Israel as a Jewish family, highlighting the importance of the receiving context to the meanings given to a move.) Like the research participants discussed in the previous section, Cato and Renata too had to manage the differences of language/culture between home and community. However, they also had to learn a new language in circumstances that involved sudden loss and violent upheaval. I examine the ways in which these individuals made sense of this traumatic disjuncture of experience and its effects on the meanings of language speaking, and on the way they experienced themselves.

The effect of inarticulacy

The process of being made refugees as young children has remained centrally significant in Cato and Renata's relationship to language and their experiences of themselves as speakers. Both addressed the effects of inarticulacy in their new language. Cato came to Britain with his mother, and following a stay in a refugee camp, he started at school where he began to learn English.

> I was quite an angry boy. I was a bit, I was fairly big for my age. But having come out of Hungary and tanks and all that stuff, I thought, talk about feeling I was a bit hard, I mean, I thought I was a bit hard, and these weedy English kids, what did they know. So, I was, I was like that, there was an arrogance, maybe not arrogance, but there was a kind of hardness. And I got into quite a lot of fights and I wasn't exactly a bully, but I was hard for a while. And it started to, it's funny actually, as, I do remember this, as I started to speak English more, I started to make friends, and make connections you know, and be able to sort of talk about myself and I suppose, a bit talking about vulnerabilities and stuff, so then, the kind of hard, tough, kind of "you can all piss off" sort of mentality that I had, started to, started to erode away. So actually, yeah, yes, I think I felt, I felt

more connected and sort of softer as I started to understand people and being able to speak.

Cato described presenting himself as a "hard" boy when he first went to school. A performance of toughness did not require much knowledge of the language, and in any case, may have been a welcome change from the sense of vulnerability and powerlessness involved in witnessing political violence and undergoing a total upheaval of his life, and indeed is a common positioning for boys who have undergone trauma to take, as others (cf Bentovim 1997) have commented. And a construction of toughness is generally given kudos by boys in schools (Frosh et al. 2002). Moving to articulacy in the new language was connoted as an ability to take up more complex positionings in his relationships.

Renata described becoming a refugee as "pretty traumatic really", a sudden unpredictable change in circumstances, from a comfortable middle-class life to a refugee camp, with the loss of all their possessions. She recalled being highly motivated to learn the new language:

I remember making some really stupid mistake and being laughed at, you know. I remember things like that, and later on in Germany I remember being made fun of because I made mistakes. I felt very isolated. [...] Very, very fast, I was fluent in writing and speaking.

Renata foregrounds experiences of humiliation as fuelling her push to articulacy in her new language. She linked her sense of inarticulacy at that time to her experience on moving into English in Britain as a young adult:

The absolute frustration and despair I felt over my, because I spoke English reasonably, but not as well. I remember locking myself in the bathroom and crying in desperation, I couldn't express myself. I couldn't stand my ground. I think something like that probably went on when I was a child.

Renata's account highlighted the perceived necessity of learning a language in order to survive in the context of school. The change of language intersected with all the other losses involved in this catastrophic change for Renata:

It wasn't just the language. It's very difficult to disentangle. [...] But I think the loss of language was also quite a big thing.

Of note here is Renata's use of the trope of 'loss of language' in relation to her difficulties in the new language. Hoffman (1989), whose auto-biography is centrally concerned with her move of country and language as a young adolescent, uses a similar construction:

> I have no interior language, and without it, interior images [...] I'm not filled with language anymore, and I have only a memory of fullness to anguish me with the knowledge that, in this dark and empty state, I don't really exist. (Hoffman 1989: 108)

What is conveyed by the notion of 'not having a language'? This trope draws on the construction and meaning of a first language – the unself-conscious relationship an individual has with their first language, a sense of being inside a language and language being inside one. A shift to a new language is experienced and constructed as placing an individual outside of the language, and the language outside of the individual. Feeling as if one does not have language also entails a loss of voice, "I couldn't stand my ground", and a disconnection from experience and a loss of self, "I don't really exist". Language no longer did what it was supposed to do, it could no longer be relied on. The relationship with language, once seamless, becomes disrupted. And Renata posited it as a major factor in her despair as a child.

> I think it probably did sort of dent my personality. I was a very confi-dent child in Hungary, and I was very shy and a rather depressive kind of child for a long time.

Cato and Renata's different narratives of becoming refugees, their different positionings in relation to a sense of powerlessness, and their relationship to language seem gendered. Renata's focus on becoming articulate and her presentation as shy, and Cato's 'hardness' and fighting, would have been brought forth in the context of boys' and girls' different emphases on ways to relate, with different pressures for articulacy.

Meanings of language and constructions of self

Cato related that he had experienced himself very differently in each of his languages as a child:

> I think the Hungarian actually connected me to that (2) how can I put it, a more kind of successful kind of identity really. And the kind of, it's not that speaking English connected me just in itself to

a different identity, but the lifestyle we had was very, very impoverished. We were really at the kind of bottom of the heap then, it was a dreadful time for my Mum. [. . .] It was an incredible struggle. And so I think the kind of lived reality was pretty impoverished here, and I think when we went into Hungarian, and actually I haven't seen it before in this way, I think when we spoke Hungarian, there was a time shift back to a time where it was very different, you know, and I was, things were Ok and reasonably easy, and I was going to do well at school. No question of any of that, and I think actually that was really helpful for me, in kind of not going under.

Cato drew on a concept of a doubled narrative of self – one in which each language became associated with a different sense of self, constructed in a different context. Cato here develops the idea that the narrative constructed in his first language had been protective, and that his first language had anchored him to his past self, in the context of considerable difficulties. This notion incorporates an idea that it would be difficult to preserve a different sense of oneself just within one language. A move to a different language created a disruption of meaning but also a preservation of it.

The meanings of his languages and of himself as a speaker had changed over time for Cato:

Things had been so kind of dreadful for us in this country that I started to kind of link Hungarian and the language with a lot of negative things, and things going dreadfully wrong.

The crossover of associations to his languages may have occurred when Cato became more successful in English, thus impacting on his relationship to Hungarian. Hungarian refugees came to be viewed negatively, and this, in turn, had its own impact on the meanings of the Hungarian language and identity for Cato and Renata. The meanings of language speaking are constructed locally, within family, as well as in wider social contexts. The impact of the dominant construction of his minority language became more influential for Cato over time.

Renata did not so much draw on a construction of doubleness in speaking about her childhood, but had thought of herself as an outsider:

When I was younger I always wanted to belong. When I was in Germany I had this really, I envied those of my friends who belonged.

This desire to claim a belonging echoed Angela and Konrad's constructions of childhood. As in the case of Konrad, a visit to her country of origin when a young woman impacted on Renata's sense of self. Although speaking Hungarian without an accent signified a sense of belonging, she experienced herself as 'different'.

> I went back, [...] which was very traumatic for me actually because that's when I really realised how non-Hungarian I was. [...] And how you know, because I came home and I had this family (indistinct) um you know family expected me to be Hungarian and I wasn't. I spoke the language but I wasn't spiritually Hungarian, I wasn't culturally Hungarian. I felt very much like a German and it clashed. [...] Um I fell back on (indistinct) it sort of confirmed my Germanness and my differentness. [...] I often wondered what kind of person I would have grown into if I had stayed in Hungary. I would have been a very different person. [...] It's a very traditional kind of society in a way and it struck me very forcefully how different it was from, you know, this was just after the 60s in Germany. I was very aware what kind of woman I would have had to grow into if I stayed there.

This visit, as it had for Konrad, confirmed her identity as 'outsider'. However, there is another construct of doubleness developed here, a lived identity and an imagined one, a hypothetical alternative identity, and a sense of contingency, that her sense of self was contextually determined. Cato's visit to his country of origin when he was an adult also had a considerable impact on his sense of self:

> When I went back to Hungary I did feel, there was a sense of coming home. [...] There was a big sense of that you know. I think it is bigger you know I mean if you don't choose to go. [...] Yeah, kind of looking around at, well again language and lots of other things are tied up. You look at people and they look more like me, facially and colouring, and you think, these would be the people I would have been, well, fantasies, I would have grown up with and getting married to or whatever.

Cato's return had acquired intensity because it was set in the context of his forced exile, and unlike Renata he did construct Hungary as 'home'. A sense of physiognomic and linguistic similarity and familiarity validated his Hungarian identity. His identity was constructed and confirmed relationally through similarity. Hearing one's first language previously used only with family in a wider context can engender a feeling of intimacy and belonging. This visit led to a re-evaluation of his identity, countering his experience of being disregarded as a Hungarian in Britain:

> In some ways I think it kind of brought the two, it helped me integrate the two bits of myself actually. Well I mean partly because [...] 'cause I still have these fantasies about it being something very, very different.

Cato constructs this visit as having had an impact on his positioning in each of his languages and cultures, but his account also demonstrates the influence of the non-evolution of the memories encoded in his first language, because of his separation from both the place and the language.

A transforming context

Britain, as her third country, had provided Renata with a context, following her initial experience of inarticulacy, in which she had developed a different and multiple sense of herself. Her description of Britain as "a bit of an in-between country", inclusive of aspects of both Hungary and Germany, mirrors Angela's description of French and France encompassing her different identifications. Renata's construction of herself as multiple, "reconciled with all my bits", seemed to accompany a reframing of being an 'outsider' as an advantage, a positioning which enabled her to think laterally.

One gets a further sense of the helpfulness of a third country, and its ability to offer a 'third space', from Cato's description of a visit to Canada where he had family:

> I mean I almost started to feel, god, I feel at home here, this is Canada. [...] it's such a kind of mixture, such a kind of hotchpotch of identities. [...] it's the kind of hybrid, they're in that kind of in-between space. [...] that kind of permission to be both identities. [...] And in a way, that's kind of I guess where I still feel, you know, I can't say I really feel Hungarian now, and I don't completely feel English either. [...] the stuff about Irish, Scottish and Welsh identities is that there is such a long, alright, alright, they're not quite English, British, but there are generations and generations of stories about how it is to be Irish here, and what it is to be English and Irish, and there aren't any stories about what it is to be Hungarian here so.

Cato encountered a context in which others presented themselves as having multiple identities, more easily lived, and which he had experienced as offering him some validation of his own sense of doubleness – something he had not experienced in Britain. As he lived in Britain, this encounter had not seemed to offer a lasting validation of a multiple identification. There were no canonical narratives in Britain he felt he could draw on in relation to his particular multiple identity. Of note is the way Cato refers to feeling 'at home' in the new context, which resonates with Angela's account of the way she felt like she had 'come home' in a French context, because of its ability to encompass her different identifications. 'Home' becomes constructed as a context of validation for those who have felt they did not belong or had been made homeless.

Cato's identity as a refugee, which encompassed a sense of loss and homelessness, remained central to his sense of self and endured over time:

> I mean you know this is maybe common to people, but I think maybe it's a bit stronger for me this thing, [...] this isn't really properly home either.

Renata conceptualized being a refugee rather differently:

> My life, you know, I suppose being a refugee you give up this idea that you can plan your life, you become more opportunistic, I think. You take opportunities when they offer them.

Renata used a construct of a stance, rather than of an identity as refugee, and had refigured an idea of home as the one she had made for her children, because then 'you become the home'.

To sum up, two research participants had fled their country of origin as young children, which involved a sudden and unpredictable loss of home and possessions. As a result, they had to learn a new language in a new country. Individuals had to make sense of a very difficult disruption in their childhood. There were gendered differences in the telling of these accounts, with Renata conveying most affect about this experience.

Their languages and identities were connoted negatively in their new country, and they struggled with this positioning. Renata placed the greatest emphasis on her push to gain articulacy in the new language, probably because of gendered peer expectations at the time. Working to claim dominant language identities was not necessarily successful.

Visits to their countries of origin had differential effects, leading Cato to positively re-evaluate his first language identity, and confirming Renata's second language identity.

Renata, like Venjamin, had moved to a third country which had offered her a changed sense of herself, seen as encompassing both her identifications, and validating her sense of multiplicity. This 'third space' (Bhabha 1994) enabled an altered engagement with various aspects of self. Renata had actively engaged in relearning her first language. Cato gave indications that another country would have provided something similar for him. Renata claimed a relatively untroubled multiple positioning, able to make use of her different perspectives. Cato's account contained a central motif of an ongoing sense of homelessness and unsettledness, possibly connected to not having found an ongoing context to provide him with a different sense of himself.

Concluding discussion

The research participants who had spoken several languages during their childhood had done so in very different circumstances, and I have explored the ways in which these different contexts impacted on their individual accounts. It is likely that children always experience learning a new language as a necessity, that they have no choice, and that they have little or no influence on the circumstances which demand this of them; however, these different contexts offered different resources and challenges.

Those individuals who had grown up in multilingual colonial contexts accounted for themselves by drawing on a postcolonial lens. The starkest difference in language speaking came from the different positionings of individuals and their languages in the hierarchies – the colonizers' children, Onno and Xandra, had stayed monolingual until their young adulthood, while Petiri had to learn the colonizers' language for his education which had been conflated with taking on colonizers' attitudes. A process of making this language his own, and reconnecting with Shona, his first language enabled Petiri to feel at ease with his multiplicity. For Xandra and Onno, coming to terms with their own and their language's positioning as oppressive was a more troubled process, carrying ongoing meanings of shame.

The circumstance of growing up in diglossic and triglossic contexts where switching between several languages were everyday practices meant that children participated in this with others. Language speaking both embedded and enacted power relationships. The meanings of language speaking were constructed in communities in relation to unequal relationships between languages, and in the context of social and political struggles, and this varied in different countries. In China, for example, Di-Yin drew fewer distinctions between her languages, while for Ffionn and Thérèse, there were current as well as historical distinctions drawn.

Childhoods speaking a minority language were mainly constructed as living in a doubled world, with home and the outside world differentiated through language. Speaking a minority language was signified as a marker of difference, and experienced as problematic in the context where an individual's claims to an identity as a dominant speaker had been refused. Individuals' racialization impacted differentially on the meanings of language speaking and on their identity claims, and I consider this further in Chapter 5. These individuals had been preoccupied with the differences in their contexts and their different sense of themselves, as well as their experiences of themselves as 'different'. The two individuals who had experienced a sudden unpredictable loss of home as children and had to learn a new language in a new country had also struggled with being positioned as outsiders or inferior and with their first language signifying their difference. However, they had the added task of making sense of a traumatic disruption and loss. Articulacy in the new language was seen as a way to survive but a sense of being am outsider was enduring.

Encountering a context which had resolved individuals' sense of their polarized identifications or validated their sense of their multiplicity was identified as crucial to developing a changed sense of self, and the lack of such a context seemed to have left Konrad troubled by his sense of his difference. Important aspects of these narratives were the external demands individuals had experienced and the way others had constructed them, and how this was mediated differently for individuals.

All of these individuals had constructed themselves as doubled or multiple in some way. Research participants drew on the notion of living in a doubled world, different languaged worlds of home and the outside world, in which they experienced themselves differently. Several individuals posited this sense of doubleness as problematic for them as children because it positioned them as different from others in every context. When their claims as dominant language speakers had been refused, these individuals had constructed themselves as outsiders. Individuals' sense of their doubleness had been structured through the unequal relationship between their languages and through processes of othering. Although several individuals struggled with ongoing tensions in their identifications, most of those whose sense of doubleness had been problematic during their growing up had found a context through which they had come to experience themselves differently. These contexts seem to have provided relational and discursive resources through which individuals could claim, make connections and use their multiplicities differently.

4
Adulthoods in Several Languages: Constructions of Self and of Language

Eighteen of the 24 research participants had moved countries and changed languages, in a variety of circumstances, in their adolescence or adulthood. For several individuals, this move had been their second change of language and/or country. Many of these individuals had moved for education or work opportunities, constructed as choice, while some had moved because of difficult circumstances – for example, escaping occupation or war. A few individuals had found themselves unable to return to their countries of origin for political reasons. In this chapter I examine the meanings given to these changes of language and context, and how individuals constructed themselves in relation to these.

Constructing oneself anew

A number of individuals now constructed their move as young adults as having enabled them to leave behind difficulties – although this had not necessarily been an explicit motivation at the time. Estelle, who had come to Britain as a young adult, now viewed this as a strategy to change:

> Estelle Because I think that for me, leaving France was wanting to leave a bit of my life behind. There was a part of me really who wanted to start again.
> CB Do you think the English helped with that?
> Estelle Yes, most definitely.

Saskia also came to Britain in early adulthood and thought this had enabled her to change:

It was one of the attractions at the time – speaking a different language and living in a different country allows you to be a different person.

Ursula too, who moved to Britain as a young adult, constructed this as enabling her to develop in ways that had not been possible previously. She described her childhood as brutal, because her mother had severely physically abused her, and she herself had been defined as incompetent and to blame. She had come to see that living in English had allowed her to take a different position:

> Because I know I am different from what I used to, how I used to be. [...] I am, (2) I don't know, it seems so odd, but it is very much related to me being me, and me being a person who can speak. I think that was it, because as a Dane, I could never speak. I think that's what it is.

Ursula draws on the metaphor of 'finding a voice' in her second language, in describing the way in which she now considered that her move had changed her. By disrupting the meanings established in her first language and relationship context, she had been able to construct herself very differently in a new language:

> I did all the development work in English. I mean I did everything in English, because I completely disconnected myself.

As a disconnection from relationships also seems to be significant, what can be said about the place of language in this process from these accounts? Estelle had found that English enabled her to express herself differently from the way she had been able to do so in French:

> Mmm, I think sometimes it's easier for me to speak English about (2) I always remember that thing where, you know, when I started speaking English I could swear. (laughs) I could say really terrible words.

Speaking a new language had been experienced by Estelle as releasing her from constraints which influenced her in French. Henka also viewed the language difference as offering her the opportunity to be different:

> I would go further, I might be more intimate in certain things in English, because they would feel so uncomfortable. It's a foreign

language. [...] it's kind of artificial. In Polish it would be very disclosing. [...] in English, it is this artificialness that the, the, the, that I've learned the meaning of the word, that gives me, you know, more of eh, um, gives me more courage to use it. I'm not really detached from it, emotionally, but in a way I am. And as if, in Polish language I grew up with those words, they got, you know, like a flesh and body and soul meaning, in a way, you know so, not just to me but all the other eh, Poles, and in English it's a way of communicating, whichever way I look at it.

The new language, English, is experienced as having enabled Henka to take more risks than she does in her first language, because it carried different meanings for her, and, like Estelle, this meant she could bypass her own constraints. This led to an interesting paradox in which because English words carried less emotional weight for Henka, she risked using them more in her relationship, which had the effect of creating more intimacy than she had found herself able to do in her first language. In a sense we can say that Henka performs intimacy in a new language more easily because of the distance which English gives her from the experience, but this in itself constitutes a more intimate relationship.

For Saskia, the difference the new language conferred was related to others' responses to her as an English speaker. She recounted that people made assumptions about her being English "middle-class" and all that entailed, because of the sort of English she spoke. This had opened up a space because these were different assumptions from those made about her in Germany, and had been discomfiting because it did not tally with her experience of herself:

> I think that's how I learned I could be someone different. It meant that you couldn't make assumptions about me in the same way as you could about somebody brought up here.

For Saskia the new language and context allowed an escape from family and cultural assumptions and constraints, through the 'permission' of the new audience, which enabled her to become different.

These individuals had constructed their move into a different language and context as enabling them to change. They had lived the idea that "you can move and start again, begin a new life". These moves encompassed a change of place as well as language, but individuals designated language as crucial to the process of experiencing themselves differently.

Learning to live in a different language had been experienced as a free-dom from constraints, individual, familial and/or cultural, and had allowed them to develop alternative narratives of self. Away from familiar ways of being, doing and talking, individuals drew on new linguistic practices, and constructed themselves anew. They saw themselves as engaged in a 'project of identity' (Connell 1987) – a notion that they could explicitly choose how to live themselves.

Inarticulacy

Effects of being rendered inarticulate in a new language had had profound effects on adults' sense of themselves – as it had, indeed, for children who had moved into a new language. For adults who came to Britain this inarticulacy intersected with their racialization and positioning to impact on their sense of themselves as English speakers. Naadir posited acquiring fluency as crucial to his ability to challenge stereotyping and racism:

> If you don't know the language you can't survive, in any aspect, in every aspect. [...] First of all the most important thing is self-confidence, you have confidence in yourself to talk, to argue, to ask for your rights, to er, speak of your mind. So I felt definitely different, I felt human.

A sense of fluency provided linguistic resources to challenge racism effectively, and, recursively, also gave the speaker the confidence to use it in this way. Privileging fluency of language in a context of discrimin-ation and racism, Naadir had become an interpreter for others. Similarly Maria's push to become fluent when she entered a school in the United States as an adolescent from South America, and her refusal to have concessions made for her as a second-language speaker, which she equated with being treated as a second-class citizen, enabled her to challenge a teacher about the school's discrimination against the Spanish speakers:

> I remember saying to her, "do you know I actually am better than you because you only speak one language and I speak two. So I've got more right to be here than you." [...] That somehow there would be something that I would have to engage through life, to prove that something that was seen as a disadvantage could actually be an advantage.

A confidence in her fluency in both languages allowed Maria to position herself to challenge negative discourses both about bilingualism and about Hispanic speakers.

There were other positions taken about inarticulacy in a new language. Henka connoted this as useful to her relationship.

> But then I thought, perhaps it's got its good sides, because where you cannot communicate you do not make mistakes, the limitation makes life easier, you might. [...] If you go for really necessary things, and vocabulary, and the explanation of solving of a, existing problems that in front, that are in front of you, and happening today or tomorrow, and with, with your limited language, or you just develop the language for that purpose. You solve the problem, you do not think too far, too much, and you do not go into analysing people's characters and feelings too deeply, because you, you haven't got the language, oh yes, you know. Sometimes not being able to communicate everything, I think it's got its good sides to it. [...] Not, not, that I don't feel limited at all, I'm just, I just feel happy that there are certain things that I do not analyse. I try, I do not try to foresee, or you know, just think about it even theoretically, because it can make your life complicated.

Henka privileges the focusing on essentials in her communications, which her non-fluency compels her to do, and posits this as enabling her to conduct her relationships in more helpful ways. Iyer (2000) has made a similar argument about the advantages of inarticulacy; he constructs his non-fluency in the language he speaks with his Japanese partner as protecting him from playing destructive word games in his relationship. Here there is a notion that fluency in language allows its use for strategic purposes, to conceal, complicate and injure, which a struggle to express oneself in a new language subverts.

Performance

Those who had moved countries as young adults or older described the processes involved in their learning a new language, something which those who had learned their languages as children could not comment on so easily. The experience of disruption of a move to a new linguistic context involved a loss of the taken-for-granted, and a disruption of meaning. Stripped of the familiar, of 'doxic' experience (Bourdieu 1991), individuals had to do something new, and in so doing, they were made aware of processes of constructing themselves through their interactions with others, processes that were invisible and had become naturalised in their first languages.

Ihsan described it as a process of observation and imitation:

> The best way I can put it, it was very exciting, number one, incredible exciting, sort of you never got tired of it because there was always something new to discover and go through and sometimes you get tired because you felt you were acting and pretending and such like, that's how I felt. [...] Yeah, English person, I am very good at it and end up having same sort of gestures and hand movements, and like always sort of monitored people in this.

At one level this description tallies with those of the processes which young infants use in entering into language, observing and mirroring those with whom they are in 'conversation'. Ihsan connoted learning English as pretending to be an English speaker, and all that this entailed, including the imitation of a physical style of speaking. This process meant trying out words, which "existed in other people's mouths" as Bakhtin (1981: 294) put it, and embodying them. This description draws on a performance metaphor and refers to an agentic construction of identity with Ihsan constructing himself as learning to perform himself in English, trying out an English identity. This has some similarities to Petiri's description of his imitation of English colonialists, described earlier. Lena described a similar process, learning through trying to be like other speakers.

> It's probably just one of my biases and prejudices. I think I'm more polite and kind of (indistinct) careful in doing things and relating to people. [...] And I suppose I try to be like the English.

Lena reported that she felt unsure of how to be an English speaker and was concerned that she might transgress rules or challenge values, and she therefore relied on stereotypes, "my biases and prejudices" of Englishness. Onno had also described himself as constructing himself as a speaker through rather stereotypical ideas of Englishness:

> I think it's about my sort of preconceived ideas about English people, and that they aren't expressive and they are much more sort of aloof or a bit stuck up and that kind of thing. And I know that those

things are stereotypes but I think maybe it's also going back to the way I grew up.

Individuals in these accounts are explicit about labelling the ideas they had about speakers as stereotypes, positioning themselves as well aware of these limitations. This points to the challenges of learning a new language and a culture – both Ihsan and Lena described initially watching television or reading about British culture in the hope of trying to get a sense of what might be culturally significant. In Bakhtinian terms, individuals attempt to position themselves in the new language, by speaking in clichés, using the 'social' of the language, and viewing the language as 'monologic' rather than 'heteroglossic' (Bakhtin 1986). These research participants are presenting themselves as individuals who know that they have done/are doing this, that their performance is almost a kind of parody, and that such stereotyping is unhelpful.

Other research participants drew on this metaphor of performing themselves in relation to each of their languages. Di-Yin described presenting herself differently in her different languages:

Usually I appear much more modest when I speak Chinese as well, so um, to be less conspicuous, I will be more modest than I usually am. In that case, then maybe, being modest also means, erase all my Western manner, [...] but on the other hand, when I speak English, my Chinese manner is easily recognised. It is very difficult for me to erase my Chinese, I do have some residual Chinese manner, especially, um, being, um sometimes I, you know, like in this professional role, you need to be a little more aggressive, especially my world is filled mostly with men, and I find I need to make an effort to be aggressive.

These ideas of 'performance' relate to ways in which Di-Yin's English-language identity had impacted on her Chinese identity, something which may only have been highlighted in a Chinese context. No longer did she use any of her languages unselfconsciously – she had to 'work' to perform herself in both her languages.

Di-Yin thought English had enabled her to 'perform' aggressiveness which was not considered permissible in Chinese culture:

Yes speaking English helps me be more aggressive.

Di-Yin was explicit about the ways in which she could 'do' emotion in English in ways she could not in her Chinese languages. This description concerns the ways in which different languages offer, allow or compel different kinds of expressions, of performance, which in turn have an effect on the way in which the speaker comes to think about themselves.

The repetitions of these performances based on imitations of others became constitutive of the speaker. Hoffman expresses this in her autobiography: "This language is beginning to invent another me" (1989: 121). Individuals both claimed agency in how they positioned themselves in the new language and culture and came to recognize that the new language was constituting them as a different kind of speaker. Researchers analysing discursive practices within one language have drawn attention to how individuals use others' speech for rhetorical purposes in their construction of their accounts and of themselves (cf Fairclough 1992; Maybin 1998, 1999, 2001b). Such practices were made explicit on entering a new language where individuals were acutely aware that they were borrowing others' words.

A sense of performance was positioned in relation to the idea of 'authenticity' in accounts. Renata addressed this in relation to the differences in her sense of self in each of her languages:

> And for a long time I suppose I felt more genuine when I was in Germany than when I was in England. Then I felt I was slightly less genuine, as if it was not quite me. I don't have that sense anymore.

For research participants, the sense that they were performing themselves, raised an ideological dilemma. It did not fit well with the claim of 'authenticity' that is so important to intersubjective relationships – what Habermas viewed as one of the crucial validity claims made in communication (Donovan 2001) – nor in their relationship with themselves.

Performance calls up the idea of individuals taking up a series of roles, or of explicitly managing their self-presentation, as Goffman (1959) proposed. But of particular interest in the use of this metaphor is its overlap with Butler's (1990) work on gender as performance. Butler's thesis is that gender identity is a set of performances, that gender is an identity constituted and signified through a regulated process of repetition. Because, on the whole, individuals live their gendered identities as if they were substantive, Butler's argument is that coming to realize there is nothing behind the performance opens opportunities for living gender in a different way; indeed, this is precisely where she locates agency. Coming to recognize that one performs a linguistic identity may have similar impact. However, unlike Butler (1990), who argued that there is nothing behind the performance, research participants privileged a sense of authenticity.

Coming to own a language

Individuals also made reference to a shift in their relationship to their second/subsequent language. This was typified by the descriptions of Ihsan and Lena of a change in their sense of themselves in the new language over time. Ihsan had constructed this as giving up his 'performance':

> After sort of one year I decided not to do that any more. [...] About a year yeah, and after it was stupid, I felt, that's not me, you know, why am I doing this, be yourself and try to be yourself, bring your own character in and carry on, so that's what I did. [...] I just got tired, something, actually I think what it was, I got tired in my mind I think, mentally I got tired of it, and gradually I said, I can't bear it, so let's stop.

The idea of 'being yourself' is significant here, with connotations that ways of speaking and living in the second language had not felt genuine, that the performance was inauthentic. Lena too made reference to being less constrained in her attempts to be English, after getting 'permission' from a friend just to be 'herself'. But what does being yourself in a new language and culture mean? Individuals noted a different relationship to the language, and to themselves in the language. Markers of fluency had been important – starting to dream in English, others no longer translated for themselves, their inner language shifted into the new language. The performance became transformed into something experienced as 'natural'.

However, learning to trust the language and themselves in the language was not always an easy process.

> Lena   I just, for a long time, and probably still sometimes now, I feel as if I'm thinking firstly, and not necessarily always interpreting but sort of searching for the words that might be appropriate to ask a question or connect with a person.
>
> CB   So you would be thinking in Serbo-Croat?
>
> Lena   Yes yes.
>
> CB   And then you'd be translating.
>
> Lena   Yes yes.

CB   And you still do that?

Lena   Sometimes. But not all the time I would say. It's happening automatically sometimes but I suppose it's because I still don't see myself as fluent enough, or not really being in the language.

Lena's fluency in English also fluctuated depending on which of her languages she had been speaking most. But belief in one's fluency may also powerfully impact on the way one positions oneself in language.

For an individual to come to feel that they 'owned' the language was sometimes impossible. Derrida (1998) writes of French, his only language, as not being his language, and of the deprivation of never learning Arabic and Berber because of his colonial education in Algeria. Individuals' connection to language and positioning in it is crucially linked to the meanings given to languages.

'Performing a linguistic identity' was a relational process which relied on others' responses. However, being accepted as an 'owner' of the language also involved complexities, as Saskia, for example, recounted:

I speak English with hardly any accent, in a way, that isn't natural. I went through a phase when I wish [...] I wish I could develop an accent [...] I am a good mimic, but I wonder whether it has something to do with identity – I was not particularly happy as an adolescent – early adolescent – but there's nothing unusual about that.

This account is concerned with a 'performance' which is too convincing, for the self or for others, or both. This is entangled with an idea that one might be 'hiding' in a second language, as Kaplan (1994) put it in relation to her entry into French, for some troubling reason; that constructing oneself differently in a new language indicates something unresolved. On another level, the experience of being able to 'pass' as a native speaker, is double-edged, with its advantages, as well as its sense of duplicity.

A sense of doubleness

The adults who had moved to live in another language all experienced themselves differently in their different languages, as those in childhood had. Many of these individuals drew on constructs of doubleness in their accounts, and I examine these usages and other constructions of self below.

One interpretative repertoire drawn on by research participants to construct themselves as doubled was that of a core identity. Di-Yin, who had lived in China until the age of 19, saw her English and Chinese languages as encompassing different and separate worlds, and defined herself as dual, with a Chinese 'core'.

> I'm not very religious, but uh (2), maybe it's quite English, because uh being not religious and doing science is part of a religion, and science is a very Western, so spiritually um (1) I have this romantic idea which is quite English. On the other hand a lot of um, spiritual, a lot of the life principles, like the goal of life, you know, what I'm after, is (2) was formed from my Chinese background. [...] But I see my difference in that the root is not English, something I formed long before the English speaking days (laugh).

Di-Yin posits a core identity as her first language identity, conceptualized as informed by the most significant values and attitudes. This conceptualization draws on the idea of the importance of early years for the development of personhood. Positioned in relation to a core, the foundation, the second-language identity becomes constructed as a layer, an addition, and for Di-Yin constructed in relation to her working life which has been entirely in English.

The construct of a core identity drawn on by individuals with its implication of singularity and cohesion may itself create tensions for individuals attempting to straddle differences of language and experience, of time periods and of place. Saskia, for example, described this as follows:

> They're different bits of my life, the first in German, second half here. [...] It was the difference between being there and here, difficult when I went back to visit. [...] I'd make an effort to hold things together, the core is the same, it's me, it probably (2) but by itself it created some tension within me, and I suppose then in relation to others.

These tensions relate to perceived demands, both internal and external, or longings for coherence in the face of discontinuities. Maria asked me at the end of the interview for feedback concerning her account:

> I don't know whether it's too incoherent. I would like feedback at some point about whether I do have a coherent story about these experiences.

Individuals' accounts are told in relation to dominant discourses of coherence and of singular core identities which offer these individuals who have lived lives with discontinuities of language and culture unsatisfactory and even troubling positions.

Some individuals who had moved countries constructed themselves as having different identities, separated by time and place. So, for example, Estelle described this chronological separateness as follows:

> I've lived half my life in both countries now, so (.) and I'm just thinking that I've lived a child's life in France and an adult's life in England. I've never had a job in France. I've never worked in France, and sometimes I feel really, and I have a whole of lot of experiences I've never had in France and sometimes I feel I haven't got a language for it because I haven't lived it.

Here the conceptualization of the differences between languaged identities is one of lifecycle stage. The experience that one's first language has not evolved poses challenges for the individual's relationship to the language, as well as rendering the interface between different senses of self in each language problematic. Ihsan, who came to Britain as a young adult, conceptualized this in a similar way.

> So you have that little amount of language and then you come out and then you go to another culture, another language, so you leave whatever you left behind, so whatever you go back to, quoting, this, it's that way. I'll tell you about capsule, time capsule, it's there, that's the time capsule. [...] And somebody actually did tell me that, I speak with them in Farsi and they said to me, "you sound like a young man."

The concept of a 'time capsule' delineated a distinct separation between his different languages and languaged periods of his life. And does Ihsan also feel, as well as sound like, a young man when speaking his first language? If so, the non-evolution of the first language could be said to be experienced, or constructed as encapsulating the non-evolution of the first languaged identity – or at least as making it difficult to update it. For Gustav, like Ihsan, this only became apparent when he had contact with his first language again; for Gustav, this was after thirteen years in exile on his return to his country of origin:

> Your memory cannot evolve. Your memory is stuck and so I had my kind of, the memory of everything was stuck, yet everything

shifted. Everything shifted sidewise. [...] The language when you listen to the radio, first time I couldn't believe they are serious. It sounded to me very kind of artificial as if they were piss taking, it was like Monty Python-ish way and it took a very long time, but it is so and it always has been, but suddenly it sounded very strange to me.

There is variation in the experience of a reconnection with one's first language. For Gustav his first language sounded 'artificial', and he uses a very English metaphor to construct his experience of it. This contrasts with the accounts of other research participants, such as Cato, who experienced an emotional connection and sense of familiarity on hearing their first language. The move of country and language is constructed as a disconnection on several levels, which was not always open to be easily reworked or reconnected. The relationship with the first language is interrupted and the narrative of self constructed in the first language disrupted, as is the process of the ongoing reconstruction of memory, which relies on the interchange between past, present and future. Ursula, who had come to Britain in her early 20s, used a construction of different languaged identities, separated by time and place.

But all the understanding that I had gained in English, I hadn't transferred to the Danish me at all. That was still the, the trouble-some teenager locked away into a world of her own there.

Notions of language which did not evolve are interlinked with those of identities that did not evolve, which became fixed. Living in a new language was considered as not impacting on a first language identity. Ursula identified a current preoccupation with attempting to find ways to connect the different periods of her life and senses of herself.

In the writing of his autobiography, Sante places language difference as central to this problem of finding interconnections:

In order to speak of my childhood I have to translate. It is as if I were writing about someone else. The words don't fit, because they are in English, and languages are not equivalent one to another. [...] It's not that the boy couldn't understand those phrases. It is that in order to do so, he would have to translate, and that would mean engaging an electrical circuit in his brain, bypassing his heart. (1998: 239)

This emphasis on the place of the difficulties of translation also constructs the loss of the past in a different language as the loss of emotional meaning. Such constructions are positioned in relation to an idea that connection to the past and the evolution of memory is straightforward within one language. The loss of language interlinked with the loss of the past heightens the poignancy and sense of irretrievability.

A different type of construction of doubleness was the one of an alternative imagined identity, a kind of shadow identity in relation to the lived self. As noted in Chapter 3, when Renata visited her country of origin she became aware of the person she might have become in her first language, constituted through a different language encoding different values and attitudes. The past self, a different self is imagined into the present. Hoffman uses such a construct of doubleness, of the hypothetical other self, in relation to a description of writing her diary in English in her autobiography:

> The diary is an earnest attempt to create a part of my persona that I imagine I would have grown into in Polish. In the solitude of this most private act, I write, in my public language in order to update what might have been my other self. (1989: 121)

The language/culture differences make very explicit the different ways an individual could have developed and emphasizes the contingency of the construction of personhood on linguistic and cultural contexts. This awareness of the sense of contingency was significant to many of these individuals and I will come back to this in the next chapter.

The differences between the identities which individuals constructed in each of their languages varied depending on the different conceptualizations of subjectivity embedded in individuals' languages. Di-Yin described concepts of identity, emphasizing role and relationship laid down in cultural sayings in her first language, different from English.

> The Chinese concepts often relate to things, a lot of proverbs, you know, a lot of um things about what you should be when you're thirty years old.

Some individuals straddled very different conceptualizations of personhood and different subject positions in each language.

With the sense of a different identity in each of their languages, individuals talked of being compelled to leave out aspects of themselves in each language. Renata spoke of this:

> You're, what you are, doesn't entirely overlap. When I was speaking German I was a slightly different person than when I was speaking English. I had a very strong sense of that for quite a long time. [...] I had the sense that there were certain things about myself in English I couldn't communicate to my friends in Germany and vice versa, when I came here, there were bits that I felt were missing.

"Bits missing" became acutely experienced because of the differences of language as well as of context – relationships and place. Sante too described this as an issue in relation to his sense of self:

> I suppose I am never completely present in any given moment, since different aspects of myself are contained in different rooms of language, and a complicated apparatus of airlocks prevents the doors being flung open all at once. (1998: 260)

Although individuals connoted having several languages as meaning they always left aspects of themselves out in each language, and as problematic, it was also seen as having advantages, in enabling individuals to present themselves ambiguously and partially and make use of this in strategic ways.

What can we make of this variety of use of a doubled identity construct? For these individuals, it is as if each language acts as a 'strange attractor' for identity, to borrow a metaphor from chaos theory – each language, a set that collects trajectories and processes (Tsonis 1992). Each language acts as a context which draws a distinction for the individual in their sense of themselves. Individuals referred more explicitly to a sense of their doubleness than other multiplicities, drawing on a notion of an inner and outer self, a doubled world or different time periods. The construction of an inner and outer doubled self (Erikson 1968) offers a less pathologizing account than that of splitting or of schizophrenia, which were initially drawn on professionally to problematize bilingualism. I return later to the question of what the construct of a doubled identity accomplishes.

Research participants also referred to themselves as multiple and as having broad identifications – "belonging to a broader world". These constructions of self were often related to a sense of place, as much as of language, connected to feelings of no longer belonging anywhere, or belonging everywhere, following a move of country. Maria drew on this idea:

I think it gives you a position of a kind of citizen of the world really.

The ways in which individuals drew on constructions of self and their ease with the multiplicity which their languages engendered were linked with their access to resources. Those who had lived childhoods in several languages seemed to have had less access to discourses or contexts at that time to make sense of or validate their multiplicity than adults did.

To sum up, research participants drew on a range of constructs of self in their accounts in relation to their experienced differences in each of their languages. In the accounts of childhood, individuals drew on a construct of doubleness linked to living in a doubled world and constructed themselves as outsiders. Adults drew on a range of versions of doubleness, referring to ideas of 'core' identity signified as first-language identities, 'performing' an identity in relation to learning to live in a new language, and 'authenticity' in a first language, and in a subsequent language when they had come to 'own' it. Another construction in use was that of a 'frozen' identity in an earlier time period and different place, and of a first language which had not evolved.

The implications of versioning the self through these different con-structions of doubleness were various. Doubleness implied challenges of interconnection. Doubleness entailed a sense of contingency, a shift of subjectivity in language. Constructs of doubleness involved a sense of partiality, viewed as troubling as well as strategically advantageous.

Constructions of self also functioned as personal and political iden-tity claims. Claims of authenticity and of a core identity were made in particular in response to disqualifications. Constructions of self were sometimes connected to place, and a sense of 'home', while others questioned the idea that identities were defined in such ways, holding identifications across countries as well as across languages.

Perhaps most striking was the fact that few individuals drew consist-ently on postmodern notions of subjectivity – of their identities as mul-tiple, fragmentary and constantly in flux.

Constructions of language

All of the research participants drew distinctions about themselves as speakers of their different languages. In this section, I examine how their constructions of themselves were interlinked with the ways in which they connoted their different languages. I consider how the meanings of individuals' languages were constructed, locally and in the wider context, as well as the ways in which individuals drew on conventions to speak about their languages.

First languages became significant in the context of another language, and their meanings were mediated through the circumstances of learning the new language. In other words, languages are constructed in relation to each other.

But how were first languages signified, what were they seen as accomplishing? First languages were signified through their prosodic elements, their sounds and rhythms, ebbs and flows of interchanges, their music, evocative of associations interwoven with the physical and emotional environment of childhood. This relationship to the sounds of a language is drawn attention to in its absence, in the context of living in another language. A common distinction, which individuals drew between their languages, was related to emotional expressiveness, with first languages mostly connoted as the language for intimacy. This meaning was constructed in the context of other languages, where it came both to signify and engender closeness. Ffionn saw Welsh as her "security blanket" in an English-language context.

An individual could also have a different relationship with two languages learned together from birth, as Justine had, as both her Dutch mother and American father spoke both languages during her growing up.

CB OK so just to think about then learning Dutch and English together. Did you or do you have a different relationship to English and to Dutch?

Justine I do. Dutch is very much the language of my family and it's the language that we will argue in if we are in public in England, but it's the language of the most important people in my life really, because my grandparents were definitely so important to me and that's the language I spoke with them. So it is a very comforting language because it's a very emotional one cos lots of love in the language, but also when you get pissed off with people, (laughs) that's the one you switch into as well but not the kind of really obscene getting angry, but just saying that's enough.

Languages gained their meanings through relationships and the domains in which they were used. Dutch was positioned as a private language in the context of English being the dominant public language.

Related to the connotation of first languages for emotional expressiveness, was its signification as the language of authenticity. For example, this was drawn on by Maria:

> I started praying in English for their welfare and then I kind of switched to Spanish, it was a kind of sense of, I don't know if it would be more powerful but it would be perhaps more genuine or something.

First languages were constructed as owned by the individual. Naadir, who came to Britain as a young adult, described Arabic, his first language, as follows:

> It's easier and closer if you say it in your own language because it means different. You put it with a flavour. [...] More intimate. So it becomes much closer.

This construction positioned individuals' subsequent languages as other people's languages. First languages were constructed as the language for play. For example, Konrad described this distinction:

> I like speaking Polish. And I don't mind not speaking well and I rather enjoy getting things wrong and creating my own. [...] To be silly and, and, provocative, which I'm not in English at all. [...] I would love to feel more, more articulate and, and, a lot of the time, I just feel stupid actually in English.

First languages were perceived as enjoying special qualities, constructed as expressive, nuanced, creative and productive, described as a language with flavour, to be used for poetry, for intimacy, for play, for 'authenticity', for 'truth', and for jokes. The meanings given to first languages were also constitutive of the speaker – the language in which individuals were expressive, humorous, subtle, 'themselves', etc.

Languages were associated with a style of speaking, with a particular embodiment, use of gestures. Bernard described his first language as facilitating his expressiveness linked to a physical style of speaking:

> Because French is a much more natural language to me, my, how can I put it, the way I express myself when I speak French is more lively,

> more um, yes more lively and expressive than if I speak English. [...]
> Yes. I've got a different behaviour, even with body movement.
> I probably use my hands, and my whole body would be a lot more
> lively and expressive than when I speak English. [...] I mean it's as if
> more subdued in English.

Here, a construction of a first language as 'natural' is also made, the language in which individuals are positioned unselfconsciously, in contrast to their subsequent languages.

First languages were considered as embedding familiar narratives of self and relationships, as a touchstone for individual's sense of self. Those with more troubled narratives in their first language often found a new freedom in their second language. The ease in a first language, noted in the context of struggle in a second, gave individuals confidence, and could provide a sense of 'being at home' in it, in the absence of being at home in their current place. A first language could engender a sense of belonging when individuals returned to their country of origin, acting as a marker for others, although this could be disrupted through loss of fluency.

Meanings of first languages were affected by loss of fluency, which, when noted, was a source of distress to individuals. This became equated with a sense of loss of the past, and of a loss of connectedness with culture. Bernard reported that he was no longer fluent in either of his languages and associated this with a sense of dislocation.

> I have got to think about it to express it in English better. Again, I've
> got the same problem expressing it in French. I am between two
> languages, I feel now.

Being rendered non-fluent in both his languages left this individual in a hazardous place between languages, no longer unselfconsciously at ease in either. It was also difficult not to take this personally or have it seen as personal failing. Cato talked of the complexity involved in his loss of fluency in his first language.

> I also feel a sort of shame now that I cannot speak Hungarian properly. It also irritated me that my father joked about it once that my
> Hungarian is atrocious, but it feels very unfair, because I had to lose
> it to become English and fit in. You are almost trying to lose your
> language to be the same as everyone around you, but never quite will
> be but then also become alienated from your own language and people.

Loss of fluency in a first language was often constructed as a personal failing, without recourse to a discourse of sustaining a language as work. Loss of fluency in a first language had relational consequences, making it difficult to evolve relationships over time. Individuals became positioned as 'foreigners' in their languages of origin, and others often interpreted their substitution of words and grammar constructions from their second language as a status claim.

In general, subsequent languages were positioned in relation to the construction of first languages, and were often viewed as more formal, constraining, and difficult to make jokes in. One of the most prevalent constructions of second languages was that it introduced distance. This took a variety of forms: individuals constructed second languages as distancing them from 'experience'; from taken-for-granted ways of being; from others; from themselves; and from language itself. As Sante (1998) put it, "no one will ever break his heart with English words". For some individuals the language distanced them from constraints they had experienced in their first language, so that they could take risks and break rules.

The metaphors used for a second language were of utilitarian articles, a thing to be used – hats, gloves, opening doors – in contrast with the notion of being inside one's first language with its richness and expressiveness. And images of "ill fitting shoes, a size too small", a "piano with keys missing" and a "net with holes in it" constructed the insufficiencies of second languages.

Second/subsequent languages had often acquired ambiguous meanings, depending on context. The colonizers' language was constructed as the language of opportunity and educational success, even as it distanced the research participant from 'themselves', and othered them. In the context of migration, the new language was the language through which one needed to claim a voice in the face of discrimination, while the first language kept connection to the absent context and the past. However, the new language was not one's own, was not necessarily 'trustworthy', and might change one's relationship with the past.

Experiences of inarticulacy or a sense of inauthenticity in a second language impacted on individuals' constructions of themselves as speakers, although others saw their second languages as allowing a greater freedom of expressiveness because it rid them of constraining associations in their first language which interconnected with a view of themselves as taking more risks as a second-language speaker.

Individuals' relationship to their languages and themselves in their languages shifted over time, although a sense of not being entirely at ease in language which endured proved troubling. Estelle constructed this as follows:

> Estelle   I think now I find it easier to speak English than I do to speak French but I find it easier to hear French than I do to hear English. So that's the position now. [...] There is something more relaxing for me to listen to French. I can really relax and I can understand.
>
> CB   Yes, and with English you have to concentrate do you?
>
> Estelle   Sometimes, and when I think that, I just think god you're really stupid, you've been in this country for 20 years and still have to concentrate. But sometimes I have to, definitely, but in French I don't have to.

An ongoing struggle in language in this account, as in many others, became conflated with stupidity.

Languages acquired meanings for individuals from local usage. Because Ffionn's Welsh-speaking parents had always argued in their second language, English (possibly to protect their children from the impact of their rowing), it became associated with aggressiveness for Ffionn, contributing to her construction of herself as 'harder' as an English speaker.

The meanings of languages were also connected to different periods of life and what that had meant for individuals:

> But when you ask me what is connected with which, my most sort of formative years were certainly connected with German, where I developed all my ideas about life and about politics and about relationships, all that is in German and I'm very fond of those memories, and I would never want to lose those. [...] I think it means that in many ways in my outlook I am German. I'm certainly not Hungarian now. I've got a sort of nostalgic connection to Hungary, but I'm spiritually more German than Hungarian.

Such meanings concern the relationship contexts in which languages are spoken and lived, the lifecycle stages involved and their particular importance for the individual. And how do we get a sense of what a German, Polish, Zimbabwean, Spanish outlook is?

Meanings were attributed to languages through relationships as well as through 'convention'. Such notions of language and of speakers came into play in the context of another language. These conventions, somewhat stereotypical notions of languages, are interlinked with ideas of what they allow, compel, and encode in relation to their concepts and grammatical structures, in relation to what other languages 'do'. Individuals also drew on these ideas of their languages which were interlinked with the ways they saw themselves as speakers. They made reference to commonly held discourses concerning their languages and speaker style, as Renata did in delineating her differences as a speaker:

> I think the German way of relating is more direct than the English way of relating.

Languages were constructed in relation to each other. For example, Saskia drew distinctions in relation to the richness of her languages, drawn attention to when she moved between them:

> It is difficult to translate – because English is so much a richer language, it is much easier to express yourself in English than in German [...] An English dictionary is much, much fatter than a German one, so it is easier to say exactly how I feel in English [...] It's a fact that there are more English words.

Here quantity is also quality. Saskia warrants this as 'fact', but what is more significant in this construction is how it fits with Saskia's experience of what English has enabled her to do – which is to find a way to express herself emotionally. Maria considered English, her second language, to be a precise language, concise and clear, in which people said what they meant, were reliable, and in which she was taken seriously. This was in stark contrast to the indirectness and extremes she associated with Spanish, her first language. In his autobiography, Dorfman (1998) too makes distinctions between his first language, Spanish, and his second language, English, in relation to the different speaker positions they offer, contrasting the Spanish impersonal passive form, 'it happened', with the English, 'I made it happen', in relation to attributions of responsibility. Such a Whorfian hypothesis of how grammatical differences compel speakers to be different is interlinked with and contributes to constructing the characteristics by which languages become known. The processes of the ways in which languages differ and encode different meanings are recursively connected to commonly held beliefs about languages and speakers. In polarized interactions, without ongoing dialogic interplay, such constructions belie the diversity and contestation of discourse use and cultural practices *within* any one language.

Languages encoded different conceptualizations of subjectivity, different values and attitudes, and were experienced as constructing individuals as different kinds of speakers. Certain ways of speaking came to signify a particular identity. Quinlan described this difference in relation to her two languages, English and Cantonese:

> Whenever I say 'please' or 'thank you' it makes me feel very English (laugh). Because it's not something we do, it really isn't.

Such signifiers of a linguistic and cultural identity would not necessarily be apparent to those who were monolingual and monocultural, for whom these would be taken-for-granted unquestioned assumptions.

Some research participants, like Di-Yin, drew few distinctions between languages they had learned when they were very young, and struggled to define any language as their first. Although neurological research would indicate age to be the crucial factor, the wider context in which few distinctions were drawn between languages seemed central here.

Meanings of language did not necessarily stay static, but could shift over time for individuals, in relation to context and in relation to each other. Meanings of language speaking constructed in a personal context could contradict the meanings conferred by the wider context. Language meanings shifted in response to sociopolitical changes, or to a change of context in which sociopolitical meanings became apparent. Onno and Xandra struggled with others' connotations of their first language as oppressive and evil. The meanings of German changed for Renata following the unification of Germany and rise of racism.

Constructions of language were also impacted by experiences of continually translating between them. Quinlan described her experience of her languages as follows:

> It's, so that's when I say, when I think, I don't think in any language, because they're so distinct, but then they're together for me as well, and I can't (tearing sound) them apart, so it's very weird (laugh).

Not only was Quinlan positioned within each of her languages but as she regularly moved between them as a translator, operating between languages was itself experienced as a positioning, in which her languages could not be separated.

In summary, the meanings given to individuals' languages impacted profoundly on their construction of themselves as speakers, and these meanings were forged, constructed and contested in local contexts as well as by drawing on commonly held discourses, and shifted and evolved in relation to sociopolitical change. Differences between languages in relation to significant grammatical constructions and the encoding of different concepts of personhood also impacted on their meanings for individuals. There were significantly different constructions of 'first languages' and of subsequent languages in these accounts. Explorations of the meanings of an individual's languages provided salient gauges of their sense of themselves as speakers.

Concluding discussion

In this chapter I have examined adults' accounts of coming to live in a new language in a number of different circumstances, which had similarities and differences from the accounts of childhood.

Constructions of speaking several languages in childhood and young adulthood mainly differed from each other because of differences in the meanings of speaking several languages, as well as the different resources available to children and adults. Children rarely experienced a move of country and change of language as choice, because adults make these decisions or other circumstances force the move. Because the moves of country and change of language had mainly been constructed as a choice and opportunity by adolescents and adults, learning a new language was experienced as changing individuals, but these differences were generally experienced as helpful. New languages were constructed as offering a new and different identity, new ways to express oneself, an ability to take risks, and a helpful disruption of assumptions. Where childhood narratives had addressed a preoccupation with differences of language and contexts, and a struggle to claim a sense of belonging or a satisfactory identity position, adults, on the whole, appreciated the differences a new language offered them, even if they experienced racism and discrimination.

Some individuals constructed learning to live in a new language as an adolescent and adult as a performance. In order to perform themselves in their new language, individuals described drawing on stereotypes as scripts, until they found a way to 'own' the language differently.

Meanings given to language speaking varied considerably in the range of contexts in which individuals lived, and were related to power and status. However, all of these individuals had to contend with a different sense of themselves in each of their languages. This was a more problematic task for children than for adults who had more resources available to make sense of themselves. Individuals drew on a number of constructions of self in relation to these differences, commonly that of a doubled self. For some this included notions of a core self and of performing a second-language identity. Those who talked of themselves as having different language identities separated by time and place, referred to frozen identities linked to language which had not evolved. Constructions of self were also made salient in their interactions with others. For those growing up with several languages the importance of encountering a context, which could provide relational and discursive resources through which they came to own their multiplicity, was highlighted.

Languages and constructions of self were interlinked in complex ways. A language could hail a particular identity and sense of self. Research participants had developed different relationships to each of their languages, and constructed these differently. First languages were usually conceived as enabling expressiveness, while second languages were often experienced as introducing a distance of a kind. These differences were constructed in relation to each other, in relation to context and to the individuals' relationship in and to the language. These constructions of language were interwoven with individuals' constructions of themselves as speakers.

5
Language Identities and Power Relationships: Strategies of Hybridization

In this chapter, the intersections of languaged identities and power relationships are explored further, and in particular the place of language speaking in racialization processes. Racialization had a powerful impact on the way in which speakers came to experience themselves in claiming identities in the dominant language. The difference which speaking a minoritized language makes for individuals is mediated through their racialized identity position. I explore miscommunications which occur between first- and second-language speakers and the ways in which these construct identities and relationships. I consider issues of sufficient contextual resources, and identify ways in which individuals have made use of their differences of language – what I have called their strategies of hybridization.

Racialization processes and language speaking

Meanings of language speaking and individuals' experiences of themselves as speakers were impacted by their racialization and the ways in which they and their languages were positioned.

This had been particularly foregrounded in the accounts of Onno, Petiri, Wasan and Xandra of growing up in colonial contexts discussed in Chapter 3, in which the meanings of becoming English speakers were very different due to their racialization and positioning. In Petiri's account the necessity of learning the colonizers' languages and its insidious part of colonizing and racializing processes were particularly highlighted. Petiri's construction of the place of language speaking in colonization is mirrored in Edward Said's memoir of growing up as a stateless exiled Palestinian attending a British colonial school in Cairo:

The worst part of my situation, which time has only exacerbated, has been the warring relationship between English and Arabic. [...] But although taught to believe and think like an English schoolboy, I was also trained to understand that I was an alien, a Non-European Other, educated by my betters to know my station and not aspire to being British. [...] To be at the same time a Wog and an Anglican was to be in a state of standing civil war. (1999: 5)

Said's theoretical work (1993) informs his construction of an embattled doubled language identity, and of the subject positions he was invited to take up through the process of 'othering'. Like Petiri, Said makes use of the idea of an 'inner' self, signified as the 'genuine' self, able to survive the stupidity and destructiveness of a colonial education.

Those research participants who had grown up speaking minority languages found this positioned them as different, and often as 'inferior', and they had mainly avoided speaking their first languages outside the home as children, wanting to claim an identity as a dominant-language speaker. This was never experienced as very successful, and processes of racialization had played a crucial role here. Quinlan's account illustrated this particularly well. Her parents had a take-away shop, and Quinlan had sometimes worked there.

I actually worked on counter for a little while where my parents have a take-away, and uh, a man came in, a Caucasian man came in, and I said, "can I help you there please", cause by that time, I had completely lost my Cantonese accent, and I have a relatively ok English accent. He took two giant steps back and said, "oh my God, you're not Chinese". I found that very, I didn't know whether to find that offensive, whether to find that, it was very difficult to take in. Because I guess um there are a lot of preconceptions about Chinese English, they always speak with an accent, they always work in take-away shops and uh, I think this man was, I don't think he was intending to be offensive, it was just pure ignorance. I don't mean it in a derogatory way.

In this account Quinlan is somewhat tentative about defining this man as offensive or racist. Such incidents were common occurrences for Quinlan. Her fluency in English was often viewed as incompatible with her racialized identity position. She described an incident which was typical of her experiences throughout her years of schooling.

> She [teacher] came up to me and she said "if you need any help with your English, or if you need any help with", just this, this preconceived idea that because I'm Chinese, I can't, and then I've had English teachers who are in total disbelief that my mother tongue isn't English. Just like, "how is that possible?" Ugh, ugh. I mean it's something I've had to deal with all my life.

Quinlan's articulateness in English and her bilingualism were rarely taken for granted as unremarkable. Her language speaking has been a site for the contestation of her identity. In a similar way, Wasan's fluency in English and his identity often came under question. His accent and articulateness were signified as English middle class, and when he spoke on the telephone he was often assumed to be white, demonstrating the ongoing exclusionary definitions of Englishness. Such challenges to their identity claims and sense of belonging, were recurrent around their speaking, due to their 'race'.

Those who came to Britain as adults also addressed the impact of their racialization and positioning on their sense of themselves as English speakers. As discussed earlier, Naadir viewed acquiring fluency as crucial to his ability to challenge stereotyping and racism. Ihsan had dealt with considerable hostility in the course of his work in the building trade – his identity was continually interrogated. He responded by changing his name, a strategy that he viewed as having been relatively successful and one which enabled him to deal with challenges there in a different manner. He commented that he was still trying to get rid of his accent which identified him as different, but that he had to date been unable to do so. Ihsan defined himself as Iranian-British:

> For a while I was thinking British-Iranian but I've come to the point now you can never be British-Iranian because, whereas my daughter, Ariana, she is British-Iranian. There's a hell of a difference, I think so. She's going to grow up even going to have a stronger expression of face than I would have, she would be one hundred percent. I mean I can see among Asians and growing up here, I can see them in the street, young girl or young lad walk with the mother, a young lad, his face and her face are very, very different compared to the mother and the mother, you should see their face, they're more submissive and, sort of, like more face up in the air, almost like begging, and when you see the youngster the head is up, the back is straight, head down almost sharp, very sharp.

Ihsan felt he had been unable to claim being British-Iranian successfully, something that was probably connected to his experiences of continually having had his identity questioned and challenged. The ability to make a successful identity claim and a sense of confidence are interlinked in this account.

Very few white research participants addressed the effect of their racialized identity position on their sense of themselves as speakers of a new language. Lena was rare in noting that although her accent marked her as 'foreign' and the neighbours in her small village kept instigating police checks of the family when they first arrived, her whiteness led others to assume she was English:

> I'm sort of queuing for tickets at the railway station, and in the queue there are black people in front of me and then the gentleman next to me says "too small an island, too many foreigners". And I suppose because I'm white he probably makes an assumption, and should I say something now or should I just keep quiet?

Passing as English was double-edged here. This man's racism addressed and implicated her as xenophobic as well as disqualifying her as a foreigner.

Their differences of language and culture were constructed by some individuals as particularly advantageous. So, for example, Bernard saw these as differentiating him helpfully, "not one of the masses", although this meaning could shift to negativity in some contexts, and Thérèse described the pleasures of this positioning.

> I like the feeling that I'm not completely English, and I see people like thinking, "oh you have a nice accent, where are you coming from?" And it's nice. I like the being different but feeling home in it.

Crucial to this positioning is the construction of feeling 'at home' – in the language and in the place – which imparts a particular meaning to difference. Neither Bernard nor Thérèse referred to their whiteness as being significant in others' responses to them, in the way their difference was constructed. Their construction as different was on the whole, although not entirely, protected from exclusionary challenges.

Others saw their difference of language and culture as disadvantageous in Britain, and Henka experienced this as powerfully constituting her:

Nobody's interested in Poland, nobody thinks that they can learn anything interesting about, or from Polish person as such. [...] There is no interest in me, so, and that automatically in a way puts you down. [...] and from that time on my confidence was plummeting, yeah, and um, I've lost it nearly completely over here, over the years.

These were not exclusionary challenging responses; rather, they reflect indifference and ignorance about Poland. Henka had found this positioning by others difficult to challenge, even when at one level she told me that it made her think she was better educated and informed than her English acquaintances. She made no reference to her whiteness at all. This construction of the disadvantage of language and cultural difference was drawn on in a different context from the one in which Henka referred to the advantages conferred by her non-fluency, discussed earlier.

Individuals were positioned very differently as English speakers because of their racialization. Speaking a minority language was always considered a marker of difference but a white identity position did protect individuals from having their language speaking and sense of belonging and identity continually brought under question. Very few of the white research participants owned a sense of this privilege.

Second-language communications and misunderstandings

Communication between persons is significantly informed by an assumption of shared meanings, as well as through the offering, taking up and refusing of subject positions in the talk. Another aspect of communication which had influential effects on meaning concerned the prosodic elements of language. Some research participants addressed the effect of tone and its impact on creating misunderstandings. Saskia described how people often misread her communications:

People sometimes think I am cross or annoyed in English, something about my tone of voice.

Xandra also reported that people often misinterpreted her when she expressed herself in English:

Somebody hears something much stronger than I meant.

Both tone and emphasis in the talk in a second language could convey meanings to others which were different from those intended by the speaker. This happened when a speaker transferred a style of speaking from their first language which carried different meanings in the second language, as in Xandra's account, where she found herself importing her more direct and passionate way of speaking in Afrikaans into English.

Having to focus more self-consciously on the speaking of a second language could also disrupt the emotional message. Because emotions are constructed and expressed differently in different cultures and languages (Heelas 1986), this also leaves considerable possibilities for misconstruing. Learning to interpret feelings (which may be communicated very differently), as well as learning how to express these are different tasks from communicating content, although intricately linked, and indeed recent neurological research (Morris et al. 1999) has found different neuronal networks involved in processing melody, tone, rhythm and the emotional content of a language from the processing of verbal content.

Accent, on the other hand, also had the effect of disrupting meanings. Others can become preoccupied with this aspect of talk which can divert from the verbal content. Estelle considered her accent to be central:

> You see if I didn't have an accent I might feel very differently. I might actually forget I'm from France.

Others' responses to Estelle in questioning her belonging unsettled her identity construction. Sounding like a 'native speaker', or being signified through prosodic elements as a 'foreigner', had powerful differential effects on the construction and claims of identity. Several individuals spoke of the significance of not having an accent in their first language when they returned to their country of origin, which acted as a signifier of belonging, even though their loss of fluency let them down in more complex communications.

Many individuals referred to their difficulties with humour in their second or subsequent language. Thérèse's description of finding humour awkward in English was typical:

> I still find joking extremely difficult, and I don't, I'm not fitting in with joking. I don't understand the jokes, and I become very annoyed about it, because I feel if I laugh, I don't understand it, and

if they see me laughing without understanding it, I would be so humiliated (laugh), but not laughing and not fitting in.

Difficulties with humour were rarely considered as the effect of speaking a second language by individuals themselves or by those in relationships with them. Rather, they became connoted as personality trait and impacted powerfully on constructions of speakers. So, for example, Ffionn saw herself as 'harder' in English, and not able to play with the language as she could in Welsh, and Onno experienced himself and described himself as "more distant and serious" in English, because of his difficulties with humour.

Venjamin reported that he honed his skills in playing with words in English – a process which he very much enjoyed. He recounted a response to a talk he had given, when he had been asked:

"How come you're so witty, because foreigners are usually humourless, so how come you are witty?" (laughter)

Venjamin's ability to be funny in English unsettled hegemonic notions of 'foreigners', which may be another reason why it gave him so much pleasure. His account also highlighted one function of the valuing of wit in Britain as a powerful way of disqualifying 'foreigners'.

Other kinds of misunderstandings occurred when individuals were fluent in English and their status as a second-language speaker was missed. Quinlan described such an incident at school:

One incident that sticks in my head was when I went to secondary school, um a P.E teacher kept asking me, "What's the magic word? What's the magic word?", meaning "please". In my household, we never have, mannerisms is considered unnecessary, because, it's sort of like, well we're your parents, we're expected to do this for you, why do you say "thank you". [...] Because it's not something we do, it really isn't. [...] I mean when that incident happened, I was about twelve I would say, I was at secondary school. And it just didn't click, it just didn't click. [...] By that time, my English was pretty fluent. I still had a bit of a Cantonese accent though, and uh (2) "What was the magic word?" and the teacher must have thought I was just being really difficult (laugh).

It was because the teacher assumed Quinlan was a first-language speaker that she constructed her incomprehension, her linguistic and cultural difference, as belligerence. This example illustrates the pervasiveness of the way in which we take language for granted, and assume that when we communicate we mean the same thing with our talk.

Second-language speakers in these accounts were engaged in miscommunications in two ways. One was when they were listened to as if they were first-language speakers, where tone and a mismatch of assumptions proved problematic. The other was when the prosodic elements of the language, the marking of their speech as second-language speakers, disrupted communication. Obviously these accounts could only include misinterpretations which were made apparent – the likelihood of such misconstructions occurring seems great. And there is obviously a danger in unequal power relationships, that such misunderstandings can construct enduring identities.

Strategies of hybridization

Except for Konrad, who viewed his languages as having split him, all the other research participants emphasized the advantages of speaking more than one language, even if they had found this problematic while growing up. In this section I want to examine some of the ways in which participants constructed these advantages. Individuals claimed that their positioning in more than one language and culture gave them a wider perspective and a willingness to engage across differences generally. Key to this stance was the way in which individuals came to think about and manage their own language differences for themselves.

I have been particularly interested to identify how individuals found ways to link their different language perspectives, given that these were often incompatible, encoded different values, etc. Here I have used Bakhtin's idea of hybridization, the term he coined for "the mixing, within a single concrete utterance, of two or more different linguistic consciousnesses, often widely separated in time and social space" (1981: 429), to examine the accounts for how individuals developed an ability to use the interplay between their different perspectives.

In the research narratives of childhood, individuals had constructed the differences between their languages as challenging to manage, and they had mainly worked to keep these separate. There had been very few, if any possibilities for hybridity, with home and the public domain both perceived as demanding a singularity. This is mirrored in Dorfman's (1998) autobiography of his childhood and young adulthood moving between South America and the United States, which is structured around the premise of his refusal of a doubled identity throughout his growing up:

> I was unable to look directly in the face the divergent mystery of who I was, the abyss of being bilingual and binational at a time when everything demanded that we be univocal and immaculate. (Dorfman 1998: 220)

Context was crucial to the ways in which research participants experienced their different languages and themselves-in-language. With no contextual support for hybridity, individuals' differences of language and constructions of self became polarised through the unequal relationships between their languages and cultures. Most research participants reported that they had come to experience their different senses of self and the differences between their languages more helpfully, once the polarisations between their languaged identities had been unsettled or resolved in some way or their multiplicities had been validated. This was linked to developing ways of using their differences explicitly.

Making use of one's own differences

Venjamin had relearned Arabic, his first language, some years after coming to Britain:

> I started learning Arabic in my early 40s. I didn't experience any sense of embarrassment about the language, on the contrary I really liked the language and was very keen to learn it and was very proud that I could speak Arabic and made the most of the basis that I had in Arabic.

The re-engagement with his first language was a marker of a transformation of Venjamin's relationship to it, which was similar to Petiri's revaluing of his first language. A shift of this kind in the affective relationship with one's first language was interlinked with a shift in one's sense of self as a speaker. Venjamin's relearning of Arabic, reclaiming it, one could say, enabled him to make use of it for his work:

> My aim is to understand the dynamics of the Arab–Israeli conflict and to do that you have to get away from looking at the Arabs as the enemy and you have to look at both societies and how Israel's

behaviour influences the Arabs and how Arab behaviour and Arab attitudes influence the Israelis, because there is a process of psychological misperception and misunderstanding which has always fuelled the conflict. So I try to look at both societies in their own terms and how they perceive the other one, and here knowledge of the language is very important.

Venjamin proposed that his knowledge of both languages involved in the conflict was crucial in trying to forge new understandings about their interrelationship. He made use of the dialogic between these two different languaged perspectives, both of which Venjamin embodied as a speaker. What Venjamin did not discuss was how his engagement with both languages for his work may have enabled him to make different connections between his own polarities from the past on a personal level. "Double-voiced discourse is always internally dialogised" as Bakhtin (1981: 324) pointed out. Venjamin's personal experience of these past polarities may also have fuelled his desire to make different connections through his work.

In the same way, Edward Said (1998) found a way to use his previously embattled language perspectives, Arabic and English, the identities which always seemed to be in conflict, in his writing and theoretical work. He described this process as follows:

> Having allowed myself gradually to assume the professional voice of an American academic as a way of submerging my difficult and unassimilable past, I began to think and write contrapuntally, using the disparate halves of my experience, as an Arab and as an American, to work with and also against each other. [...] though it was difficult, it was also exciting. (1998: 6)

Said's argument here is that one has to find a way to 'own' all one's voices/languages in order to be able to use their different perspectives. This again raises the question about how one does make a language one's own – owning a language and using it in one's own voice. The ability to use his professional voice and his perspective as 'exile' (Said 1993) to helpfully deconstruct taken-for-granted assumptions in English literature presumably had an effect in coming to own it.

Research participants also identified ways in which they made use of their different languaged perspectives in their everyday lives. Ihsan talked about instances when he made use of his two languages to help him to think through issues for himself:

Analysing, yes I analyse it in Farsi and feel I understand it in a different way than when I analyse in English, and then it does affect me. [. . .] Yeah, two different ways of thinking and looking at it, and it does help me in a certain way, yeah.

Ihsan explicitly drew on both of his languages to generate new perspectives for himself. But he also talked of finding that he used his different languages in a more implicit way. Ihsan identified himself as very good at developing hunches about people and situations, and he noticed that this happened in Farsi, while speaking in English. His two languaged perspectives operated at different levels in his interactions with others.

Justine's family switched between their two languages as part of their family style of talk, developing links between their two languages to play:

Ya at home we're always having these cross-language jokes because, we make so many puns. We spend lots of time, just in any language, and between the languages that, like friends who spend a lot of time kind of wind up groaning when another one gets mentioned. But there are just so many. So there's this extra humour level that you get from knowing two languages, and being able to play between the two.

This is a recognition of an increased richness of the bringing together of languages. This was not a context in which one language disqualified the other, or tried to obliterate the other, but one in which a 'lightness of touch' engendered creativity and fun. Xandra described a different kind of switching, a switch from one language to the other in her internal language when she was on her own:

It was a physical like, you know literally changing channels, it was like changing, you know, turning the knob.

For Xandra this had been a "profound physical experience", a marker of a switch between her languages which she had never noticed in this way before. She had begun to try to take note when she switched languages internally, and to discern what it might indicate concerning her differential responses to individuals or situations. This growing awareness of her internal code switching was enabling her to make more explicit use of the interaction between her different languaged perspectives. In her memoir, Hoffman (1989) described learning that her different perspective was one of the most valuable assets in her professional life, and also starting to use the interplay between her two languages explicitly to debate personal dilemmas in her life.

Petiri described a different strategy of using his differences. He saw himself as presenting different aspects of himself, strategically, to 'fit' with different contexts, aware that he held different views and attitudes in his different languages.

> I can still have a conversation with somebody, even sometimes when I think to myself, I wouldn't do that. I've become very curious about it, but I know I'm being Western. I think, this is a Western concept, but when in Rome.

Petiri reported that at times he explicitly shifted his self-presentation, but now without feeling that he was disqualifying himself, as he thought he had done as a schoolboy in Zimbabwe. This self-presentation is what Bakhtin termed, taking a heteroglossic authorial position, maintaining different distances from a variety of languages in order to use them in 'refracted' ways and to work their interplay. 'Heteroglossia' is the ability to refract intention through the differential use of different languages; the metaphor of 'refraction' of light rays used to illustrate the ways in which authors take up other voices and already claimed territories, to produce their authorial discourses (Bakhtin 1981). This kind of positioning entailed Petiri to be able to take a self-reflexive stance, an awareness of his relationship to his languages in their different contexts.

Lena described how the interplay of each of her languages sometimes gave a perspective on the other, and highlighted "her own prejudices":

> I think that I have become much more sensitive to my own prejudices and thinking and saying, slow down, you don't know that and it's ok not to know, and it's ok if you show just kind of respect and curiosity.

This allowed her to identify how she dealt in "ideologically freighted discourse" (Bakhtin 1981: 333), and Lena thought this enabled her to achieve a self-aware position in her relationships and her work.

Further ways to use different perspectives were identified by Renata who had come to appreciate a positioning of 'outsider', something she had previously considered as a loss:

> I think being an outsider has got advantages and disadvantages. I mean the disadvantages are that you never really belong. [...]

I could never really belong. I was sitting on the fence. That's the disadvantage, also an advantage because you come in from the outside. It's sometimes an advantage in getting jobs. I think I've got jobs because I was an outsider and was less aware of what the hierarchies are, and didn't really care about them. [...] I sort of cut through things in a way. [...] There is an advantage in coming in from the side.

This ability to maintain a different perspective to a dominant discourse because of another language, that there is never just one way to think about anything, was claimed by many of these research participants – as it had been by Hoffman and Said in their memoirs. This is a claim that their ability to value their own multiplicities enabled them to challenge dogma. Many made similar arguments to the one advanced by Renata, positing their own experiences as informing their stance in relation to inequality and singular ideologies:

I probably am politically intolerant of nationalism and racism and those exclusive kinds of ideology, partly because of my experiences of my own I think.

Maria linked her construction of herself as multiple as helpfully challenging her own ideas about certainty:

I think it gives you a position of a kind of citizen of the world really, because you can't take a position of knowing.

This position comes with the ability to find a way to own one's own different perspectives as well as 'work' them for oneself. The certainty within one languaged perspective is challenged through the other language. This is a complex positioning – a confidence about the helpfulness of 'not-knowing'. Hoffman (1989: 275) described this as follows:

Because I have learned the relativity of cultural meanings on my skin, I can never take any one set of meanings as final. I doubt I'll ever become an ideologue of any stripe.

These claims made by individuals about the usefulness of the interaction between their different languaged perspectives concur with Bakhtin's proposal that the use of two languaged perspectives relativizes consciousness and that this can decentre language and ideology. The realization of the contingency of their sense of self, and the relativity of their languages, also changed individuals' relationship to language generally – an issue I address in the final chapter.

Rhetorical use of different languages and identity claims

Code switching was another way individuals used the differences between their languages, a strategy of hybridization at a different level. Several research participants described the way they switched languages for rhetorical purposes. At times this functioned as a claim of identity in their interactions with others.

Individuals chose to incorporate particular differences from one language into their other. Lena described how she had introduced English expressions into her family conversations in Serbo-Croat:

> During the weekends in the house I would speak Serbo-Croat all the time, but picking up here and there English words, and saying much more "thank you" and "please" than before. [...] That's one of the things I liked about um the language here and saying that even to tiny little kiddies, and when you say that, it affects you really, you start to appreciate what's been happening. It's not something we would do back home.

Here, a 'performance of appreciation' through the introduction and use of English expressions into Serbo-Croat brings it forth and impacts on the 'doing' of family relationships.

Di-Yin and Wasan, whose languages encompassed very different ways of expressing emotion, had also developed strategies of using their different languages for different purposes. Di-Yin presented herself differently in each language. Di-Yin saw English as enabling her to perform assertiveness/aggressiveness which was not considered permissible in Chinese culture. She also described experiencing different feelings in English from those she experienced in her Chinese languages:

> Angry, yes, also in English. Especially in Chinese culture, being angry you should suppress it. So it's much easier to express it in English. So even if I don't need to express it, sometimes I keep it to myself, nevertheless I feel it in English (laugh).

Because Di-Yin could only express anger in English, she only experienced it in English. Her different languages (and cultures) named, differentiated, and 'allowed' different emotional states. This illustrated some of the processes of the social construction of emotions. As Volosinov (1986: 85) put it: "it is not experience that organises expression, but the other way around – expression organises experience". Just as Slobin (1996) proposed that we learn "thinking for speaking", to pick out salient features of an event which are encodable in language, we could say that Di-Yin had learned "feeling for speaking" in English in ways that were different from the way she did so in Mandarin or Shanghai Dialect. Her speaking in turn had an effect on her feeling/thinking. Di-Yin gave other examples of things she could only express in English.

> It's partly in the language. For instance in Chinese you don't say, "I love you". You know it is a very strange thing to say and uh, so I don't say, "I love you" in Chinese, but I will say it in English. And even to this day, to my daughter, I never say, "I love you" in Chinese. If I want to say that, I will say it in English. Because it just feels *so*, like your skin feels weird to say that in Chinese.

The idea of what a language can compel you to say or not say is persuasive here. Di-Yin presented herself as being acutely aware of the constitutive nature of language, of knowing that she feels and expresses herself differently in profound ways in each of her languages. Her sense of what her languages could and could not do seem to have engendered an 'ironic' stance to her languages, an ability to make explicit use of the differences between languages for rhetorical purposes. Of all the research participants, Di-Yin commented on her use of her languages in the most self-reflexive way.

Wasan also talked of his languages embedding very different concepts and modes of expression and he reported that he used English to speak about feelings in his conversations in Gujarati:

> And if it's more in terms of emotions and feelings, it's more likely to be in English. I would have very few Gujarati words for expression of emotions.

He talked of incorporating untranslatable English words, such as "depressed" and "angry", into his Gujarati conversations:

> I would be talking Gujarati and then I would say, "I got angry" in English, and then I would go back into Gujarati, or something like that.

Within his conversations in Gujarati, Wasan would report in English that he had become angry, and it seemed that he would not express anger in his interactions in Gujarati. Wasan, like Di-Yin, talked of making explicit use of what each of his languages would 'allow' him to express, and of employing a mixture of his languages to address his differential experiences.

As well as using different languages to express different emotions, individuals brought their different languages into play for rhetorical purposes and made different identities salient in their interactions. Angela, who had found her difference problematic during her childhood, reported that she began to claim her Italian identity in her adolescence, a development that was linked to a change in the status of Italians in Britain:

> The association was like power, almost. It was a powerful thing. Like, people jokingly said, "I suppose you know people in the Mafia", and you'd say, "well if I did I wouldn't tell you". You know. So the secrecy (laughter) and we played on this, and the fact that you did, I wasn't going to tell them. (laughter) Cause they had this romantic idea of the Mafia, you know.

This was 'performance', a strategic usage of a particular construction of Italian identity, which echoed Phoenix's (1998) finding in her study with Tizard (1993) that black boys in Britain sometimes made strategic use of certain constructions of black masculine identity. This claim of identity, an active positioning of herself, challenged some of the earlier negativity Angela had experienced, when she had considered herself positioned as inferior.

Venjamin talked of having claimed different national and cultural identities for himself over time. Currently, he talked of his languages as engendering different identifications for him. A switch of language brought about a switch in Venjamin's sense of himself, although this may also have been evoked by context. He talked of the different effects of presenting his views in Hebrew or English in Israel.

> In Hebrew I'm probably seen as more aggressive and more provocative um, outside consensus, because it is not common for an Israeli speaking in Hebrew to use such strong language in condemning Israel.

The impact of Venjamin taking a critical position in Hebrew had a different impact on others from doing so in English, and taking this position in Hebrew may also have been a different experience for Venjamin. He talked of the ways in which he made identity claims:

> I find that I have problems with terminology when I'm in Israel. When I'm in England I would always speak of Israel, I would never say 'us' or 'we'. So I would be a detached observer. I may have strong feelings but here is the conflict and there are Arabs and there are Israelis and I'm not part of this dispute. I am commenting on it, I may be taking sides, but I stand outside. Whereas when I'm in Israel and speaking in Hebrew, I sometimes slip into saying 'we'. Even if I'm criticising Israel's behaviour I would say, "we were quite wrong to do that, we were the expansionists, we were the aggressors, it wasn't the Arabs who set the pace, but it was we who kept clobbering them on the head". And then I sometimes catch myself and say, "why am I saying 'we'? I should say 'you', 'you' are the aggressors".

Venjamin described changes in the way in which he claimed identity depending on the language he was speaking, as well as the context in which he is speaking. The question of whether he was seen to be Israeli or not was heightened, because of polarizations between the stances of the Middle East conflict. He did not report these shifts as explicit decisions, but his use of language may be viewed as a rhetorical device to enable his critique to be accepted. To position himself as an insider may make it harder to be discredited, despite his view that it comes across in a harsher way in Hebrew. A switch of language also engendered a switch in Venjamin's own identification. The interplay here was between his Israeli and his English identities, with Venjamin's Arabic identification remaining invisible, perhaps because this would be seen to disqualify his position. Following Widdicombe's (1998a, 1998b) ideas about the ways in which individuals make their identities salient in interaction, we can see how Venjamin used Hebrew to make his identity as Israeli salient, in order to strengthen his critique, and then, disingenuously, claimed an identity as outsider, "why am I saying 'we', 'you'", perhaps to confound its use as a rhetorical device. Although Venjamin described the way in which he changed terminology, he did not refer to using this explicitly, in contrast to Di-Yin, who reported that she switched languages strategically in her Chinese relationships:

> There's a lot of good things in Chinese and a lot of bad things in Chinese. And I like to get the good things, and I don't like to get the bad things, and in order to get the good things I speak Chinese with

them, and in order to avoid the bad things I speak English with them. So that's how I do it. Yes. So for instance, in Chinese, usually women are looked down upon, so if I'm dealing with Chinese male friends and I don't want to be looked down upon, I speak English. (laugh). [...] So, and also Chinese are very, very friendly. They are very, very willing to do something, because it's like a kinship type of thing, and sometimes, um, also, they feel like to help women as well, so sometimes when I need help (indistinct) then I speak Chinese. (laugh)

Di-Yin is clear about the ways in which she makes explicit choices about which language to speak with whom. She knows that she makes use of her different languages as a rhetorical strategy in a number of ways – in order to make different identity claims in her interactions, and, in particular, to unsettle and challenge gendered interactions. Ihsan too reported switching between languages in conversations with his brother in order to make use of their differences:

And I keep telling him, "don't speak in English, speak in Farsi to me, because that way you can express yourself in a general way about Iranians or parents, because we've still got parents", and I said, "don't speak in English about parents because [...] because that way you and I can decide a better way for them, if you do it in English then you might as well alienate them and let them go. But in Farsi you come a bit more connected, caring and let's decide better things for them." That's what it is and I often tell him, have a go at him, "don't speak to me in English, speak to me in Farsi. Decide about your family in this way."

Ihsan persuaded his brother to speak Farsi in order to invoke cultural expectations of family relationships and to create family obligations. Indeed, Ihsan declared this strategy to his brother rather than using it without making a meta-comment in the way that Di-Yin did. He explicitly worked to make his and his brother's identities as Iranians salient through speaking Farsi, and it did indeed have this effect, despite declaring his stake, demonstrating the evocative nature of language. Like other research participants, such a claim of identity was made in relation to a particular context.

Renata similarly talked of making identity claims differently depending on the context and in response to how others were trying to construct her:

Well I think the worse thing about it is that England is very prejudiced against Germans. And that is pretty unpleasant when you come, especially when I see myself as a left liberal German. And being sort of associated with the war is quite ridiculous and irritating. I suppose in a way I sort of re-adopted my Hungarian identity. Although internally I never felt that I was more Hungarian than I was German.

Renata used her identities as a resource, and made claims for strategic purposes to protect herself against hostility, although that did not always correspond to her self-definition. Her construction of identity was negotiated differently within different interactions. Renata suggested that her sense of her own identity had changed over time through living in English, although this did not necessarily match what she would want to claim:

I think I've probably become more English generally as a person, although I would never call myself English. I would never even take on English nationality, but one gets used to [. . .] You get used to a certain way of being.

Living in English is itself constitutive. However, constructions of self also function as claims of identity in interactions with others. Such constructions of identity can be considered as drawn on in relation to a particular imagined audience, or to make political claims. Issues of claiming identity were complicated for Lena because of the dangerous politics of identity involved in the war in the Balkans to which she was passionately opposed. Lena defined herself as a Yugoslav, in opposition to the redefining of identities, the claiming of singular identities and disowning of multiplicities, in the conflict in the Balkans. This was a significant claim which would have different meanings in Britain and in the former Yugoslavia. Lena continued to speak her first language and name it as Serbo-Croat, in the face of its evolution into different languages, Serbian, Croatian and Bosnian, as part of nationalistic movements. The connection of language and identity is here powerfully in evidence. In Britain Lena's claim also had another function because it worked to disidentify her as Serbian, those constructed by the media as responsible for genocide, although these constructions impacted profoundly on her sense of herself:

Oh there's a lot of media coverage which is saying that everybody hates us over there and they're horrible people over here. [. . .] I'm very, very sort of sensitive and paranoid initially. I think once people realise who I am and my background no one will speak to me. I knew it would not be the case, but it's really hard to resist that.

Like Onno and Xandra, Lena faced issues of refuting a troubling identification with those in her country of origin with whom she had passionate differences. Such claims entwine personal and political identities.

Thérèse spoke of another kind of self-presentation, of using her multiple identifications as a resource:

There's something nice about that, I feel, you're not really part, and it creates a mystery a bit, like, "where is she coming from, where is that coming from?" You can relate but you're not the same. I like that position.

Thérèse enjoyed the point that others could not identify her easily. A multiple identity could enable an ambiguous positioning. An appreciation of the potential of ambiguity is the other side of the sense that each language only allows a partial self-presentation. This is a stance in which it is possible to play with absent and missing aspects of oneself.

To sum up, almost all of these individuals viewed their languages and their different perspectives as creative and helpful. Individuals had found ways to position themselves in their several languages in order to use the differences between their languages in their everyday lives. It allowed them to generate different perspectives from those with whom they were in interaction, and also new perspectives for themselves. Some research participants noticed the interplay between their languages without setting out explicitly to use this, while others 'worked' the differences between their perspectives in explicit ways.

Individuals used code switching between their languages and other rhetorical strategies to claim identities and make them salient. Individuals claimed both multiple and singular identities within their interactions and in different contexts, which depended on how others responded to them, and what they themselves wanted to accomplish. The ability to use several languages and the differences between them gave individuals a wide range of linguistic resources to draw on in a number of ways, including a capacity to make use of ambiguity.

Concluding discussion

The meanings of language speaking were constructed in power relationships, and were contested as part of social struggles at local as well as wider societal levels. Individuals' racialization impacted powerfully on the ways in which they were constructed as speakers, and challenged in their claims of identity.

The prosodic aspects of being a second-language speaker were found to have a significant impact on the construction of individuals and on their relationships, often through misinterpretations and misreadings.

Individuals reported a variety of struggles in relation to working their differences of language and senses of self. An ability to make use of the sense of multiplicity engendered by their languages to their advantage was an ongoing challenge. Individuals were found to have developed strategies of hybridization in which they switched between languages for themselves or in their interactions with others, and I return to examine these strategies in the concluding chapter.

6
Language Use and Family Relationships

Two different perspectives on language use and family relationships were given in the interviews: interviewees' constructions of their experiences as children within their family of origin; and adults' views of their relationships in their family of creation. In the following chapter, I draw on both of these perspectives to identify pertinent themes and constructions in the talk of family and language, with the aim of elaborating the complexities in family relationships when family members live their lives in more than one language.

Three significant areas were identified in the analysis concerning family relationships as follows: (1) language and power in family relationships; (2) parenting and language use; and (3) claiming identity and creating alliances. Some of the challenges families face in sustaining the speaking of several languages are identified.

Language and power in family relationships

When children become more fluent than parents

Research findings and professionals working with families, such as family therapists, have indicated that there are significant issues for family relationships when children learn the dominant language faster than their parents, when families move from one language/culture to another (Burck 1997; Lau 1984; Papadopoulos and Hildebrand 1997; Raval 1996). There are many reasons why children learn languages faster than their parents, perhaps one of the most important is that children are obliged to attend school, a context in which they need to communicate in order to survive, so that the necessity to learn is immediate. Children are usually constructed as less shy of trying out a new language and making mistakes than adults are. The younger the child the more likely this environment will replicate something of their initial language-learning environment, the trial and error of continual use, rather than more 'rational' second-language learning situations offered to older children and adults, in which formal aspects of the language are taught (Lamendella 1978). Children are often less organized by loyalty to their first language and culture than adults, which also impacts on the way in which they engage with a new language.

Angela, Cato, Konrad and Quinlan had all become more fluent as children in English than their parents, and Bernard addressed this issue from his perspective as a father whose children became more fluent than he was.

Cato, who came to Britain with his mother as a refugee, and Quinlan, who had moved to Britain as a young child, had both been pushed into taking on adult responsibilities and forced into relating to the outside world for their parents because of their relative fluency in English. Both remembered this as having been very difficult. Cato became the translator for his mother, and had only recently constructed this as a common reversal of power relationships for children in this position:

> I was thinking, you know, maybe some of the kind of contempt, and this and that difficulty I had with my Mum has some quite simple root, reason for it, that a lot of other people have experienced too, being thrust out and become responsible far too young. And I always blame, that's right, I always blame my Mum for making me so bloody responsible before I was old enough to do it. I think she had no choice, really. It wasn't really her fault. What else could she do? I was becoming better at the language. It wasn't just her making me do it. I would do it. I was probably asking to do it, because I wanted to show off anyway.

In this account, Cato placed his remembered feelings of contempt and blame of his mother into a frame of 'inevitable' consequences for families moving language. This reframing gives the past difficult relationship between Cato and his mother a more benign explanation. The double-edged nature of the positioning offered children through fluency in the dominant language – the resentment, and the enjoyment of the power involved – is constructed as a central dilemma.

Quinlan's main recollection of translating for her parents was of terror:

> Because you'd be put into a situation when you were 10 when you're translating for two adults. [...] There would be words that I wouldn't have understood in both languages, and so I'd go, like, "I don't really know how to do this", but you just struggle through. And uh, and at that age as well, you're just like intimidated by, by strangers first of all, and than having to speak to someone you don't know, and then having to translate for your parents, and uh it's a nightmare. (laugh) It is a nightmare. But as you grow older, now, I've lost that fear (1) It *was* fear, actually. [...] Even when it was on the telephone, like if we were making an order for something, I would feel very timid and very frightened and I shook, I physically shook when I had to do things like that. And as I've grown older, cause I've had to do it, and it's actually become a skill now that I've acquired because I've had to do it.

Quinlan constructed a 'trial by fire' developmental narrative, of very difficult experiences leading to competence in both her languages and in translating. She posited an increasing sympathy with her parents' ongoing struggles in English and an awareness of her Chinese peers' loss of Cantonese, as key to her appreciation of her own language skills and of how helpful it had been to be 'forced' to develop these.

Both these accounts identified the stress and difficulty involved as children, when expectations of who should take responsibility in the family were disrupted through a move into a new language and culture. Cato and his mother had been made refugees, with all the accompanying losses and upheaval, while Quinlan, as a young Chinese person, had to manage exclusionary and racist responses alongside the stress of having to manage adult conversational settings. There are also differences of emphasis in their narratives. Cato's highlighting of his past resentment of his mother related to his construction of his mother's responsibility, while Quinlan's emphasis on the advantages gained from her difficult experiences linked to her focus on her own difficulties. Quinlan had been able to share these experiences with her younger brother, while Cato had to manage this on his own.

Konrad, born to Polish-speaking parents, had also become more fluent in English than his parents. He remembered helping his mother with her English speaking. His father, who had a good knowledge of English, had been very worried about not speaking well enough, and Konrad recollected feeling anxious about him.

I remember having enormously sort of emotional feelings about my father doing something wrong and being laughed at by somebody. And I think every child has that, you know, if your parent slips, or, or makes a mistake, or might be laughed at by somebody, you just want to swallow them up and protect them from it. I remember that feeling and that may have been to do with language as well. [...] going out with my father was like, I didn't really want people to know he was my father for some reason. I wasn't proud of him for some reason, but now we're also going onto deeper psychological problems.

Konrad constructed his lack of confidence in his father as an indication of 'deeper psychological problems'. It did not seem that he had considered this in the frame of language, that he may have been very sensitive to his father's uncertainty about living in a new language/culture. This was an unbalancing of power relationships in the family at a more subtle level than the two earlier accounts, also double-edged, with his childhood feelings constructed as both shame and protectiveness. Interestingly Konrad who was a rather articulate man, was himself preoccupied with concerns about his own fluency.

Angela, who was born in Britain, had also become more fluent in English than her Sicilian parents. However, she reported that it was because her parents spoke Italian and were very emotional in public, which drew attention to their difference, which she had found difficult. Angela's parents were embedded in an Italian network which may have buffered issues of fluency for them and Angela.

Bernard gave an account as a parent whose children were more fluent in English than he himself was:

Bernard   They were very aware that they had a father who was from a different culture and they probably liked that and they still like this, being a bit unique in a sense. What I have noticed is both my son and daughter if I make a mistake in English they look at me and they say "Daddy, how long have you been in this country?" and it means, speaking English better.

CB   So they correct you?

Bernard   They correct me when I talk then in a way English and it's a U-turn and I then become shameful of not being able to express myself better or making a big mistake. I feel like I am in a stupid situation.

CB   Are they only teasing you or?

Bernard It is almost shameful, yes. If they have their friends, they say "I think my father is a bit thick" you know. They say "excuse him" but they don't like it. It's like, "Daddy how can you?" I don't blame them because I should speak better.

Bernard reported that his children are embarrassed and contemptuous towards him about his language speaking, which echoed Cato's responses to his mother as a child. This reversed his parenting relationship with his children, and as their responses confirmed his own view that he should be more competent, he did not challenge them and this contributed to unbalancing this relationship further.

Children's greater fluency in the dominant language introduced contradictions into family relationships, in relating to the outside world. Children were put in positions of carrying adult responsibilities on behalf of their parents, and parents delegated power to their children in ways they may not have done in their first language context. Fluency in English conferred competency in spheres outside the family, and indeed, non-fluency, the opposite, as in Bernard's account, was connoted as 'thick'. Parents' struggle with learning the dominant language unsettled ideas in families about who should be competent, carry responsibility and hold power, and this intersected with the ways in which minoritized parents were positioned in relation to class. None of these parents were privileged enough to counter the loss of status experienced through their language difficulties and discrimination. Ideas about parents' competence could be perturbed in subtle ways because of their uncertainty in the new language and culture. As Bernard's account demonstrated, a parent could be profoundly responsive to and organized by their children's contempt, which contributed further to an unbalancing of family relationships.

Adults recollected that they had been embarrassed, anxious, contemptuous or resentful of the way they had been positioned by their parents. These accounts suggested that as children they had experienced these difficulties as personal. Neither they nor their parents had explicitly addressed these as a common aspect of moving into a new language, and this frame enabled a more benign account than they had held as children.

Unpacking the effect on family relationships of issues of language fluency could unsettle ideas of personal failing or family dysfunction. Adults' feelings of inadequacy in the dominant language, differentially experienced in relation to their resources and status, may dovetail with their children's responses. An explicit consideration of the effects of a change of language on family relationships may avoid these being translated into personal failures, and enable parents to support their children in these new tasks as well as facilitate their connection and respect for their culture of origin. Helping parents challenge narratives of incompetence constructed through inarticulacy could potentially recalibrate these power imbalances so they could offer support to their children and the challenges they face. This could mediate the construction of these processes and contribute to a parental sense of competence, and children's developing skills. Suárez-Orozco and Suárez-Orozo (2001) for example, found that a parental sense of authority and respect is crucial to supporting their children's bicultural competencies, an ongoing connection to their language/culture of origin and a helpful positioning in the dominant one.

Partner/marital relationships and language use

Differences in fluency had an effect on the relationships between parents and children, and it also affected marital and partner relationships. Twenty out of the 24 research participants were (or had been) in part- nerships conducted in English, their second or subsequent language. It had been taken for granted that relationships would be conducted in English with an English-speaking partner, and research participants had also been living their lives mainly in English. This in itself testifies to the dominance and status of English in Britain.

When neither partner's first language was English, decision-making about which language to conduct their relationship in was an explicit issue. Questions about who would learn whose language were negoti- ated in relation to issues of power within the relationship, as well as in relation to differences in the status of the languages. I examine this later in this chapter in relation to the claiming of identity.

The status of English was taken for granted in the other partnerships formed in Britain. A few individuals had set about learning their partner's language at the beginning of the relationship, and this had been important in itself, as Maria put it: "He went to classes and everything, and said all the right things", and for Renata, the fact that her partner could speak her childhood language was one of his attractions. However, these relationships were all conducted in English.

There was considerable variation in the ways in which research participants constructed their experience of conducting an intimate relationship in their second/subsequent language. Henka, Saskia and

Venjamin thought they were able to be more intimate in their relationships in English, connected to a freedom from constraints they had experienced within their childhood languages. Maria felt that she was taken seriously in her relationship in English, in contrast to those she had had in Spanish. Ffionn saw English as introducing a helpful difference into her relationships, having described her previous relationships in Welsh as follows:

> Yes. It was a brother and sister sort of relationship (laughs). It was funny, it was like family, because the Welsh community is so small, it's like going out with somebody in your family. (laughs) No, I don't mean that in that sense.

Bernard and Estelle both presented themselves as excited about engaging across differences of language and culture in their relationships. These are constructions of the difference a second language helpfully conferred, either in how it enabled them to be in relationship, or in relation to the attraction to difference. Others found it more challenging.

Individuals' partners were portrayed as varying in how they constructed being in a cross-language relationship. Saskia and Cato relayed accounts of their white English partners being rather dismissive of their languages, which had impacted both on their sense of themselves and on their relationship. They had both separated from their partners, actions that were perhaps connected to these attitudes in some way. As on the whole, little if any discussion about language seemed to have taken place in many of these relationships, views about language may only have become apparent over time.

Cross-language relationships, even when based on attraction of difference, often ignored the impact of language differences in the relationship.

> Estelle I am sure looking back now there was a lot of misunderstanding between us. There were genuinely, which you know I probably thought actually this guy doesn't understand me, actually it was probably a lot of, yes, misunderstanding.
>
> CB So that now looking back on it you'd think ah well that must have been something to do with language. At the time you might have taken it for something else?
>
> Estelle Well, I mean I'm sure there is no doubt something to do with language. That was an attraction for me there.

When such differences are ignored, misunderstandings are put down to other dimensions of relationships.

Interactions around issues of language sometimes became constructed as problematic in relationships. Thérèse's white English partner had learned a bit of Flemish but they conducted their relationship in English, and she described his impatience when she struggled with English words:

> Sometimes I didn't use the right word and I tried to explain and that he would use them against me, like taking it literally, and I would say "you know I can't find", or he would joke with it, like when I'm tired I could say, "can you take that thing out of the thing", and he would say "oh my god, you with your things, name it", and that he is impatient about. And still now, I can have, when I'm tired and I don't find the word, and "that thing that you do that thing with it" (laughs) and that can cause some, some, that he gets like, "you're now ages here, you should know the word", and, or he can't do what I've asked him to do and he gets annoyed about it, because I don't explain myself properly.

In Therese's account the issue of her non-fluency in English becomes problematized and material for marital tension, and in this description her husband comes across as insensitive to her second-language status. Differences in competence in English are likely to impact on whose versions of issues and events come to be accepted in the relationship. Therese (like Bernard) found it hard to refute the idea that she should be more competent in English. Maintaining an awareness of each partner's different positioning within English as a characteristic of the relationship seemed challenging. And it is likely that other issues in the relationship may get emptied into questions of language.

Ffionn referred to similar interactions in her relationship with her husband, but these had acquired a different meaning than in Thérèse's relationship.

> Sometimes I can't express myself, and he says "Why don't you just say it?" and I say "Well, I just can't, because I can't say it in English, because I can't think of the words". I think he is beginning to realise what it is. It took him a while to understand that it is difficult for me sometimes to express in a language that I can't express in. So yes, so I think he understands.

Ongoing acknowledgement of difficulties of expressiveness in a second language avoided constructions centred around personal failure and problems. Ffionn believed that her husband being Irish was crucial to his attitude to language. However, she also reported that he often commented on her lack of a sense of humour, which he did construct as a personal characteristic, rather than an effect of being a second-language speaker.

Differences of language and of fluency in English in the relationship could also heighten individuals' sensitivities to the possibility of mistaken assumptions and misunderstandings, and focus them on the ongoing struggle to understand the other. Thérèse described beginning her relationship in a new language:

> Emotionally you were more intense in trying to understand each other and there would be more effort to listen while the communication was difficult, and it was extremely tiring too.

This is a heightened awareness of the need to work between language differences in the partnership, of the need to struggle in language with the insufficiencies of language. The value of this awareness has led some authors (DiNicola 1986; Steiner 1998a) to propose 'translation' as a helpful metaphor for any communication.

As discussed earlier, in Chapter 4, several research participants talked of the usefulness of the honing down of their own talk in their second/subsequent language with a concentration on 'essentials'.

If we consider English as a first language and English as a second language to be different languages, coordinating these has the potential for creative dialogic interactions as well as the danger of producing monologic discourse, in which difference is dismissed and disqualified (Bakhtin 1986). In monologic discourse, differences, such as those of expressiveness, are problematized; in dialogic interactions, they are validated. And if an individual's other languages are ignored in the relationship altogether, significant aspects of their experience and of themselves might never be brought forth in the relationship. These individuals' relationships moved between resisting and being captured by English-language dominance. There was some variation in the ways in which these relationships acknowledged and worked the differences of language, and individuals' different positioning in English. Significantly, these processes often seemed to be left implicit.

Parenting and language use

Issues of language within adult relationships became re-contextualized when individuals became parents, and raised questions concerning language not previously considered. In this section I identify these issues and analyse the ways in which women and men constructed their parenting and language use in different ways.

Seventeen of the research participants were parents, and 13 of these had parented for some of the time in their first/childhood language. As only three of these individuals were speaking this language with their partner at the time, it highlights the significance of this choice of language for their parenting. Women and men gave rather different accounts of their use of language for their parenting.

Mothering and the use of language

In the context of becoming mothers in Britain, most of these women had spoken their first/childhood languages to their babies from birth, and this was a significant aspect of mothering and language use. The two women, Angela and Thérèse, who had spoken English to their children, positioned themselves in relation to reasons why they had not used their first languages.

Women drew on a range of constructions in giving their accounts of themselves as mothers. Saskia, who was living her life mainly in English when she gave birth to her first child, told me:

I talked German to my son naturally when he was a baby.

Ffionn had found herself "having" to talk Welsh to her baby when she first picked her up after her birth:

When my daughter was born, in the hospital when she was born, and I saw her for the first time and I picked her up and talked to her, I had to talk to her in Welsh. I just couldn't speak to her in English and I still can't.

These women draw on a construction of the 'naturalness' of using their first/childhood language for their interactions with their babies. Inter-linked with this construction, is the way individuals constructed their first/childhood languages in the context of mothering. Interestingly, research participants who used their second childhood language to parent constructed these in the same way as others did their first language, indicating a blurring of subjective distinctions between languages learned when young. Renata described this:

> With my children there was a kind of intimate vocabulary and that's probably why with my daughter I spoke a lot of German because that kind of tender playfulness came much more naturally in German, playful, what you do with little children, that sort of thing.

Constructions of first and childhood languages as 'intimate', 'playful' and 'emotionally expressive' in relation to mothering, echoed the way in which first languages became constructed in the context of living in subsequent languages, as previously discussed. The use of a first language as a mother was also constructed as allowing access to aspects of self not available in the language learned later. Estelle said the idea that she would not be able to speak French with her children made her think:

> It would be like losing a part of myself in my relationship with my children.

Such aspects of self could encompass expressive abilities as well as ways of thinking and perceiving. Mothering in one's first language was also considered a way to create a context for speaking this language when no other opportunities existed. As Estelle put it:

> I probably talked French to him because I had no one else to talk to.

In this way, mothering could keep one's language, feared to be atrophying, alive.

Neither Angela nor Thérèse spoke their first language to their children, and they talked about mothering in English as if they needed to defend this choice. Angela cited the lack of a supportive context, away from her mother and a language community, but at the same time, defined herself as lazy, for using English to parent.

> I was lazy. But I couldn't teach them pure Albanian. I couldn't teach them pure Sicilian dialect. [...] And I couldn't even teach them Italian. [...] Because none of it was my mother tongue, you know

Angela positioned her account in relation to the idea that she should have used her 'mother tongue', and made use of this construct in a somewhat ambiguous way. One construction is that being brought up with many languages precludes one from having *a* 'mother tongue'. This may draw on a notion of the importance of the 'purity' of language use, in relation to which speaking a mixture of languages is not considered proper. Cromdal (2000) has pointed out how this idea of 'purity' is a monolingual norm which constructs successful bilingualism as monolingualism in each linguistic setting.

Thérèse had found herself speaking English to her son from the moment of his birth, although English was still a very new language to her.

> And my first words to the baby were English. [...] And I'm still annoyed with that, because I started to speak English already, so I adapted so quickly to the environment that it was not natural anymore to speak Dutch to the baby who was born, and therefore I have always spoken English to the children.

Thérèse referred to the idea of having assimilated 'too quickly', which disrupted the 'naturalness' of mothering in one's first language. She constructed herself as having mistakenly privileged assimilation, indicating a change in her perspective over time, or perhaps some tension in her self-account, because she also presented herself as someone who challenged rules and conventions, with which this account did not fit so easily.

These accounts indicated that women positioned themselves and were positioned in relation to the idea of the 'mother tongue' – that one mothers in one's first language.

Alongside an interpretative repertoire of the 'naturalness' of using one's first language for mothering, many of these women drew on a discourse of 'language as work'. Women proposed that speaking their first language to their children in the context of a different dominant language needed commitment and ongoing attention. Ffionn said:

> I think if I don't constantly speak the language to her and say, this is the language I speak and that's what you have to speak to me, she won't learn it. [...] So I have to sort of like say that's it, that's all I hear, I don't speak English. She knows I can because she hears me but she knows that I don't speak it to her. So we have a special language.

This interpretative repertoire of language speaking as work was drawn on more often when children's own perspectives became influential, as I go on to examine later.

Fathering and the use of language

Fathers used their languages in different ways to the mothers, and this was connected to the way in which they constructed their languages in their accounts of their parenting. Seven of the research participants were fathers. Only Naadir had spoken Arabic, his first language, with his children from birth and he was the only father with a same language partner. Four fathers had shifted to speaking their first language to their children when they were somewhat older. Two fathers used only English for their parenting. Unlike the women, none of the men referred to ideas of naturalness in relation to their own parenting and language.

Ihsan described switching to speaking Farsi with his daughter when she was a couple of months old:

CB   Tell me when your daughter was born did you think to speak with her in Farsi?

Ihsan   I still find it very difficult to speak to her in Farsi. I speak to her in Farsi, you know, it's sort of like talking to my best friend and I don't want to do that, so I don't think it's right she's going to learn a bad language, that's the way I look at it, a strange language, so I find it very difficult to do it. But I'm doing it because if you do it, you must do it.

CB   And you decided that from the moment she was born?

Ihsan   About 2 months, a month and half after...

CB   After she was born. Did you start speaking English with her?

Ihsan   I was speaking English all of the time, yes but then I'm stopping it, now, I speak Farsi to her now.

In contrast to being 'natural', Ihsan constructed speaking Farsi to his daughter as difficult, and drew on an interpretative repertoire of 'language as work', an ongoing effort and duty, "if you do it, you must do it". Like Angela he referred to a notion of 'purity' of language, connoted as necessary for child rearing, not speaking a 'bad language', a hybrid language he had developed with Iranian friends – once again impacted by monolingual norms.

Petiri switched to speaking Shona with his daughter, when she asked him what language he was speaking, and wanted to learn it. The switch in his use of language for fathering was driven by his daughter, and, in fact, Petiri did not speak Shona to his son. This change in his language for fathering also reflected a different positioning from his earlier decision to parent in English, which I discuss below.

Naadir had spoken Arabic to his children from birth, as had his wife. However, he saw his children as having difficulty sustaining their Arabic speaking, and finding it impossible to learn classical Arabic. Naadir raised concerns about this, in terms of their relationship with Islam:

> You see the problem is, if you don't speak Arabic properly, you can't read the Qur'an.

Naadir here constructs his first language, not in terms of emotional expressiveness, but in relation to relaying religious knowledge and facilitating cultural continuity. Bernard explained that he read in French, his first language, to his children, rather than speaking this with them:

CB   Did you decide, OK I'm going to speak French to her, or what did you do?

Bernard We never actually spoke French. Um, except for reading, which we read with a loud voice and I would, well I was teaching her French, yes, but we didn't speak French in normal conversation. We had our little sessions, but (2) I never forced that on to the children. It was not a natural thing to do in a way, like the mother tongue. A mother who is, say, born in France and come to England and marry and had a first baby, she might tend to speak French to her children when they were babies.

CB   Did you ever have that feeling?

Bernard No. Never had that feeling. I didn't feel very comfortable speaking it to my babies in the language in the context. For me it was out of context in a funny way.

This is a construction of language use as educational rather than as relational. Bernard drew explicitly on the notion of 'mother tongue' here, which he saw as not applying to him, because he was not a mother. Bernard also makes reference to his experience of the constraint of the context he is in, and Gustav placed this as central to his decision to parent in English:

> Czech didn't come into it, because my partner doesn't speak Czech and I thought it was just ridiculous to speak Czech because there was no kind of context for it anyway.

The construction by fathers of a lack of context in which to speak their first language to their children stands in contrast to the women's accounts, who make reference to this only when their children are much older. Ideas about the importance of context for fathers' language use links to the ways in which fathers often come to rely on their partners' relationship with their children as the context for their own fathering relationship, often only highlighted after marital separation (Burck and Daniel 1995b). The fact that their wives/partners did not speak these men's first language to their children may therefore have acted as the most significant context for their decision-making, rather than the wider context as such.

When fathers did shift to speaking their first/childhood languages with their children, they remarked on the difference this made to their relationship. Venjamin had switched to speaking Hebrew with his daughter during a year in which they lived in Israel, when she was a young child, and noted that:

It brought us closer together. [. . .] And I remember that she woke up one night in the middle of the night and she um said "Abbale," which is in Hebrew, her first word was Dad, sort of in kids' language. [. . .] Abba is father, abbale is Dad, and I remember that, she obviously had become Israeli to the extent that when she woke up in the middle of the night she would use a Hebrew word and call me, rather than use an English word and call my wife.

For Venjamin, the context acted as a resource for his switch to parenting in his childhood language, because both the wider society and his wife were very supportive of his language switch. A first/childhood language conferred intimacy to fathering relationships. This would also be related to how individuals experienced their first language themselves – associated with a sense of familiarity, as much as of ease of expressiveness. Speaking a first language also signified and brought forth connectedness at another level – that of cultural similarity. Petiri's description of the shift to talking Shona with his daughter in Britain at her request was constructed in similar ways:

It's brilliant. It's really feels so good [. . .] So when I'm with my daughter it feels like, we could be in Zimbabwe, it's as relaxed as that. And she's very very keen and very interested.

The shift into fathering in his first language both engendered and conveyed a different kind of connectedness between Petiri and his daughter than had existed in English. An important aspect of switching to his first language in his relationship with his daughter concerned its evocation of other aspects of his sense of self and of his country of origin. It may, therefore, have a similar function to Estelle's parenting in her first language had in keeping it alive in the context of its absence elsewhere. Conducting their parenting relationship in their first language could serve to construct home away from home, a way to bring the past into the present.

Of note, then, was that none of these fathers constructed their first languages as those for intimacy and play for fathering, but when they switched to speaking their first/childhood language with their children, after parenting in English, they experienced this as conferring intimacy and connectedness. This may mean that there are many similarities in the experiences of parenting in a first language across gender. However the different ways in which women and men construct their use of language for their parenting and their languages in the context of parenting are connected to different choices of language with their own effects.

Constructions of parenting and language

Because family relationships are gendered it is perhaps no surprise that issues around language use within families are significantly interlinked with gendered constructions – in particular, how mothering and father-ing have been conceptualized. Although there are considerable cultural variations between the research participants, mothers generally talked about language use differently from fathers.

In this context, it seemed important to interrogate the term 'mother tongue' which, as noted earlier, has remained in common usage in the literature, with all its assumptions of parenting arrangements. In the perusal of these accounts, it has become apparent how much the con-cept of 'mother tongue' operated as an implicit idea drawn on by both women and men. Given that these research participants were living in Britain and most were conducting their intimate partner relationships in English, the fact that most of these parents parented, at least for some of the time, in their first/childhood language seemed striking, and interconnected in interesting ways with the concept of 'mother tongue'.

The notion of the naturalness of using their first language to mother referred to by many of these women, in contrast to the way men talked of using their first language to father, related to the notion of 'mother tongue' although very few used the term itself. Mothering itself has, of course, predominantly been constructed as 'natural' (unlike fathering), despite feminist work that has deconstructed this notion (cf Phoenix and Woollett 1991). These overlapping constructions of 'naturalness' – of mothering, and of a first language – underpinned the concept of 'mother tongue' in these interviews.

Beliefs about 'mother tongue' embedded in these accounts were influential, but what were these beliefs? What is a 'mother tongue'? In a different language context, one's first language and its familiar sounds are given an emotional investment and meaning, in which the feeling that one will understand and be understood is central, as well as signifying identity. In the context of parenting, a 'mother tongue', signified something much more specific. The implicit meaning, which research participants drew on in relation to the notion of 'mother tongue', was that the language one was mothered in is the language one mothers in. These meanings are generated in relation to an idea that one's first language, one's 'mother tongue', facilitates drawing on one's own experiences of being mothered in order to help one mother. First languages were experienced and constructed as offering a way to feel connected to one's family of origin, a sense of the familiar and to the past, across distance. They could be experienced as providing a sense of home, 'being at home' in the language, in the absence of any geographical place that one could identify as home.

The women constructed their first language differently from the men, connoting it as one for intimacy and playfulness, as relational. The use of a first language was also seen as a way to access aspects of self that were unavailable in a second language, as well as providing an opportunity to speak it. The meanings of language for parenting did not stay static, however, and could shift with sociopolitical changes as well as changes at personal and family levels, and impact on decisions about language choice. For example, Renata talked of how an increase in racism in Germany following unification changed the connotation of German from a language of intimacy for parenting, to one that exposed her mixed-parentage children to danger, and that this had led to her decision to parent her younger daughter in English.

The notion of 'mother tongue' was understood as excluding fathers. Why is a first language constructed as belonging to mothers, and what relationship with their first language does this construct for fathers? In these accounts, it constructed fathers as individuals who didn't use their first languages with their babies for intimacy and play. In relation to an idea that a 'mother tongue', that is, the language in which you were mothered, helps draw on those experiences to help you mother, this constructs men as unable to learn to father from their mothers.

And what meaning is given to the language you were fathered in, which, in any case, is often the same language as you were mothered in? 'Father tongue' in these accounts was not named, but was constructed as a language for educational purposes and for carrying cultural identity. This construction of the language for fathering mirrors constructions of fathering which have emphasized 'role' rather than relationship. When fathers did switch to speaking their first/childhood languages with their children after having parented in English, it was experienced as changing the relationship.

Women may implicitly draw on the notion of 'mother tongue' to warrant a change in the language practices within the family. When women become mothers, they can lay claim to the importance of their first language, ignored in the context of their partner relationship. This may also function to place their partner in the more disadvantageous position in relation to language, which the women themselves may have experienced in the dominant language. The idea that it's 'natural' to use one's first language to mother, the signification of 'mother tongue' as important, makes this difficult to refute or challenge.

If we can deconstruct the notion of 'mother tongue' which has been so powerfully constitutive of choices made by both men and women interviewed for this research, this could enable a reconsideration of language use and parenting arrangements in families, alongside a consideration of the value of speaking several languages. For these parents, fathers as well as mothers, speaking their first or childhood language with their children increased their sense of intimacy and closeness in these relationships, for whatever reasons, as well as sustaining minority language speaking both as parents and for children.

Code switching as rhetorical strategy in parenting

Individuals who used their first language to parent had the potential to switch between languages – to code switch. It is likely that a lot of code switching within family relationships would take place without any conscious awareness of its function or meaning, which is why research into its use tends to use observational methods. Nevertheless, research participants reported on instances of code switching which they used explicitly as parents in various ways or had noticed.

Some individuals reported that their families had developed a style of code switching in their conversations. Certain concepts or phrases in their first/childhood languages came into common usage in English conversations, because they encompassed ideas and feelings which could not be translated, and English terms were used in their first language interactions.

Di-Yin and Naadir both described an explicit use of code switching in their parenting, moving from their first language to English for rhetorical purposes. Di-Yin described how she switched to English at times in mothering her daughter:

> Because in day care the teachers were disciplining her, saying, "you're not allowed to do this," and teachers always discipline much better than mothers (laugh). Because sometimes when I really want her to do something, I say it in English, and also because her language is just developing, and she doesn't understand Mandarin as much as English, because eight hours of English in day care, she understands more. So when I really want to discipline I say, "you should not do this," and I lecture her in English (laughs).

Di-Yin used English, strategically, to back up her sense of authority with her daughter. English enabled her to 'perform authority', similar to the way English helped her to 'perform anger', discussed earlier. In using English, Di-Yin may also have created some distance in her relationship with her daughter, from which position she could 'do' discipline differently. This switch also involves the use of 'appropriated speech', where an individual reproduces another's words in a different context (Maybin 1999), invoking the day care teachers through the use of English, with the added dimension and weight of a switch to the dominant language.

Naadir thought he needed to know English well as a father and to use it on particular occasions:

> When I have to explain to them something really important, I have to speak English, because it's so serious, I want them to understand. For example, if I teach them anything, mathematics, language or reading things or doing things for them, I have to do it in English for them to understand. If I have to discipline them or teach them things in life I have to speak in English to them, so that they understand what I'm talking about. Otherwise the Arabic for them is like fruit.

Like Di-Yin, Naadir could be said to use English to 'perform authority' in his relationship with his children. He also used the code switch to make a metalanguage communication, to mark the importance of the content for himself and for his children. Naadir felt strongly about his need to speak English at times in order to connect to his children's concerns, and linked this to the way he thought about himself as a father.

> You have to have two different hats and a third hat in-between, because poor children have two different lives. For us as adults, I know which is right, which is wrong and how to behave, because I came as an adult to this country. I still have lots of carrying with me a whole culture and customs and language, a whole life behind me, or with me. They don't. So sometimes, for example, they have to behave in the school like English, to be accepted among the English, or this is the only thing they know. When they come home, they have to behave a different way according to us, and our religion. So sometimes you have to behave with them as a father, as an Arab father, and sometimes you have to talk to them as an English father for them to understand me, and that hat in the middle, to differentiate between this and that. So it's very difficult.

Naadir saw his children as needing to manage two different worlds (very similar to the childhood accounts). This is code switching articulated at a different level – a switch back and forth between languages and between the kind of father he is in each. Naadir code switched to offer a way to enable his children "to be accepted in both and understand both and be respected in both". Naadir's work as an interpreter seemed influential in his construct of fathering as also managing the in-between, the difference between the languages. Was this the kind of resource lacking in some of the childhood accounts? Naadir went on to elaborate on the place of language in problematic relationships between Arabic-speaking parents and their children, from his experience as an interpreter:

> For the Arabs not to lose their children in this country, the parents should learn the language and the culture here and the mentality here, because your children are going to have this mentality, if you don't understand their mentality through their language, you won't be able to discipline them or bring them up properly as you wish so.

The position Naadir was elaborating here was not so much one of assimilation, for which it could easily be mistaken, but one of a strategic use of code switching with the aim of parenting in the way one wanted.

These uses of code switching – developing the use of their different languages as 'heteroglossia', to use Bakhtin's term – demonstrated its sophistication as a rhetorical strategy, similar to other research on code switching which had countered its previous negative connotations. It also demonstrated the self-reflexivity of the individuals who made use of it. Di-Yin and Naadir switched languages as a marker of affect, to grab attention, to emphasize, to indicate a change in relationship, and to invoke the authority of others. They both used English to 'perform' authority in their relationships with their children and, in doing so, they relied on associations their children would have to English, including its status in Britain.

Parenting in a second language

Some research participants had chosen to parent in English, and many of the others had gradually switched from parenting in their first language to parenting in English. I examine the ways in which individuals warranted their decisions and the ways in which they constructed the advantages and disadvantages of parenting in a second language.

Some accounts of parenting in English were positioned in relation to ideas of what parenting in one's first/childhood language would have entailed, or in which it should have occurred. There are notions here of first languages encompassing a richness and complexity not possible in a second language. Petiri constructed parenting in English as follows:

> One can only do one's best, but it's always, like an analogy of an ill fitting shoe, it will do, but it's never quite as good fitting as a proper shoe. It's a size smaller so you always know there's something that's not quite right.

Petiri presented himself as someone who now regretted his choice to parent in English, but warranted his initial choice to enable his children to 'fit' into and be successful in the community. This was important to Petiri as a black man, because he knew his children would experience racism. He also proposed that parenting in English was protective of his relationships with his children.

> The children can identify with my values because they don't see them as alien. Whereas if I had parented as an African father, certainly there would have been a lot of clashes, and I would have been the loser because at the end of the day, you can only go so far, you can't force children to do what they don't want to do. So parenting

in English has helped me to be aware of all that, to be very respectful of where they're coming from, to go for collaboration really, rather than leading them, to go for authoritative parenting rather than authoritarian parenting.

Petiri saw his children's assumption of English values and attitudes as inevitable and that his parenting in English allowed and enabled him to father in a way that fitted in with the context his children inhabited, to make sense of the perspectives they took on. This is a similar position to that taken by Naadir, that using their children's dominant language to parent, for at least part of the time, could subvert the polarizations that so easily occur between language and culture differences. And just as individuals described being different in each of their languages in other contexts, they also experienced parenting in each of their languages as being a different kind of parent, embodying different values encoded in the language, including different conceptualizations of 'parenting' and 'children'.

Angela parented her children in English, and, as commented earlier, had taken up a somewhat defensive position about this. She talked of how aware she had been of issues for her children around identity:

> But again, my children went through what I went through, especially my son, he did have an identity crisis. He didn't know, he said to me, I remember, at the same age as I did, "I don't know whether, I'm not English, I'm not French, I'm not even Italian." They have a third one. "I don't know who I am", you know.

In the context of her own struggles as a child in relation to her languages, through which she continually experienced herself as different and an outsider, Angela's decision to parent in English could be viewed as an attempt to protect her children, although she did not name this as such.

Venjamin gave up speaking Hebrew to his daughter and switched back to English when they returned to Britain:

> I didn't think that it was important to keep up her Hebrew, but my wife did, and my wife was disappointed with me for dropping Hebrew and not trying to, not continuing to speak to her in Hebrew, um. I think that even if I had made the effort for a year, two years, it would have been an uphill struggle and she wouldn't have been able to retain her Hebrew. I wasn't motivated. I didn't attach much

importance. I tend to be more matter-of-fact and more utilitarian. She lives in England, she goes to an English school, she doesn't learn Hebrew at school and uh, she, uh, was learning French at school, so the thing to do was to concentrate on French rather than Hebrew. [...] So I, I suppose, I felt it's up to my daughter if she wants to learn Hebrew, I would make, provide teaching for her.

Venjamin constructed his decision as pragmatic, drawing on an interpretative repertoire of 'language as work'. He proposed that the wish to learn Hebrew should come from his daughter (which is how Petiri came to speak Shona to his daughter). Like Angela's stance, if we juxtapose this account with Venjamin's childhood narrative, this may be considered an implicit wish to protect his daughter from the difficult experience, the shame he had experienced about his first language throughout his growing up. However, he too did not construct it in this way.

What was explicit in these accounts was that these parents privileged their children's ease in the dominant language and context over their ability to speak several languages – examples of the dominance of English alongside the devaluing of the advantages of multilingualism. This was mirrored in Wasan's account of his parents' position in relation to his language learning on arrival in Britain when he was a young child:

> It was more a sense of this child 's got to be up there with the others and what can be done to make sure that that happens as quickly as possible [...] At home we spoke in Gujarati. The first sort of value was in secondary school, when I started secondary school, and having a headmaster I think had fought in probably the last bit of the Second World War, through India and Burma I think. So the message from him was make sure that you at least speak to your child at home in Gujarati [...] if it wasn't privileged by the headteacher we would have continued in that sort of way, that you should be teaching your child English [...] I think that's what gave the permission to my parents to keep it going or validate it then, otherwise there was a sense that you shouldn't be doing that [...] you have to kind of get your child established and forget about Kenya, India and that kind of thing.

A dominant discourse concerned the importance of a child's fluency in English for success, and in Wasan's account it was only an authoritative professional who could counter this prevalent interpretative repertoire.

Estelle's account as a parent further illuminated the effect of dominant discourses around bilingualism. She recollected a significant intervention by a health visitor:

Estelle   I remember the health visitor saying to me "Oh you must speak." and my son spoke quite late. And I just thought well, you know, because he used to speak a word of French, a word in English, and I knew what he was talking about, [...] and then and I remember the health visitor saying, "you mustn't do this, you mustn't do this, you're gonna confuse him, he is going to have speech delay"
CB   She was saying you mustn't do what?
Estelle   You mustn't speak two languages to him. Speak one or the other. You must speak English to him because otherwise.

Estelle had initially talked of switching languages for parenting as a personal choice and only later in her interview did she remember this professional intervention, which had impacted on her language use as a parent. Her daughter speaks little French. Saskia's decision to move to parenting in English was also taken in relation to concerns that her son was language delayed:

I was worried that he was actually quite slow in speaking and I made a conscious effort not to speak so much German to him. [...] but I remember it being more gratifying speaking German to him.

Constructions of bilingualism in children causing language delay were dominant professional discourses at the time, and these accounts demonstrated how insidious professional hegemonic negativity about bilingualism could be, and the ways in which it contributed to language loss.

In parenting in a second language, individuals experienced themselves as positioned differently from when they used their first language. Ursula switched to parenting her second child, a son, in English, having parented her first child, a daughter, in Danish in Denmark. In exploring the effect of mothering in two different languages, Ursula described keeping a physical distance from her daughter to try to protect her, because of fears of repeating her own mother's abusiveness. She thought that mothering her son in English had been different:

CB   I just wanted to ask more about whether you felt uh being a mother to him in English made it easier to be a different kind of mother from your mother, because it was in a different language?

Ursula   That could be, it could be, I mean, it certainly, in my very down moments, I actually, when I spoke Danish, I heard myself as my mother. I thought God, and so I think, yes it was always a relief to get out of that mood, so, it allowed me to distance myself from myself, I suppose. [...] Yes I didn't know what my driving forces were, but it certainly, yes English, doing it in English was easier.

Of note here is the difference that a second language was experienced as bringing. The experience of repeating their own parents' phrases (the appropriation of others' speech) unselfconsciously, which many parents report, is disrupted here because of the switch in language. The disruption is constructed as acting at two different levels – the second language provides a distance (from experience, from the self, from the relationship) and it aids self-reflexivity. As Ursula constructs this account in the process of the interview, she links the distance English provided her from her mother with her ability to be closer to her son.

Oh yes I think it did, with him I was much, much closer, so the whole thing was, I was actually, I felt close to a human being for the first time in my life.

Other factors undoubtedly contributed to the experience of such a different relationship, gendered differences of mothering a son and a daughter, parenting in a different country, mothering a second as opposed to a first child. However, I found Ursula's construction, of how the language difference aided her in her parenting, to be compelling, and it was echoed in others' accounts.

In unpacking the effect of parenting in English with other parents, it emerged that it had helped to avoid a replication of unhelpful patterns from their families of origin at different levels. Gustav spoke of wanting to be a very different father from his own father:

My father was more kind of domineering in that and because I really [...] disagreed with his way of parenting if you like, [...] I have definitely tried to avoid consciously in any language. Fundamentally father is always good at putting you down whatever you did, because you didn't do what he wanted, whatever else you do was bad by definition, which I think is a terrible thing to do to a child. So with my son definitely we kind of set ourselves a sort of agenda.

Exploring the effect of his parenting in a different language and context, Gustav described how his relationship with his son was reversed, because of his unfamiliarity with English cultural/linguistic practices.

CB   I was just thinking about things like nursery rhymes, songs, I don't know whether there were a lot of that when you were growing up, that your mother would do for you? Obviously now you're doing something very different?

Gustav Well I'm picking them from him as opposed to the other way.

CB   Yes exactly, he's teaching you?

Gustav Well it is actually quite sweet, [...] stories and so on, which I had no party to, so now it's quite fun that I'm beginning to read Winnie the Pooh for example (indistinct)

What parenting in English accomplished for Gustav in his 'agenda' to father differently was that, in contrast to his father, who had always taken a stance of a critical expert, he could not position himself like that, and he became a father who learned from his son.

Zack thought his parenting in his second language was very different from how he did this in his first:

It encourages me to be more ah measured about um (4). I have the feeling when I am speaking to him that um, I am more careful about what I say, and what, what I'm thinking about what I say to him, whereas I might say more things which are just sort of instinctive, or intuitive, just firing from the hip.

The construction of the effect of parenting in a second language makes reference to the introduction of distance which enabled this father to take up a reflexive observer position to himself. One could say that a second language is experienced as creating a space between feeling and acting. The long pause in this extract indicated that this was a new idea to Zack. Many of these research participants had not considered such effects of language on their parenting. Parenting in a second language had not been chosen explicitly for these reasons.

The major losses involved in not parenting in a first language was language loss in the next generation and a loss of complexity and diversity for the individual and the family – a loss of emotional nuances, and of historical and local knowledge. Parents saw themselves as leaving out aspects of themselves in their second language, and of not being able to draw on the richness of their first language and its interconnectedness with their culture, with resultant losses for their children. However, some parents constructed parenting in their second language as supporting their children to be successful in the dominant culture. And what emerged in the analysis was that a second language had enabled some parents to be more like the kind of parents they wanted to be. This mirrored individuals' experiences that moving to live in a second language had helped them to construct themselves differently.

Using language to claim identity and alliances in families

Another dimension of language use within families concerned the ways in which language speaking was signified in the construction of identities. In this section I examine this aspect of language use in both partnership relationships and family relationships. Language speaking and identity claims have been linked in other studies (Bucholtz 1995; Haarmann 1986; Mckay and Wong 1996; Miller 2000; Sebba and Wootton 1998). This study has relied on individuals' reports of their own, their partner's and their children's use of languages within the family context. Individuals continually make claims about their identities in their interactions with others, without necessarily identifying these as significant. In these interviews, individuals have selected particular interactions as important markers in the way in which language speaking evolved in their families.

In marital relationships in which neither partner's first language was English, decision-making about language was more of an explicit issue, in contrast to those where one partner was English. Petiri had married a woman whose first language was French, and they spoke English together and to their children:

> She was not prepared to learn Shona, no way was she going to learn Shona, and I knew that learning French would make me again more of a foreigner. I was foreign enough being in English, speaking in English and doing things in English, I was still a foreigner, but to then to become an even bigger foreigner by acquiring another

foreign language. I thought it was just too much, so I decided to go for the safe option, which was English.

Decisions about language speaking are here explicitly linked to questions of identity in relation to the wider community. Petiri's claim of belonging in Britain was continually under question and challenged in his everyday interactions because of how he was racialized as a black man. Claims of identity were also crucial within the relationship, where differences in the status given to English, Shona and French were also in play as were gendered differences.

Wasan's first language was Gujarati and he had married an Indian woman who had Hindi as a first language. They spoke each other's language and Wasan described their relationship as being characterized by teasing and disputes about whose speech was correct – his East African or her Indian version. Although they could switch back and forth between their languages and did so with their respective families, they conducted their relationship in English, which each spoke well.

It is likely that English was chosen for both Wasan's and Petiri's relationships because it is easier in Britain to do so, because it is the dominant language with high status, and because mostly their living was conducted in English. English could also be viewed as an equalizer within the marital relationship, in that each person had a similar relationship to it and neither partner had to privilege the other's language or claim of identity for the family.

The status of a language could also be used rhetorically, to warrant a claim for an individual's first language. Naadir began his relationship with his Moroccan wife in English, because neither knew each other's version of Arabic, and they later switched to conducting it in his Arabic. He gave the reason as follows:

> Because we all prefer the Middle Eastern Arabic even the North African. [...] Because it's more beautiful, higher status, definitely, because it's nearer to the Qur'an. The Northern Arabic, either Arabic French or Arabic Spanish, which is disliked by the Arabs, it's a broken Arabic, it's a mixture.

Questions about who will learn whose language within the partnership were given meaning in relation to claims of identity both within the relationship and within the dominant communities, in relation to issues of power. Differences in the status of languages also impacted on decisions and were utilized in individuals' claims and negotiations.

Choosing to parent in one's first language may be considered a claim of identity at a time when definitions of self are experienced as changing. When Saskia became a mother:

> I got really homesick, I went home for a month when my son was very little. [...] that's when I felt really unrooted, when I first had my son. [...] and I really didn't deal with that terribly well, um but again I can't really blame my husband for that, but I certainly didn't get any help and encouragement from him. It remained very polarized I guess, my husband and me and Germany.

For Saskia, becoming a parent raised questions of identity and belonging for herself. Speaking one's first language to one's baby can constitute a claim of identity both for oneself and for one's baby, and can be considered as such by a partner. Such claims are made at a time when couples are negotiating their differences of parenting and what they want to carry on and give up from their families of origin.

When one parent parented in a language not spoken by the other, families were faced with issues of managing inclusion and exclusion, and of living with alliances created through language speaking. I use the concept of an alliance here, as a relationship experienced as closer than other relationships in a family, formed through something shared, or in opposition to another individual or relationship.

In some families, one parent spoke with their children in a language not understood by the other. When everyone privileged the importance of speaking this language, exclusion did not become an issue. Ffionn felt supported by her Irish husband, in speaking Welsh to their daughter, because he viewed maintaining linguistic/cultural connections as important:

> CB   Does your husband understand any Welsh?
> Ffionn He is understanding bits and pieces. He is picking it up and he doesn't mind at all. A couple of times he has got a bit funny about it. He is very good really. My husband, he is really really supportive, and thinks it's really important that she doesn't grow up to be a monoglot (laughs). If he spoke Irish he would definitely teach her Irish.

Despite the mutual agreement of the value of bilingualism, this is not altogether straightforward, as implied in Ffionn's comment that her husband "got a bit funny about it" at times. Ffionn, in contrast to some other parents, was not influenced by concerns about exclusion in the presence of other English speakers when she spoke Welsh to her daughter, perhaps because of her husband's support, as well as her family's and her community's historical tradition of persistence in Welsh language speaking and claims of identity in the face of English encroachment.

Maria and her white English husband had received advice about how to manage language speaking when they became parents:

> Unless my husband was completely fluent in Spanish we should speak one parent, one language. Now that created some dilemmas for us, because it meant when I was talking to our daughter, it excluded my husband. And so the rule we evolved was that I would speak Spanish with our daughter when I was on my own with her.

The principle of inclusion became the highest context marker in the family for language use. It was constructed as Maria's task to switch to English to avoid a language alliance with their daughter in the presence of her husband. Maria thought her husband: "understands everything [in Spanish], but he pretends he doesn't", yet she did not speak Spanish in his presence, so that he would not feel left out. In this way, Maria's husband became aligned with English dominance, and Spanish became a private language between Maria and their daughter.

Saskia gave up speaking German to her son altogether, because of concerns about exclusion, which were heightened because she had experienced her husband as dismissive of German, so that she held sole responsibility for her language choice.

> I think that I found it just too difficult to hold together, the speaking German to my son in that one to one, and having another relationship when we were altogether, so either we had to speak English, or my husband wouldn't understand, so I abandoned it really.

If exclusion was an issue in families, the task of inclusion fell to the parent to switch to English in the presence of their partner, rather than to their partner to learn the other language. As discussed earlier, men in this study were more tentative about speaking their first language to their children and those who did, had partners who were actively involved in supporting their language speaking, so issues of exclusion did not arise in quite the same way. For the women, the privileging of inclusion may have connected to the common construction fathers make of themselves as excluded from mother–child relationships when children are young, so that mothering in a different language would confirm such a construction.

Alliances created through language, acquired racialized meanings both inside families and outside them. Petiri had decided to parent in English because of concerns about exclusion in the community, as well as concerns for the relationships within his family:

> I think there was something about fear of difference, and if I was going to teach them Shona or anything to do with my cultural background that would highlight the cultural differences between myself and my wife, and myself and the host community.

Petiri posited inclusion within the family and in the community, in the context of racism, as primary in making decisions about language. His choice of English served to stake a claim to identities for his children as English.

Yvonne, a white mother, talked of the pleasure she had in speaking Dutch to her son in the presence of others:

> I'm aware now that if I speak to him in Dutch, when there are other people around, in a sense it's reinforcing the bond I have with him. [...] It's almost like saying to people I have something unique with him. [...] Which is so silly really. Another reason why I try not to do it. (3) Very complicated actually.

This account illuminates some of the contradictions experienced in speaking a minoritized language in the public domain. Unlike Ffionn, who had a family tradition of maintaining Welsh speaking in the face of English dominance, Yvonne, in common with other parents, found it troubling to contravene social expectations related to inclusion and exclusion. Speaking a minoritized language acted as a marker of difference for parents. However, in contrast to the accounts of childhood this difference was not to be avoided because of its stigmatizing effects, but rather to be celebrated as a mark of specialness and intimacy. This construction of speaking a parent's first language as conferring intimacy to the relationship had, however, also been present in some of the children's accounts, alongside other constructions, as Cato described:

> What I more remember is a sort of a specialness really. A little bit of a sort of secrecy between you know, my mother and I.

The meanings of the alliances constructed through language changed depending on context, and whether inside or outside the family, and over time.

Claiming an identity for oneself as a parent and for one's child through the use of one's first language for parenting was not always straightforward and could present other dilemmas. Ihsan described some discomfort he had in speaking Farsi with his daughter, in relation to certain sayings he found himself using with his daughter:

> My daughter, Ariana, cuts her bread into small pieces, I say "don't cut your bread in small pieces, it's bad luck you know. [...] Don't cut your bread into small pieces it's a sign of lots of children, don't do that." You know, it's a lot of rubbish.

Like many individuals parenting in the same language in which they had themselves been raised Ihsan had found himself repeating the precise words his parents had used. For Ihsan, parenting in his first language in an English context had the effect of creating and highlighting contradictions between his languages and cultures. Until that time he had been conducting his relationship with his partner in English. This would entail having to manage the interface of language and culture differences – an aspect which may otherwise have been kept separate.

Children's claims

Children themselves were significantly involved in decisions about language use within families. As reported by their parents, children made identity claims of their own, by refusing or choosing to speak a parent's language, and turning down or confirming a shared cultural identity with them. English, the dominant language, made inroads into families' talk that itself impacted on children's identity claims.

Bernard's children had differential responses to reading French with him, with his daughter enjoying this, and his son refusing to do it:

> My son didn't want to learn French like that. It was extra lessons and they had enough. My son said, "I was born in England. I am English, so I don't want to do French". But that was a reaction. My daughter didn't have this reaction at all but my son did.

Bernard's son made a claim of an English identity, through which he refused to speak French. This claim also served as a rhetorical device to avoid what he saw as unwanted work. This was not a claim for a language alliance within the family, as Bernard's wife was not English, but a claim as a dominant-language speaker. Saskia's son took a similar stance:

> But my son also said things like, he didn't want to speak German when he was little, "I'm an English boy, not German". He's been much more the one voicing that. I don't know whether that's to get at me, or because that's the imperialistic notion, "I don't need to speak German, everyone will speak English".

Claims for alliances through language and culture, as well as gender, may be staked within the family, as well as in relation to the wider dominant community. In this account, Saskia's husband was perceived as dismissive of German and therefore as supporting the dominance of English, while Saskia's daughter became motivated to learn German, although born into a much more established English-speaking household. Estelle too saw her children as having quite different cultural identifications and engagement with her first language.

> My son is French, I always think of him as being French. He has a lot more connection with France. He loves everything about France. He goes and stays with my mother. Not my daughter, though, she is an English girl.

Of interest here is how these identifications get taken up or refused within family relationships, and how they become constructed over time. What are the effects of these different identifications when they involve languages which constitute their speakers differently? When Petiri's daughter asked him to teach her Shona, his son refused to take part and began to learn French, his mother's language. Family alliances became demarcated through language, with each parent–child pair using a language the other pair did not understand, experienced as claims of shared cultural identity. Such alliances formed by and through language also raise questions about how to avoid creating rigidity in family relationships.

Naadir's children moved to speak English within the family, while Naadir and his wife continued to speak to them and to each other in Arabic. Naadir described that they frequently claimed their identity as English:

> My children, if someone asks them, "where are you from?" they say, "my father is from Iraq, my mother is from Morocco and I am

English." (laughing) I say, "no, you are Iraqi," they say, "yes I'm Iraqi, but I'm English."

In this instance the children's language choice accompanied and performed a claim of identity as English, in spite of the counterclaims of their parents. The negotiations of cultural identities were ongoing processes inside families as well as outside them, and language speaking was very much intertwined in these. These are influenced by shifts in the wider context, where certain identities become constructed as more or less desirable in relation to sociopolitical events.

Language speaking became conflated with identity claims. Because speaking a minoritized language signified a different cultural identity, often problematized in the context of Britain, English identities were constructed as monolingual, correlating with dominant discourses of Englishness. In working to claim an English identity, children often refused other languages. The status of languages was also significant, as English was not only the dominant language but has a high status throughout the world, conveying this to the speaker. Although parents varied in relation to their capital resources, which have been found to be crucial to the ways individuals from a minority group can establish themselves in a different society and support their children's language maintenance, it was challenging for all of the parents in this study to counter these dominant meanings. As children brought the English language and their English friends into the household, and siblings spoke English together, there was an increased alignment with dominant values about language speaking.

There was no easily discernible gendered pattern that emerged in the reported language speaking of children within families. Firstborns generally had a better chance of learning their parents' first languages than subsequent children, because of the gradual move to use English in many of these families, often precipitated by the children. Language speaking was centrally interconnected with children's identity claims. Language choice by children formed alliances and claimed shared identities in interaction with their parents, and sometimes with grandparents.

Decisions made about language use within families demonstrated a variation in comfort with alliances delineated through language. Partners' attitudes to languages and not being able to understand were considered to be significant in supporting the speaking of several languages in the family, even though they rarely felt impelled to learn the other language themselves. However, the dominance of English encroached on family's language use even when a partner in rare instances did learn a language. In Justine's family, her Dutch mother spoke English more fluently than her American father spoke Dutch, which influenced which language became dominant within the family, even when they were committed to living bilingually.

The privileging of English identities by many research participants' children perhaps reflected the longing for singularity and belonging addressed in the childhood accounts. Research participants' own ease with their own multiplicity and their claims of the advantages their languages gave them was not necessarily persuasive for their children.

To sum up, issues of language speaking in families were conflated with claims and counterclaims of identity, as well as claims of alliance. It was unclear whether these meanings of language speaking, and of claims of belonging and not belonging to the dominant culture, had been explicitly considered within families. The ways in which children in families constructed language speaking raises questions about how families can best sustain their speaking of several languages. What is evident in these accounts is how actively both parents need to be involved in supporting and enabling their children to be able to live in several cultural and linguistic contexts in Britain.

Complexities of speaking several languages within families

The identification of the constructions of language and family relationships in these accounts allows a consideration of the complexities for families when adults do not share a first language.

In forming their adult partnerships, individuals and their partners, on the whole, took it for granted that their relationship would be conducted in English, the dominant language. Very few partners decided to learn the other language. In ongoing negotiations of constructions of personhood and relationship, each individual drew on different cultural and linguistic resources and contexts, and partnerships varied as to how they took individual's different positioning within the dominant language into account or not. Issues of fluency in English were open to being problematized. Differences of language and culture could also keep relationships more focused on the struggle for understanding. One could view these cross-language relationships as being characterized by the challenge to make use of the dialogic interaction of differences, and to avoid monologic communication, and they varied considerably in managing this and over time.

Becoming parents recontextualized issues of language for families, and other constructions came into play – of mothering, fathering and children. Many individuals parented in their first/childhood languages for at least part of the time. Having children may powerfully highlight the potential of loss of language and culture, and raise previously overlooked questions about identity. It was a dedicated task to pursue parenting in a minoritized language in the context of Britain. Despite the proliferation of languages in Britain, languages other than English are still considered largely irrelevant, with the emphasis being wholly placed on articulacy in English. The 'bilingual' parent had to operate in two different languages and cultures, and also to find ways to help their children manage this positioning, and their partner's stance seemed crucial in this task. Perhaps unsurprisingly, many research participants drew on a discourse of maintaining their first language as 'work', in their parenting, as they did in relation to keeping their own fluency in their first language.

The gendered differences in the ways in which men and women parented in their first language and constructed this, highlighted the impact of the concept of 'mother tongue', and the ongoing construction of women as those who taught language to their children. This construction made it likely that most mothers would use their first language with their babies, in spite of other constraints on speaking minoritized languages. It also made it less likely that fathers did so, if both they and their partners considered mothers to be responsible for language. Fathers needed some external intervention/permission to speak with their children in their first language. And women and men constructed their first languages differently in relation to parenting, shaped by and contributing to constructions of mothering and fathering.

Parents balanced the importance of sustaining their first language with the importance of fluency in English and the need for children to 'fit in' to the community. Some shifted between these two positions, or they and their partner held different positions with some danger of polarization. Professional discourses had emphasized the importance of fluency in English, as did children themselves. Many parents who had begun parenting in their own childhood language described this changing over time, as they switched over to English, influenced by children themselves.

Children made identity claims in refusing to speak their parents' language, drawing on discourses of the irrelevance of these languages, and seeing language as a marker of difference. However, first languages were also constructed as conferring intimacy and specialness by both parents and children. Giving up a language involved considerable losses.

7
Positioning the Researcher

Qualitative researchers see self-reflexivity as being central to the research processes. This stems from the adoption of a social constructionist stance in which knowledge is considered as constructed and situated, and therefore calls on the researcher to take responsibility for their own positioning (Lincoln and Guba 1994). The importance of scrutinizing one's personal and theoretical assumptions and values as researcher and of examining their impact throughout the research process has been addressed by a number of qualitative researchers (Burck and Frosh 1994; Steier 1991; Wilkinson and Kitzinger 1996), and it is particularly crucial in researching questions personal to the researcher. Indeed, it is through the maintenance of self-reflexivity that qualitative research has legitimized the exploration of questions personal to the researcher.

In this chapter, I address ways in which I have attended to personal–professional links as a researcher, at various different stages in the research process. This may allow the researcher to be scrutinized alongside the research participants, and for the reader to judge the persuasiveness of the analysis.

The rationale for this research was personal as well as intellectual and professional – a curiosity about my own experiences, as well as about the literature, and about the multilingual individuals and families I have encountered in my work:

> It wasn't until I read Eva Hoffman's *Lost in Translation*, several years ago, an account of her move at age 13 from Poland to Canada, from one language to another, that I began to reflect, explicitly for the first time, on my experience of my languages. I live my life mainly in English. I swan about in it with great ease, this language which is

insinuating its way into the entire world's discourses. However, many of my family relationships are conducted in Dutch. And I always swore in Quebecois, because it is gutsy, outrageous, and irreverent in ways which I thought English and Dutch just could not be.

As someone who has grown up speaking several languages, I was positioned as a researcher exploring experiences similar (at least in one aspect) to my own. It was therefore important to identify the contexts which contributed to the choice of the research question and its focus. Being interviewed about the area of the research can help to forefront a researcher's implicit assumptions and beliefs and enable a different relationship to be taken to these. I decided to conduct the research interview with myself, to bring forth my own experiences, to highlight personal connections to the research alongside my theoretical interests, and to facilitate a comparison of similarities and differences with other research participants. I wanted to make explicit my own hypotheses, rather than have these organize the research in an implicit way. I did not want to 'discover' what I already knew or believed. Aspects of my own interview that seem particularly pertinent are included here.

Personal contexts and researcher hypotheses

I moved when I was four from Holland with my family to live in a bilingual French/English community in the province of Quebec. I took it for granted that there was a different language for each context – my parents spoke Dutch at home, we spoke English at school and with friends, and Quebecois French was spoken everywhere else. I cannot remember anything about learning English and French at the age of 4. Our family always talked across languages, as my parents continued to speak Dutch to each other and to us throughout my growing up, while my brother and I switched to English as soon as we were in school. My mother always worried about the extent of my vocabulary in English, and made me study long lists of words when I was in high school. My parents switched to speaking English or French when other people were present, except if they wanted to tell me off which they always did in Dutch. This was a double-edged experience, a marker of having done something wrong, but in a secret code no one else could understand.

Language speaking was politically loaded in the community I grew up in. The north of Quebec in the late 50s and 60s was divided by language: there were separate school systems for English-speaking and

French-speaking children (further divided by religion). Although each school system taught the other language from the age of eight, we were not allowed to speak Quebecois French, the language of the community, at our English school. The education system in combination with other structural factors constructed the relationship between the English and French Canadian languages (and cultures) as unequal, and contributed to the polarizations around language use which continue in the province today. The devaluing of French Canadians and their language by the minority English-speaking population laid the grounds, alongside economic inequalities, for the separatist movement. Indigenous and immigrant languages remained invisible.

When I went to an English-speaking university and then later came to live in Britain in my early 20s the only language I spoke regularly was English, and my working life and further training has taken place in English. Neither I nor anyone else paid any attention to my knowledge of other languages.

Whenever I travel back to Holland and hear Dutch everywhere, it engenders an uncanny sense of familiarity, even intimacy. I feel a warmth towards everybody I encounter. I experience a connectedness, but at the same time, I have a sense that this may at times be misplaced.

A few years ago I gave a presentation at a conference in Holland. As this was the first time I had had the opportunity to work in the country of my birth and of my first language, I had decided that I would make my introduction in Dutch. When I began to speak in Dutch, I suddenly became overwhelmed by a powerful physical sensation, and could hardly go on. The chair of the session looked over at me anxiously, uncertain how to respond. Switching back to English, I 'recovered myself' and I continued the presentation without a problem. I was very puzzled by this experience.

My accent marks me as different in each of my contexts, Holland, Canada and Britain, and I seem to have a different concept of 'home' to those who have lived in only one place. When I am pressed to define myself this shifts depending on the context, but such definitions do not mean much to me, although I am aware that I do not often need to respond to exclusionary processes because of my whiteness.

I recently took formal Dutch lessons for the first time in my life, and becoming aware of grammatical constructions I had never previously noticed, had a startlingly paralysing effect at first. I began to read in Dutch, and noticed that I have to verbalize (silently) to myself, as I do in French, as if I have to process this aurally, rather than through the written word. I have difficulty deciphering spoken numbers in English. There are some concepts in Dutch for which I cannot find adequate descriptions in English.

I didn't consider language explicitly when I became a parent. I brought up my son in English. It never really occurred to me to speak Dutch to him and I was living almost entirely in English and speaking very little Dutch, and my monolingual English husband did not seem supportive of his learning Dutch.

My personal context of growing up in several languages contributed to my choice of research questions as well as informing my ideas about what to explore with research participants. I have been influenced by the idea that many individuals, such as myself, would not have reflected on their experiences of different languages. I considered it likely that many individuals would experience each of their languages differently, and I was curious about these effects. I thought that there would be untranslatable concepts between languages, and that this could affect cross-language relationships. My experience of my languages is interlinked with my moves of country, and I thought that these kinds of interconnections would be important to explore with others. My growing up in a community with two languages with unequal status made me want to explore the effects of this with others. I was aware of the negativity associated with bilingualism in common discourses and in the research literature, and wanted to deconstruct this. I was very curious about the effects of switching between languages on individuals sparked by the experience of my presentation in Dutch.

Co-constructing the research accounts

The examination of interactional processes in the research interviews can highlight researcher effects and ways in which the interview is co-constructed. Within the interview, researchers inevitably pursue certain areas and close down others. In such circumstances posing questions about the questions used in the interviews when examining the transcripts has been helpful: Why shift topic at this point? Why persist in this area? Why question this statement and let that one pass? How can one make use of similarities and of differences?

An examination of the research interview transcripts revealed that I asked questions to invite individuals to consider contextual influences whenever they had constructed a 'self-blaming' account. I have concerns that individuals often construct issues as personal failure which seem related to context. For example, when Saskia described herself as not valuing her culture and language enough, I responded by asking about her context:

CB: But do you think there were people around who would have contributed to your valuing it?
Saskia: Yes.
CB: You did have people?
Saskia: No. Not here. I didn't have any German friends.
CB: So pretty hard, hard to value it?

I have been concerned to explore links between personal experiences and wider social contexts. Because of my awareness of the negativity still associated with bilingualism, I wanted to elicit alternative experiences which had been neglected.

When Venjamin used a double negative and positioned himself in relation to a negative connotation, I asked the opposite to reverse this frame. When he persisted with the term 'problem', I stayed with the reversal:

Venjamin: I don't think language was an inhibiting factor in that relationship.
CB: And you said there wasn't ever a problem, do you think there were any advantages?
           [...]
CB: Do you think it freed you up in a way? Do you think um doing it in English, if it wasn't an inhibiting factor, that it was the opposite, it freed you up in some ways, or not?

This is explicit interventionist questioning. I took a position as researcher to try and elicit alternative experiences and perspectives in contrast to the negative ones of dominant discourses.

Because these research interviews touched on various aspects of research participants' lives, for some this included significant losses and difficulties, and there were moments when it was important to acknowledge poignant experiences and to consider the scope of my questions. I was concerned to pace the emotional intensity of the interview, and to wait to explore more sensitive or difficult issues until later in the interview when I had a sense that the research participant and I had established more of a rapport.

Constructions of new meanings

A research interview seeks to explore issues of interest and relevance to the researcher, while the agenda of research participants can be varied – sometimes involving a wish to explore issues for themselves, sometimes having a desire to put a strongly held point of view, sometimes involving a wish to be helpful. Research participants in this study seemed keen to explore the issues for themselves and I experienced most of the interviews as ones in which mutual learning took place. I formulated many of my questions to connect to research participants' individual responses with the effect that individuals constructed new links and perspectives. Many of these individuals had never talked of these experiences in this way before so they were actively constructing their accounts for the first time.

One example of this occurred when Cato spoke of his experience of his languages when he first settled in England as a child refugee, an extract I discussed in Chapter 3:

> And so I think the kind of lived reality was pretty impoverished here, and I think when we went into Hungarian, and *actually I haven't seen it before in this way*, I think when we spoke Hungarian, there was a time shift back to a time where it was very different, you know, and I was, things were ok and reasonably easy, and I was going to do well at school. No question of any of that, and I think actually that was really helpful for me, in kind of not going under. (*my emphasis*)

He ended the interview by reflecting, with some surprise:

> It's an evocative experience this. It's interesting you know, one's relationship with language is, well loaded with feelings, isn't it?

Konrad too indicated that he had formulated a different meaning during the interview process, in an extract examined earlier on growing up with a minoritized language:

> *I was just trying to make a sort of language connection to that.* [. . .] I mean by the end, I suppose the problem for me could have been, was I this English person, or was I this Polish person? [. . .] *That's what I'm sort of forming in my mind at the moment.* [. . .] And I think this was, this was, *I've never thought about this*, but this whole issue

was something to do with this English person and this Polish. [...] *That's really interesting. That's really useful for me. (my emphasis)*

Konrad explicitly commented that this description, which was a new one, offered a helpful perspective for him. My own thinking about this shift is that using a frame of his different languages and the wider context enabled Konrad to generate an alternative idea from the ones he had held previously which had been more de-contextualized.

At the end of her interview, when I asked what, if any, effect the interview had produced, Thérèse identified a dilemma she had formulated through the research process.

Yes especially towards my children so I was thinking I have to take the Flemish lessons a bit more seriously, like do I want it or do I not want it, or do I?. *What am I doing actually*, uh, driving the poor children with their 10% commitment (laughs). And maybe I should do a bit, if I want that they have access to that part of, of their background, maybe I should do a little. *(her emphasis)*

It is evident that the research interviews were contexts in which new constructions were being formulated, and that I as the researcher was influential and need to take responsibility in developing these.

Similarities and differences in the research relationship

It is easy to replicate processes of 'othering' and of colonizing others' experiences, even when that is not one's intention (Borštnar et al. 2000; Wilkinson and Kitzinger 1996). Going back to the research participants for comments on the interview or the analysis is not always a straight-forward way of managing the dilemmas of power in the researcher–researched relationship (Borland 1991).

As power dynamics are subtle, and positionings in interviews complex, it has been particularly important to try to pay attention to these. Researchers have power; they both take it and are given it, to make evaluations.

In some interviews I became aware of the way a research participant would test out my position before going on to elaborate their experience. As noted earlier, Quinlan seemed rather hesitant about naming an incident, in which her fluency in English had been questioned and her identity challenged, as racist. We ended up constructing it as such in the interview. I was unsure whether Quinlan's tentativeness was in relation to me, the researcher, or whether she rarely used this frame for such experiences, common during her growing up. At times, she was ironic or would qualify her comments about her beliefs or experiences, which I took not only as her clarifying her thinking for herself, but also as a way for her to judge how I positioned myself, before she would go on to elaborate these in a more definite way. This made visible some of the social power dynamics between us, me an older white woman researcher and her, a young Chinese woman. It suggested that there were also complex positionings in the other interviews that were less obvious.

There were also times when research participants and I made reference to some similarity in our positioning such as in this interchange with Renata:

> Renata   Probably, I think I've probably become more English generally as a person, although I would never call myself English. I would never even take on English nationality, but one gets used to...
>
> CB   It happens (laughing).
>
> Renata   You get used to a certain way of being. (indistinct) You must know that yourself. (laughing)

These positionings of similarity and difference and of unequal power relationships influence what is said and what remains unsaid. And I can only guess at the hypotheses research participants held about me in relation to the research question, which would have had its own impact on the way in which they constructed their accounts.

Evaluative aspects of the research interview

It is also important to take into account the evaluative aspects of the interview itself. As discussed earlier in the book, at the end of her interview Maria asked whether I had found her account of herself coherent. I found this query very helpful in two ways: in highlighting the importance of a perceived demand for coherence, and the ways in which this can be troubling, and in reminding me of the way researchers are given power to make evaluations.

Bernard told me he had found the interview difficult and that he had been very self-conscious throughout:

> I'm not comfortable at all. Apart from my accent being appalling, um, I can't even talk like I normally talk because I don't feel very easy

about it, about the interview. [...] I don't feel very at ease and it gives me a bit of perplexion in my mind in the way of finding the why's.

The interview had highlighted Bernard's dissatisfaction with his lack of fluency in both his languages, and he had talked of his children's contempt of the way he spoke English. Perhaps the interview tapped into a concern about being judged – experienced as a test of language ability, rather than an exploration of meaning and experiences. Bernard and I had known each other in a different context for many years, and the research interview brought a different punctuation to our relationship.

Self-reflexivity throughout the research process

A researcher can maintain a stance of self-reflexivity during the analysis process by asking others to scrutinize their analysis of texts to help identify researcher assumptions. What I have come to learn through this process is that I had been bolder in my analysis of those aspects of experience that were more similar to mine than I had in my analysis of those which were more different. My researcher community have helped to highlight my absences and reluctances, in order that I could pursue other ideas from the data.

Maintaining a stance of self-reflexivity throughout the research process is challenging as this needs to occur at so many different levels. Making explicit personal contexts for oneself and for the reader is important in order to take account of how they have informed this project. As a researcher, I co-constructed the accounts produced in the interviews, in both explicit and subtle ways. I have highlighted my tendency to contextualize individual accounts which focused on self-blame, to unpack what I considered to be unquestioned negativity about bilingualism, and to ask questions which enabled individuals to make new connections and develop different perspectives. I have tried to take into account some of the subtleties of power dynamics in the research relationship. There is an evaluative component to any presentation of a self-narrative, and this is heightened in a research context which, despite attempts to make this a collaborative process and challenge such associations, can be associated with ideas of the normative and judgements.

Recursive influences of the research and personal context

Although I was prepared for and paying attention to the effect my personal and professional contexts would have on the research project,

I had not anticipated that the research process would have an impact on my constructions of my experiences:

When examining the challenges for families of children learning the dominant language faster than their parents, I became aware for the first time of the protective effect of my parents' prior fluency in English and French on my own migration experience.

During the analysis, I became intrigued by the 'protective function' of a second or subsequent language, and the distance it could provide from difficult and traumatic events, and I suddenly made a connection back to my parents. My parents had always warranted their decision to move to Canada as providing opportunities for us children, and for my father, his longing for open spaces. I now began to think about their transition to living in a new language/culture in a new way. During WWII, both my parents had been Japanese prisoners of war; my father was sent to work on the construction of 'Death Railway' connecting Burma and Thailand, my mother imprisoned in a camp with other Dutch women in Indonesia. Back in Holland after the war, they never really settled, and decided to immigrate to Canada. I now started to consider their move to a new language/culture as a survival strategy, a way to give them a distance from their past experiences, to enable them to live productively. They did however parent us in Dutch, perhaps because these relationships began in Dutch because we were born in Holland. It may also be the case that Dutch escaped meanings of abusiveness because their captors had spoken Japanese.

I have come to realize, like others in this research study, how much I enjoy ambiguity, not being easily defined, that I can emphasize one language identity, leave out another. I notice that I can use this to avoid responsibility and that this is not helpful and often indeed not possible, and that I am positioned (white, middle class, etc.)

Finding my personal narratives changing as a result of the research process has been an unexpected effect. Carrying out this research has sensitized me to the ease with which language is lost, as I became acutely aware of the insidious effects of the dominance of English, and the advantages of sustaining languages at the individual, family and sociopolitical level. I have had to face my choice to parent in English and that my son does not speak my first language, and have come to regret my decision to parent in English, my contribution to language loss in my own family. I had a sense when I began this research that the negativity attached to bi- and multilingualism so prevalent in the linguistics literature and in common discourses was misplaced. I have found the constructions of multilingualism as creative and radical in some of the literature and in these accounts, persuasive, although it is obviously not straightforward for individuals to develop ways to make use of their differences of language. I find these constructions particularly persuasive as a multilingual individual myself. It has fuelled my passion at a professional level to find ways to enable individuals and families to sustain their languages, or, at least, to reflect more explicitly on the issues of language speaking.

8
Concluding Discussion

So what can we conclude are the significant aspects of living multilingually from these accounts elicited in the dominantly monolingual context of Britain? And what can we extrapolate from this more generally about the interlinking of language and subjectivity?

These research participants readily accepted the invitation to reflect on their relationship to their languages. I take this as an important effect of being positioned within more than one language system, since this facilitates assuming an observer stance to oneself and one's language. One can more easily look at a language, and oneself in that language, when one has a position outside it – that is, from a positioning in another language (although it is impossible for any of us to be 'outside language'). Kristeva (1969/1986) once remarked that when one looks at language one is declaring oneself a foreigner. Many of these individuals had had little opportunity previously to talk about issues of speaking several languages, and viewed these as highly significant to their lives.

These interviews have been particularly well suited to analysing research participants' constructions of identity and the ways in which they made use of discursive resources in their interactions with others and for themselves. It has allowed an examination of the advantages and challenges of living in several languages, and of their implications for individuals and families.

Of central significance to individuals, no matter what the circumstances of speaking their different languages, were the multiplicities engendered by their languages. This enabled an examination of how individuals conceptualize and live with these multiplicities. The book has been able to elaborate findings from those previous research studies discussed in chapter one (Ben-Zeev 1977; Bialystok 1988, 1991, 1997; Carringer 1974; Grosjean 1982; Lambert 1977; Romaine 1995; Saunders

1982; Scott 1973; Swain and Cummins 1979) that in supportive circumstances being bilingual promotes individuals' mental flexibility, divergent
thinking and creativity. All these individuals, bar one, confirmed how
advantageous they found it to live in more than one language. Their
positionings in more than one language generated complexity and
flexibility, which other studies have found to be correlated with resilience
in living in ever-changing contexts (cf Falicov 2002). At the same time
these accounts demonstrate how the ongoing devaluation of languages
other than English in Britain contributes significantly to the difficulties
of maintaining minoritized language use, and highlights the ease of
language loss in the face of the dominance of English.

A prevalent idea in Britain is that only certain people have a 'natural'
ability for learning language, and to some extent this has been reinforced
by the linguistics research on individual competence in language speaking.
When ways of being are connoted as 'natural', their construction as
such becomes invisible, as does the accomplishment of such constructions.
The interpretative repertoire of a natural ability for languages locates
language speaking as an aptitude inside the individual rather than
within social processes, making invisible the circumstances and power
relationships that shape the ways languages are learned and used. It is
the case that some individuals are drawn to learning languages and
seem to have a particular facility, but many people in Britain draw on
this notion to warrant their monolingualism by constructing themselves
as having no talent for languages, facilitated by the dominance of
English throughout the world. Everyone in this study had learned their
languages through necessity, highlighted most starkly in colonial contexts.
And, indeed, a number of research participants made a point of defining
themselves as not good at languages, as if to trouble this discourse of
natural language ability.

The meanings that language speaking acquired for the individuals
interviewed for this study were forged in different relational contexts as
well as through social and ideological struggles in the wider societal
context.

As those with least power came to speak the most languages in
colonial contexts, bilingualism and multilingualism became associated
with those of least status. Other writers (cf Abley 2003; Amati-Mehler
et al. 1993) have pointed out the way in which many read the story of
the Tower of Babel as constructing the diversity of the world's languages
as punishment, as shame, rather than as richness. In spite of the
increasing number of languages spoken in Britain, such connotations of
multilingualism are still in play.

Living with multiplicity

Whatever their histories and circumstances of language learning, whether they grew up with several languages or learned their languages later in their lives, the research participants described experiencing themselves very differently in each of their languages. Living in several languages meant that individuals constructed different meanings within each of their linguistic/cultural contexts, which included, significantly, making different meanings of themselves.

This has also meant, put at its most simple, that those who learned to live in another language later in their lives, found that this changed them profoundly: "To change your language is to change your life" (Walcott 1969).

These accounts of subjective experiences of difference tally with the research cited earlier in the book which had found differences of diverse kinds when individuals used their different languages: presented different values and affective content (Ervin 1964; Grosjean 1982; Pérez Foster 1998), recalled events very differently (Javier 1996), were able to be simultaneously psychotic in one language and coherent in another (Hughes 1981; de Zulueta 1990), and which involved different cortical networks in the brain (Kim et al. 1997; Pinker 1994; Binder et al. 1997; Pouratian et al. 2000).

Clearly, there is something at work here which is not 'simply' connected to the use of language to claim identity (although individuals also did so). Individuals used their languages in different relationships and contexts. They developed different associations and networks of meanings in each, and positioned themselves and were positioned differently in each. Individuals also constructed their languages differently. Linguistic contexts make 'a difference that makes a difference' (Bateson 1979) to individuals, and one which can be noted explicitly, and therefore allow an exploration of living with multiplicities.

It has also been possible to identify in these interviews what cultural resources and narrative forms are available to individuals with which to construct their accounts. Individuals drew on different canonical narratives in each of their linguistic and cultural contexts, and had to find a way to position themselves in relation to their differences. Many of the research participants had experienced discontinuity and disjuncture between their languages and contexts.

Childhoods in several languages were mainly constructed in relation to challenges of moving between different language contexts. Those who had grown up in a family who spoke a minority language had to manage distinctions of language and culture between home and the outside world, with little confirmation of the complexity of these experiences. Those who had fled their country of origin as children were organized by an immediate need to position themselves in the new language to counter experiences of powerlessness, as well as having to make sense of disjuncture in their experience, a disruption of meaning, in the context of traumatic loss. Claims to an identity as a dominant-language speaker were often unsuccessful and individuals had to position themselves in relation to the inequitable relationships between their first language and the dominant language. These accounts were often underpinned by a notion of an ideal of an unproblematic singularity. As Linde (1993) had pointed out, constructing a narrative of self as a claim of identity predisposes an individual to experience a pull to find resolution to disjuncture and contradictions.

Those who were older when they moved languages and countries constructed this as a transition through which they developed a different sense of themselves: for some there was a sense that they could invent themselves in the new language, released from familial and cultural constraints; for others these was a sense of losing their bearings/meanings and the constraint of being rendered inarticulate and having to manage hostility and racism. Changing languages and moving countries is disruptive of individual and family narratives, of expected storylines which have been important in individual's self-accounts. Individuals had to 'work' the disjuncture between their different experiences in each language, across time and in a different place, and construct identifications with each of their 'imagined communities' (Anderson 1983), absent as well as present, which were rarely untroubled. Narratives in first languages were constructed as remaining static and separate from developments in the new language.

For those who did not have ongoing possibilities to speak, the attrition of their first languages happened imperceptibly over time and, when noted, this phenomenon distressed or shocked individuals. A loss of fluency in their first language became equated with a loss of the past, and a loss of identity. Sometimes an individual's first language had not evolved past a particular life stage after they had moved into a new language. No longer 'at home' in their first language, individuals became positioned as foreigners for themselves, and on returning to visit were often considered by others as claiming a status identity when they interspersed words from their second language. Noting a loss of fluency had precipitated some individuals to relearn their first language and was often accompanied by a reclamation of their first-language identity.

Constructions of self

How did these individuals construct themselves as speakers of several languages? Research participants presented versions of themselves and claimed particular identifications through their reflections on their experiences of their languages in the interviews. Very few individuals seemed to have well-worn, often-repeated narratives about themselves as speakers of several languages, and the many uses of the phrase, "I've never thought about it this way before", indicated that research participants were actively constructing new meanings in the interview. The discursive work identified within the accounts accomplished solutions to certain problems and dilemmas and created others.

One of the striking features of these accounts, given my choice of a heterogeneous group of individuals in terms of their 'race', ethnicity, culture, class and circumstance of learning their languages, was the way in which women and men made use of a construct of a 'doubled self', differentiated by language, in the accounts of childhood and in their current descriptions. Of note, too is how a number of autobiographies and memoirs addressing moves between languages and cultures (cf Dorfman 1998; Fitzherbert 1997; Green 1987; Hoffman 1989; Kaplan 1994; Said 1999; Sante 1998; Stavans 2002) also draw on this concept of doubleness.

What can we make of the fact that so many individuals draw on a notion of 'doubleness' to elaborate their experiences of their language speaking? The use of a construct of 'doubleness' seems particularly striking at a time when the conceptualization of multiple subjectivity has become commonplace in the academic literature. Several of the research participants were clearly familiar with these postmodern discourses of subjectivity, and several spoke more than two languages. So why doubled? Is this reflective of the continued pull to dualism, the predominance of constructions of binary opposites, so persistent within western discourses?

A century ago, W.E.B. Du Bois (1906) developed the idea of 'double consciousness' in relation to African American identity: "two souls, two thoughts, two unreconciled strivings". He can be considered as providing a canonical narrative of identity. He posited this to address the difficulties for black people in the United States who internalized an American identity which excluded them, thereby experiencing a double marginality. There is a distinction, a doubleness, inherent in western self-consciousness between 'I' and 'me' – an awareness of oneself (me) by oneself (I), and an awareness of oneself (me) from another's perspective (other), propounded in theories of identity by James (1890) and Mead (1913) and informed by philosophical, political and social scientific scholarly work. The notion of doubleness further elaborated by Laing (1965) through his concept of the divided self, through which he drew distinctions between the true and false self, and by Winnicott (1960) through the idea of false selves formed to protect the hidden true self have informed popular discourses on subjectivity. However, postmodern theorizing of subjectivity as multiple (Brah 1996; Henriques et al. 1984) with subjectivities conceptualized as shifting and dependent on contexts is currently more prevalent.

Doubleness was referenced in the interviews in a variety of ways, as discussed in Chapters 3 and 4. Some individuals posited their doubleness in terms of an 'inner core' and an 'outer self'. 'Inner' and 'outer' are powerful metaphors for making distinctions between the private and the public, between thoughts and self-presentation. This may have become a prevalent metaphor for those who learned a language later in their lives, describing a period when their internal language and external language were different. This usage also becomes conflated with the discourse of a 'true' and 'false' self, with inner first languaged experiences given connotations of authenticity, and the second language self considered a performance.

The notion of a doubled self may have particular salience in a context in which an individual's first language and culture have come under attack. This was the case when the idea of an inner and outer doubleness was employed in relation to the effects of colonization through language. Here an inner first-language self was considered authentic, encompassing a cultural identity which could counter the processes of colonization, while a false self was considered as that constructed through subject positions offered in the colonizers' language. Important identity claims can be made with this usage, and it offered a way to address and challenge colonization and racialization processes. The ways in which individuals used a construct of a genuine inner self overlapped with a notion of an essentialist self. This entailed dangers inherent in claiming essentialist characteristics of cultural/racial identity, of which other writers (Bhavnani and Phoenix 1994; Hall 1989; hooks 1989; Said 1993) have warned, disavowing heterogeneity, contradiction and ongoing processes of identification. However, claims to essentialism are often made to challenge disqualifications and can perhaps most helpfully be viewed as discursive work and part of a process over time (Burck and Daniel 1995a).

Not all of the research participants used an inner and outer distinction; some of those who grew up with several languages conceptualized their doubleness as being linked to an idea of a 'doubled world', two separate contexts – most often of home and the outside world. The differences of language and all this entailed accentuated the differences between these domains. These individuals used a construct of doubleness that did not include a primary sense of self, as the idea of a core self did. One usage of this doubleness was of a 'neither/nor' identity (rather than a 'both/ and' identity), which was constructed as outsider-ness in every context.

Doubleness was also structured temporally and spatially, by those who had migrated, with some individuals drawing on the idea of a core self, signified through the importance of language in the early years of life, an idea that "the first language seems to be attached to identity with a kind of absoluteness" (Hoffman reported in Zournazi 1999), while others did not identify a primary languaged self. Another version of doubleness was that of the 'lived' self and the 'imagined' self, the hypothetical self who would have developed in the first language and place, a kind of doppelganger as Stavans (2002) put this in his memoir, different from the lived self in the second/subsequent language.

Some academic literature also draws on a construct of doubleness in its theorization of bilingualism. Pérez Foster (1998) has conceptualized the 'bilingual self' as doubled, and argued that there are two different "language-bounded inner representations of the self", with each language operating as a separate code, with its own "psychic structures" (1998: 75). Of course, it was the conceptualization of doubleness which was originally used to argue that bilingualism was detrimental, leading to split minds and personalities (Adler 1977), the construct of doubleness becoming conflated with and signifying madness.

Doubleness as trope

How can we unpack doubleness as a trope? What does the use of a construct of a doubled self accomplish? Many of the individuals in this study had lived in predominantly monolingual countries and tended to switch language when they changed context. Only a few individuals had lived in a diglossic context, where it was common practice for everybody to switch between languages. Many of these accounts are therefore concerned in one way or another with discontinuities in the switch from one language to another, and some individuals had experienced major interruptions through moving country and language, entailing disruptions in their narratives of self. For these individuals, living with disjuncture and contradictions, constructing themselves as doubled I want to argue, accomplishes a sense of coherence.

Narrative theorists and feminist critical theorists have highlighted the many demands for coherence in giving an account of the self, in the form of narrative itself (Irigaray 1985; Kristeva 1986; Linde 1993; Ricoeur 1984). Writers from many different theoretical orientations have addressed the difficulties of sustaining contradictions and fissure in identity, how easily individuals and communities erase these and become attached to dogma, the myth of unitary identity, in the face of fragmentation (cf Rose 2001; Said 2001). Individuals work hard to maintain a sense of their own continuity and consistency. A change in language and country makes fissures very explicit. The use of a construct of doubleness can be viewed as a way to work fissure and discontinuities, paradoxically both attaining cohesiveness and sustaining differences. The use of a construct of a doubled self serves as a device to keep differences separate, and invokes the ideal of a coherent unitary monolingual identity, through constructing two. Because a developmental narrative is privileged in our culture, a doubled construct transforms discontinuity into two distinct developmental narratives.

Despite the availability of postmodern interpretative repertoires of multiple subjectivities, persons live with notions of their own and others' enduring and singular identities. Despite ever-increasing migrations and displacements of peoples in response to which conceptualizations of diaspora space and diasporic identities have been elaborated (Brah 1996), individuals still come under question from others, are still asked to define themselves simply. Justine's self-reflexive comment concerning such requests/demands demonstrate how individuals have to manage this for themselves in their relationships:

> Usually when I discuss what I feel I am, I now say that I only ever think about that question to be able to give other people an answer.

However, individuals in this research study did not draw only on constructs of doubleness. They also referenced themselves using other notions of multiplicity. There was considerable complexity in the ways in which individuals made identifications and constructed themselves, and positioned themselves in their languages, in their different relationship contexts.

Performing linguistic identities and owning language

The question of how individuals take up language to construct themselves is one that can be examined explicitly when individuals enter into a new language.

The move from a sense of an ontologically referential identity to one of a conjunctural play of identifications (Stam 1998), as individuals enter a new language and learn to perform themselves in it, challenges individuals' sense of what is important to them. Individuals often conflate authenticity with what is usual. Doing something new becomes constructed as inauthentic because it does not fit with ideas about the self or other. It appears that individuals learning to live in a new language are forced, through the necessity to communicate, to stay with their 'performance' despite its disruption of their sense of authenticity. These reiterative performances in the new language became constitutive of the speaker, who becomes a different kind of speaker from the first-language speaker.

Butler (1990) has argued that it is the awareness of performance that enables a challenging and subverting of gender identities. Others hold that individuals shift between authenticity and performance in everyday practices and that these discourses are drawn on for claims and counterclaims in interactions involving affect and desire (Frosh et al. 2002; Horton-Salway 2001). I was interested to explore what effect the explicitness of performing themselves in a new language over time had on these individuals, an awareness more prolonged than those of more everyday performances within one language. This sense of performing oneself differently in a new language linked to a growing awareness of the contingency of self on language, which I go on to discuss further below.

Some research participants retained a sense of themselves as performers, of themselves 'doing a linguistic identity'; several had this sense of themselves in all of their languages. For others, their performance became experienced over time as 'natural' – a "mask merging with skin" is how Sante (1998: 259) described it in his autobiography. This is a shift in fluency and subjectivity, recursively linked – a switch of internal conversation to the new language, an experience of speaking without translating, finding a different positioning within the language.

The word in language is half someone else's. It becomes 'one's own' only when the speaker populates it with his (sic) own intention, his (sic) own accent [...] adapting it to his (sic) own semantic and expressive intention. Prior to this moment of appropriation the word does not exist in a neutral and impersonal language [...], but rather it exists in other people's mouths, in other people's contexts, serving other people's intentions; it is from there that one must take the word, and make it one's own [...] [But] expropriating it, forcing it to submit to one's own intentions and accents, is a difficult and complicated process. (Bakhtin 1981: 293–4)

The processes of making a language one's own involves a struggle. It also entails the ability to say "I am me" in someone else's language, and, in my own language, "I am other" (Bakhtin 1981: 314–15). The question of whether one can come to 'own' another's language through which one is positioned as 'other', to make it one's own, is contested. Some have argued that it is impossible to use a dominant language, in particular the oppressors' language, in order to create a different paradigm (hooks 1989). Coming to own a language was linked to the ways individuals were positioned in and through it, and therefore to its meanings forged within social struggles. The ability to take a reflexive stance towards language, and oneself-in-language was significant in these accounts. So, for example, in drawing on postcolonial discourses to reflect on the ways language had constructed them, individuals presented themselves as having developed a different relationship to themselves in their languages.

Initially, individuals did not seem to consider a new language as encompassing diverse discursive practices, or a new culture as heterogeneous and contested. Individuals could be considered as attaching themselves to a particular storyline, and ignoring complexities. Here I follow Hall's attempt to unpack the processes of the suturing of a subject to a subject-position. A performance is not a suture, but reiterative performances produce a suture of a kind. This carried its own costs and dilemmas. I have come to see an individual 'owning' a new language as no longer just being 'hailed' by it (Althusser 1971; Hall 1996), no longer only taking up certain subject positions, but using the language as heteroglossic.

It was also the case that others could challenge an individual's performance as a dominant-language speaker, and then different kinds of claims of identity became necessary. Speaking a minoritized language in Britain acted as a marker of difference, helping to construct ethnicity and cultural identity. Speaking with an accent also affected interactions at a prosodic level and could call a performance into question. Individuals' positioning in language intersected with their 'race', and had significant effects on the meanings of language speaking and on themselves as speakers. The Chinese, South Asian, Israeli, and Zimbabwean speakers' language and identity came under continual scrutiny. White research participants sometimes had their whiteness signified as an English identity, but, with a few exceptions, they did not present themselves as aware of the privileges of their positioning, particularly if preoccupied by their construction as different. Some individuals claimed an identity as an outsider, and came to enjoy this positioning, and also their ability to present themselves ambiguously. However, during childhood individuals mainly recalled longings to belong and be similar to others. Adults generally had more resources with which to make political as well as personal claims of identity.

Languages and family relationships

The ways in which languages were spoken and given meaning within family relationships were heavily influenced by the meanings in the wider context, in which language speaking intersected with the construction of ethnicities, and cultural and racialized identities, and with power relationships and inequities.

In the context of language choice for parenting and childrearing, discourses concerning women and men's different relationship to language as well as to parenting came into play. It was striking how many of the research participants had done some parenting in their first language in a context which worked against this. First languages were generally perceived as conveying intimacy to the parent–child relationship, which indicated how important, among other reasons, it may be to support its choice.

What has also been highlighted is how accounts were positioned in relation to the concept of 'mother tongue' and the signification of women as the guardians of language with which it was associated. Although implicitly underpinning women's choice to parent in their first/childhood language, it worked against fathers using their first languages to parent their babies from their birth onwards.

Second languages were sometimes privileged in families to try and ensure children's success at school, to enable them to fit in and claim belonging. It became the language of the present and future while the language which the parent often considered richer and more emotionally expressive and which carried historical continuity, came to signify the past and absences. 'Doing parenting' in a second language was seen as changing parents' values and attitudes, positioning individuals alongside their children in the dominant culture. Although it entailed language loss for both parents and children, some individuals constructed their second language as enabling them to be more self-reflexive as parents, thereby helping them to parent in preferred ways, and to avoid repeating unhelpful patterns from the past.

The analysis of research participants' accounts also identified how language choice was interlinked with identity claims and was central to the politics of family relationships in everyday life. However, if this research group is anything to go by, this is only rarely discussed explicitly.

Individuals used their languages to make salient their own and others' identities. Because language speaking was a marker of cultural identity, language choice was used to claim identity and to make alliances. The way in which individuals used their identities as a resource in their interactions was complemented by the way in which they made use of their languages as an identity resource. Through their language choice, parents made identity claims for their children, as well as for themselves. Individuals took up or resisted membership categories within the family, created or dissolved alliances, claimed membership of the family culture or refused it, claimed one cultural identity over another, through their language speaking. Individuals' claims made through their language carry meanings of loyalty and disloyalty, and of continuity and loss within families. A switch to a first language could invoke cultural expectations of family relationships and bring forth particular identifications. Use was made of the dominant language by parents in order to perform authority and to warrant their own position. These claims and counterclaims of identity and of relationship within families were interwoven with claims of membership of their imagined communities.

Claims of identity were made in response to racism and othering in the wider context, with individuals refusing identity claims made on their behalf or concealing aspects of their identities and presenting themselves in ambiguous ways. Such claiming of identities for strategic purposes to disrupt unhelpful interactions with others did not always map on to an individual's self-definition. Individuals code switched between their languages for metalanguaging purposes, although in monolingual contexts this could only occur in circumscribed situations. Speakers switched language to position themselves as an insider in order to increase the saliency of their argument, to claim status and to challenge ways in which others positioned them.

Many of the research participants' children were reported as staking their claim to an English identity, by refusing to speak other languages.

Some families developed cross-language talking between the generations, with parents and children claiming different linguistic identities through their choice of language. It was not easy for parents to provide a validating context for their children's multiplicities in the face of dominant discourses in Britain, as children became captured by a desire for singularity and belonging.

This study has analysed adults' constructions of childhoods, and parents' descriptions of their own children. The effect of context on children's sense of their multiplicity was of particular importance. Analysing children's own constructions of their experiences with several languages in different contexts would add other perspectives of relevance. A different kind of question is posed when considering how speaking several languages as a young child affects the development of a 'theory of mind'. Research has indicated that a crucial development in young children is learning that other people have different perspectives (Hobson 2002). As speaking several languages entails holding different perspectives oneself, one could hypothesize that this facilitates such development in young bilingual and multilingual children, affecting their relationships with others. Such identification of further advantages of living multilingually may help contribute to building contexts to sustain it.

Some language choices by parents demonstrated ways in which languages are lost at a family level. With parents giving up their everyday use of their first language and children never learning to speak it, families move to monolingualism, losing expressive capabilities, ways of thinking and perceiving the world, and the flexibility and hybridity which living in more than one language engenders. These are the processes at a micro-level through which language loss and the loss of diversity which accompanies it occur, mirroring the processes of dramatic language loss at micro and macro levels worldwide.

Contextual resources

Individuals' ease with their sense of their multiplicity shifted over time and according to context. Holding identifications in several linguistic contexts, individuals both lived with traditional notions of cultural identity and simultaneously challenged these, sometimes captured by stereotypes of themselves and others, sometimes developing a hybridity which unsettled such ideas. Individuals had to find ways in which to manage the discontinuities between their languages and the contradictions these encompassed, and had to find ways to translate themselves back and forth between their languages. As discussed earlier, constructs of multiple subjectivity were not necessarily easily available or drawn on. Context was crucial to whether individuals had found ways to develop a self-reflexive positioning to make use of their language differences.

In some of the childhood accounts, individuals described experiences of feeling disqualified or being denied recognition. One could say that they had been unable to achieve what Wilkinson and Kitzinger (1996) have termed, an adequate 'fit' within an officially recognized narrative. They did not have access to a coherence system rich enough to encompass their multiplicities (Linde 1993).

What kinds of contextual resources are helpful to individuals? One answer might be the accessibility of discursive resources to draw on to describe, attend, encompass, construct one's multiplicities, and the structural and material support to live them. The identification in the accounts of childhoods, troubled by a lack of validation and unhelpful polarizations, of an encounter with a 'third space' (Bhabha 1994), a transforming context, which had provided a different way to bring together their multiple identifications, seemed of this order. These had provided a shift in individuals' sense of themselves and offered them a different kind of positioning, an acknowledgment of their multiple identifications which disrupted polarisations. These were not so much 'significant turning points' in individual narrative accounts (Riessman 1993) but the beginning of processes of developing ways to live their multiplicities proactively and make use of their differences. In a discussion of the kinds of canonical narratives available in our cultures with which individuals can construct themselves, Bruner and Gorfain (1991) proposed that it was the cultural stories that were most open-ended, ambiguous and paradoxical and which therefore enabled dialogic and emergent co-construction of personal narratives which become most significant and helpful for individuals. This speaks to the importance of dialogism, as well as the contextual resources needed to enable these processes.

Relationship to language and place

A pertinent question to ask of all these research accounts is what else may get emptied into language? Or, indeed, what is specific to language? In exploring the question of language, I have employed a particular lens through which individuals could construct their experiences in the research interviews. But other issues may have become constructed as language issues. Culture and language are inextricably intertwined.

Language speaking and racialization processes are entangled with each other and difficult to separate out. Diasporic identities are theorized as multiply constructed and constituted relationally, with shifting contexts triggering shifts in subjectivity, as different facets of individuals' 'race', gender, class, culture and ethnicity and their intersections are emphasized and privileged (Brah 1996). Mama (1995), for example, had shown how black British women used multiple subject-positionings dependent on their relationship context, varying their use of dialect and speaking patterns accordingly.

When individuals move from one country to another, one culture to another, without a change of language, they also have to manage the dislocations of place, loss of relationship networks, and disruptions of meanings. What is the significance of geographical place as contrasted with language in the construction of identity and of memory? The longing for place is particularly powerful in the context of exile. Place is itself a complex notion, constructed and signified through ideas about rootedness, 'home' and nationalism, and is gendered, racialised, and classed (Uguris 2000). The concept of diasporic space has worked to denaturalize 'home' as 'location', and challenged notions of geographical origins while at the same time making claims to representation and belonging (Brah 1996; Radhakrishnan 2000). Place and language can come to stand for each other, in the context of a political claim, as when Darwish, the Palestinian poet, claimed his language as home in the context of exile (Forché 2001). Individuals in this study too had conceptualized home in a variety of ways: many spoke of feeling they did not belong anywhere, or that they could belong everywhere. Some had also conceptualized language as a home in the absence of place, a notion of being 'at home' in their language. This resonates with Abley's definition of home in his study of endangered languages as "a place where knowledge resonates with meaning" (2003: 273).

Perhaps one cannot say what is different about shifts in linguistic contexts, from other shifts of context, only that the ways in which these individuals living multilingually constructed their multiplicities will overlap with others, and is of significance. Living in several languages constitutes multiple subjectivities. Perhaps one can say that one distinction we can draw between language and other shifts in context is that because language enters individuals and their internal conversations, individuals can themselves switch linguistic contexts, and all that this entails, in their self-talk. We can perhaps also argue that it is only a move between languages which creates a different relationship to language itself.

On entering a new language, individuals moved from being in language unselfconsciously to noticing language, its effects and its limitations. This acute awareness of what language can and cannot do and of a plurality of meanings eschews the illusion of shared assumptions and predictability with which we communicate most of the time. This is an experience of the 'centrifugal of language'; language without a centre that holds (Bakhtin 1981).

> How astonishing it is that language can almost mean, and frightening that it does not quite. (Gilbert 1994)

These are the dangers of exposure to the limits of language of which the translation literature warns. However, the necessity of communicating leaves individuals with no option other than to use language in the knowledge that it will no longer really suffice, if indeed it ever did.

Advantages of speaking several languages

What did the sense of their contingency on language, noticing their difference senses of self, offer individuals in this study? It has been noted that the ability to identify the cultural genres which have been available and of the ways in which one has taken them up to tell the story of one's life (Ricoeur 1985) can enable individuals to take an ironic position, conscious enough of the discursive cultural order to make transgression, critique (Freeman 1993; Willig 1999) and change possible (Burck and Daniel 1995a). Experiencing the contingency of oneself on the language one is speaking seems to be of this order. We can say that living in several languages overtly decentres subjectivity. Such acute awareness of their sense of contingency on language challenged a dominant western interpretative repertoire of individualism, the conceptualization of the individual as autonomous and independent.

The philosopher Rorty (1989) has argued that a sense of contingency creates the potential for making new meanings. Because individuals held dissimilar and even contradictory language perspectives, they lived with a sense that there was never just a singular truth, and that they always had what Rorty termed ongoing and radical doubts about their "final vocabulary". This, Rorty argues, allows the possibility not to try and escape from contingency, but to acknowledge and appropriate it, and to find new descriptions. This is the continuous flux between a sense of contingency and a sense of agency.

Individuals had to find ways to 'work' their different perspectives. They developed strategies of hybridization, bringing these perspectives together to create new meanings. Although hybridity can be seen to be ubiquitous because notions of 'purity' have long been discredited, challenging unitary ways of seeing and finding ways to live with contradictions continue to be difficult. Said addressed this difficulty in his academic writing, while at the same time arguing for its use for creativity:

> Our model for academic freedom should therefore be the migrant or traveller: for if, in the real world outside the academy, we must needs be ourselves and only ourselves, inside the academy we should be able to discover and travel among other selves, other identities, other varieties of the human adventure. (Said 1991/2000: 403)

Said seems to be saying here that multiplicity is possible in the academy, but not in everyday living. But what does he mean by the phrase to 'be ourselves'? Perhaps this is what Hall (1987) termed living the 'necessity' of identity – having to position ourselves because we need to act. At times, individuals live their multiplicity as serial singularity; at other times, they engage with their own diversities and contradictions.

Hybridity has often been characterized by ideas that 'anything is possible' rather than with an engagement in subverting inequitable relationships structured through dominance (Radhakrishnan 2000). But, as Stam (1998) noted, hybridity was always entangled with colonial violence, and was centrally concerned with asymmetrical power relations. Bhabha (1994) and Benjamin (1998) have both emphasized how fraught the recognition and negotiation of difference can be in any particular encounter.

Holding the relationship between disjuncture and continuity is complex. Phillips (2000) pointed out that Marx proposed that it is in simulating continuity that rupture, radical change, is made possible. Here, the proposal is that from the conditions of rupture something radical can be created. Braidotti (1994) argued that it is a 'lightness of touch' which is required to make connections between things which are disconnected, accompanied by an accountability for one's own positionality.

Many of these individuals addressed the way in which they used the differences between their languages. Venjamin's use of both his Hebrew and his Arabic perspectives in his work to escape the linear explanations on both sides of the Middle East conflict in order to examine their interrelationship mirrored Said's (1998) description of how he came to use the differences between his Arabic and English perspectives in his writing, 'contrapuntally', each positioned and changed in position in relation to the other in turn. Such a strategy of hybridization involved being embedded within each language perspective and being able to take a relationally reflexive position (Burnham 1993), by which I mean, able to maintain and use a relational and interactional view from within the relationship itself.

Others also used their language differences to switch between their different perspectives both in order to generate new ideas for themselves and also in their interactions with others. Those whose languages encoded different ways of constructing emotions moved between them to perform or express particular emotions. This made tangible how their feelings were contingent on language, that 'doing' emotions was a discursive practice, which developed individuals' self-reflexivity further.

It was through the development of reflexive practices that individuals made use of the contradictions and the sometimes irreconcilable tensions in their different language perspectives, and, indeed, came to celebrate their multiplicity. All of these individuals, with one exception, considered the multiplicities engendered by their languages as highly advantageous, and of which they made creative use, and positioned this in relation to a construction of the limitations of monolingualism. What is evident from this study is that a positioning in several languages facilitates the development of reflexive practices of the self – that this is a recursive relationship – that self-reflexivity is a technology of the 'multilingual self'. However, the contexts in which individuals are situated enable or hinder the development of such reflexivity. In contexts where individuals were positioned in relationships where differences were polarized, they were less able to use their own differences dialogically. However, when individuals develop reflexive practices this in turn enables the development of relational reflexivity with others.

The research participants moved between claiming singularity, doubleness and multiplicity, for playfulness as well as for protectiveness, and made their different identities salient in particular interactions. At times, individuals were compelled by a language to leave out significant aspects of themselves, at other times they enjoyed playing with their multiplicities, and the sense that others found them difficult to define and to place. Their positioning in more than one culture/language enabled individuals to present themselves ambiguously, and to claim or subvert different constructions of identity in different contexts to considerable benefit. This sometimes posed its own dilemmas, as the pleasure of presenting themselves ambiguously and the sense of manoeuvrability this engendered were countered at times by the troubling sense that their 'doubleness' and multiplicity was a profound ambivalence, which somehow should be resolved. The stance of holding multiple positions can involve the dangers of relativising and distancing oneself (Hoffman 1989). Defining oneself as more significantly connected to another, absent context can also be a way of sliding away from taking responsibility and committing oneself. At the same time the flexibility and adaptability engendered by having a number of languages and perspectives were constructed as helpful.

Implications for individuals, families and professionals

There are important implications raised here for both bilingual and multilingual individuals and families, in a context of ever-increasing migrations and displacements and at a time when the world faces an accelerating loss of languages and diversity (Abley 2003). Instead of taking the languages in which we speak for granted, or, indeed, regarding them as a neutral media, this study has highlighted the differential effects of language on subjectivity, and the ease of language loss.

Language use had profound effects at two levels – as a claim of identity and on the experience of self. What is clear is that when an individual's languages are ignored, significant dimensions of living are left out. This is most likely to happen when individuals can get by or are fluent in the dominant language.

It is also clear that languages carry a range of meanings which shift over time and in different contexts. We cannot make assumptions about what a language will mean, or what a language will evoke or encode for an individual. As others (cf Thomas 1995, 2001) have argued, an examination of the meanings of language is particularly crucial in the context of colonialism and racisms. The effects of a dominant language on the ways individuals can position or reposition themselves benefit from explicit attention, as do the ways language speaking becomes a site of contestation for individuals because of their racialized identity positions.

Issues of language are entangled with other transformational processes involved in migration, characterized by ambiguous loss, and tensions between presence and absence (Falicov 2002). Family members who move to live in a new language and culture have to renegotiate their sense of themselves and their relationships and face dilemmas of continuity and change. Language speaking comes to signify loyalties to the past or present, and claims of identity. The task of balancing the importance of speaking in a first language, and the advantages a second and subsequent language can bring may be crucial.

Being able to speak in one's first language may be significant for individuals because of the meanings it has acquired in the context of a new language, as well as what they can do in and with it, alongside problems with translation. The significance of individuals' idiosyncratic use of language easily gets lost in translation (DiNicola 1997), and concerns are likely to be constructed in dissimilar ways in different languages.

Equally importantly, if individuals lose their first language, they also suffer the loss of the positioning in-between languages. Both Derrida (1998) and Deane (1998) have spoken eloquently about the loss of this 'in-between' in the context of never having had the opportunity to learn what should have been their first language because of colonization processes.

A second (or subsequent) language offered opportunities to individuals in this study to construct themselves differently, and to parents to help them to parent differently. In this way, the use of a second language offers considerable potential for change and for experimentation. However, being rendered inarticulate and experiencing ongoing difficulties with humour in a second language also had profound effects on constructions of self and on communication.

There had been comparatively little explicit attention to issues of language within some of these families. Would knowledge of the advantages of being multilingual have an effect on language choices in families and challenge dominant discourse? Examining language choices and their effects explicitly may enable family members to make more use of their languages, more flexibly, as well as preserve languages. In considering language choice for parenting, unpacking the notion of 'mother tongue' as well as of fathering, might enable more fathers to parent in their first languages. If women are constructed as the carriers of language, men need to take a very proactive stance in the context of dual-language parenting. If they are dominant-language speakers, they have societal backup, but as speakers of minoritized languages they do not. Unquestioned use of this interpretative repertoire is likely to contribute to language loss within families and the exclusion of significant aspects of individuals' experiences and expressiveness.

For many in this study, language speaking was interwoven with claims and counterclaims of identity and of relationships within their families and of membership of wider communities and in response to racism and exclusions in the wider context.

Those who spoke minoritized languages as children remembered the challenges of moving between the differences of their language of home and of their communities, and of finding a satisfactory definition for themselves as onerous, and one to be faced on their own. This raises challenges for parents trying to support their children in sustaining their languages. The challenges involved when children become more fluent in the dominant language than their parents were identified in several accounts. These circumstances developed children's confidence, resentment, contempt, or contrivance. Adults' feelings of inadequacy in the dominant language, differentially experienced in relation to their own resources and status, may dovetail with their children's responses. Challenging narratives of incompetence constructed through inarticulacy can be key for parents, to recalibrate power imbalances and to offer support to their children, and their bicultural and bilingual competencies.

Constructing a milieu which enables living with multiplicity is particularly challenging when residing in a context in which the derogation of values, language, sense of self, and perspectives are frequently experienced. Enabling the development of multiple perspectives without mutual deprecation within the family means finding ways to counter dominant discourses, a different way to work across the differences between languages. Having several languages is a resource, as well as a site of contestation, for individuals and families. Speaking several languages within the family entailed the bringing forth of different and, at times, contradictory values and attitudes. Tensions about how to interrelate the different cultures and identifications can be played out within the family, as much as between the family and the communities in which they reside. Different languaged perspectives can lead to intense embattlements. Families often run into trouble when claims and counterclaims, which are often lodged in differences between parents and children, have become polarized. It is likely that there may be more possibilities for fruitful use of language differences if held by all family members, rather than polarised between them. This is a particular challenge when children take up dominant ideas about the irrelevance of other languages and refuse to speak their parents' minoritized languages. A more explicit consideration of issues of identity constructed through living multilingually may unsettle demands for singularity. The challenge to hold together the multiple perspectives and social realities in dialogue and to subvert and escape polarisations, requires the encompassing of disruptions, discontinuities and fragments, without having to go for coherence or closure (Byrne and McCarthy 1998).

For families who chose to include all their languages, there are questions of who will learn whose language and who needs to adapt to whom. If some family members speak a language not understood by others, individuals need to find a way to position themselves in relation to the inclusions and exclusions this creates. A belief that alliances will mainly be benign seems important in supporting the speaking of a language not understood by everyone, alongside a commitment to the value of multilingualism. For those in this study, privileging inclusion above multilingualism, alongside monolingual norms, often resulted in language loss.

Although individuals had become multilingual in very different circumstances, there was a commonality in their experiences of multiplicity, which almost unanimously they had come to see as extremely advantageous. They also faced inherent tensions in living in several languages, challenges of managing the discontinuity and contradictions between their languages. Despite warnings others have raised, of the dangers of striving to erase fissures in their self-narratives (Rose 2001; Said 2001) or of using languages to repress or split issues unhelpfully (Amati-Mehler et al. 1993), none of these research participants had taken a rigidly dogmatic position in relation to their discontinuities and contradictions, and indeed they mainly positioned themselves as anti-dogma. On the other hand, one research participant considered himself unhelpfully split by his languages. These ways individuals in this study came to experience their multiplicities were linked to the different kinds of relational and contextual discursive resources they had had available.

In the research group, there were considerable variations in the development of individuals' self-reflexivity and the ways in which they made use of the differences of their languages, as noted earlier. Taking up a self-reflexive stance to their languages and their effects opened up a range of resources for individuals. An increasing awareness of the accomplishments of their different languages had developed the potential to make use of these differences. This may have considerable further potential for bilingual and multilingual individuals who have not had the opportunities to reflect on their language differences.

There are important issues here for teachers, youth workers, GPs, health professionals, psychologists, social workers, counsellors and therapists, working with bilingual and multilingual individuals. It is evident that professionals can – and often do – participate in the silencing of other language experiences. If we do not consider languages explicitly, significant aspects of self and relationships are missed. Professionals can choose to contribute to the unavailability of such experiences of self, excluding significant perspectives and constructions of the world, or they can work to include individuals' languages as significant dimensions of their lives.

In cross-cultural interactions, it is helpful to be able to explore the 'doxic' (Bourdieu 1991), aspects of lives which are not explicit, the social and cultural patterning of meanings and contexts, but, as Krause (2002) has pointed out, we need to learn to ask questions which make sense to individuals. What I am arguing here is that explorations concerning an individual and family's languages are a particularly fruit-ful way to do so.

Asking about language is important, but monolingual professionals may also facilitate the inclusion of individual and family's languages in talk. The experience for individuals of speaking in their first language and then translating themselves into another language, elicits different perspectives and affective descriptions for the individual themselves as well as for the professional who is inquiring. Green (1987) has described this process in his writing, translating his articles from French to English and from English to French to access his different perspectives and feelings.

On the other hand, the distance often conferred by a second lan-guage can be enormously helpful when individuals have undergone traumatic and difficult experiences which they have not been able to bring into language. The distance from affect created by a second language can be protective and enable talk that is impossible in a first language. Such description in a second language may allow individuals to develop another view on these experiences, without feeling too over-whelmed. For example, the elaboration of children's narratives of their experiences of war, through the use of their second language, enables them to develop multiple perspectives, resilient alongside fearful ones, of these traumatic events (Smith 2005). While others have argued that a second language can sometimes introduce an unhelpful distance from significant affective themes (Pérez Foster 1998), this can often be used for considerable benefit.

The distance a second and subsequent language provides may also prove useful for professionals in certain aspects of their work. Working in a second language may safeguard the professional from the impact of powerful expression of feeling, such as extreme anger (Burck 1997). And, paradoxically, an individual working in their second language, who may experience a sense of protection from the emotional impact of a narrative, may find it easier to listen to accounts of difficult events others would find much harder.

For some of these individuals, speaking in a new language had honed their communication, forcing them to concentrate on essentials, which they saw as beneficial to their relationships. This aspect of communication in a second language can sometimes elicit significant issues quickly. Individuals cannot dissemble so easily in a new language. However, the identification of the kinds of misunderstandings which occurred in interactions between first- and second-language speakers point to the importance of taking the effects of being positioned in a second language into account, to avoid mistaken ideas about persons and personalities being constructed.

It is clear from this as well as other research (cf Sebba and Wootton 1998) that individuals use code switching to construct meaning. The ability to use this as a linguistic resource in a monolingual context is somewhat constrained, but multilingual professionals who engage with individuals who speak the same languages can tap into the different experiences, values and meanings each language carries, and use code switching in their interaction as a communication resource.

Professionals who are themselves bilingual or multilingual and have been educated in their second languages may have experienced the exclusion, or even the disqualification, of significant dimensions of themselves through the training and in their work. Multilingual professionals themselves may need to find contexts to validate the differences of their languages and their different experience of themselves in order to make use of the differences their languages bring. Professionals too can make explicit use of their language differences to generate alternative perspectives for themselves in their work. Being able to reflect on dilemmas in several languages can generate new perspectives, which may in itself be helpful in dissolving impasses.

Concluding implications

Claims were made by these research participants, as by other bilingual and multilingual writers (cf Anzaldua 1987; DiNicola 1997; Dorfman 1998; Dyson 1994; Fitzherbert 1997; Hoffman 1989; Kaplan 1993; Maalouf 2000; Mukherjee 1999; Said 1999; Sante 1998; Stavans 2002; Steiner 1998a, 1998b; Wierzbicka 1997), that no matter how challenging experiences of discontinuity and contradiction have been, the multiplicities acquired by living in several languages engenders creative, even radical change. Hybridity, the generation of perspectives not available to others, and the ability to present oneself ambiguously are seen as special resources, and individuals on the whole construct themselves as committed to challenge and subvert unhelpful dominant singularities. This is the value of 'obliquity', able to enter a language perspective and then to trouble it, "to learn that conventions can be exploited and subverted" (Cowley 2003: 8).

The ongoing challenge, as Radhakrishnan (2000: 3) outlined, is that of "opening up hybridity as an allegorical and second-order space" finding ways to generate and facilitate the processes of hybridization without fixing these. This challenge is addressed by Said in a rather different quote from the one examined above. In the last pages of his autobiography he described himself as follows:

> I occasionally experience myself as a cluster of flowing currents. [. . .] These currents, like the themes of one's life, flow along during the waking hours, and at their best, they require no reconciling, no harmonizing. They are "off" and maybe out of place, but at least they are always in motion, in time, in place, in the form of all kinds of strange combinations, moving about, not necessarily forward, sometimes against each other, contrapuntally yet without one central theme. A form of freedom, I'd like to think, even if I am far from being totally convinced that it is. That scepticism too is one of the themes I particularly want to hold on to. (Said 1999: 295)

As Said's quote highlights, the tensions inherent in living with multiplicity are ongoing ones, of which the ability always to take another position, to generate another perspective, "the scepticism", is an integral and invaluable part and process. This is most certainly not a relativistic position, as Said's own passionate political stance in relation to the Middle East demonstrated.

The idea that it is those individuals who themselves tolerate and embody differences, in this case those with several languages, who can best develop ways to work across differences has been proposed by Dorfman (1998). These claims of multiplicity as generating creativity or radical change may shift between coming to fruition, and functioning as desire – the "hope of a Global soul [. . .] that diversity can leave him (sic) not a dissonance, but a higher symphony" (Iyer 2000: 121). These claims themselves may provide some narrative resolution to difficult contradictions and support the ability to sustain, and live multiplicity and complexity. But in the meantime, language slips away.

Appendix 1: Protocol for Research Interview

The following questions are those I was interested to cover in the research interviews. As I followed the feedback of the research participants, the questions were not asked in any particular order, nor did I necessarily cover each question, if it did not seem appropriate.

How many languages do you speak? with what kind of fluency? spoken/written? Which language/s do you consider your first language?

Circumstances of learning and speaking languages
Could you tell me the circumstances of learning your languages? (age, relationships, contexts, by choice, 'forced', moving countries/cultures)
Where did you use which language?
Which language were you educated in?
Which languages used at home? with parents? with siblings? with grandparents?
Within community? other contexts? private/public domain differences?
What about religious affiliation? Is this connected to your language use?
What was this like for you? Any issues around language use? What were the constraints and/or opportunities in this experience?

Wider contexts in which language spoken
How were your languages valued? Did your context value languages? Issues of colonization? What effect on you?
How do you think languages are valued here in Britain? (Are you aware of a hierarchy of languages?) What effect?
Experiences of racism, marginalization, exclusion? Effect on your language use?
Would you use your language/s to manage/challenge this?

Self-definition
How would you define your ethnicity and describe yourself culturally?
Has this changed over time?

Fluency of languages
In which language do you feel most fluent currently?
Has your ease in your different languages changed over time?
Does it change dependent on context?
If you have lost fluency in your first language, what do you think the effect has been?

Relationship contexts of language speaking

Current family relationships
(If you have a partner) what language/s do you speak to him/her?
How was this decided? issues? effects on relationship/s?

What kinds of issues are there in your family around language use?
(If you have children) what language/s do you speak with them?
How was this decided? issues? effects on relationship/s?
Do you ever find yourself repeating/translating phrases of your parents?

Family of origin
What language did you /do you use now with your family of origin?

Other relationships
Which languages use for other important relationships? choice or no choice? cross-language relationships?
Do you have friendships which you conduct in both/all your languages?
Issues? effects on relationship/s? similarities or differences in relating?

Language use
Are there particular circumstances/contexts in which you use your languages? (choice or no choice)
Have you worked in all your languages? experiences and issues?
Can you write in all your languages? experiences/issues
Do you ever change languages (code switch) in any of your relationships or contexts? for what purpose would you do this?
Do your languages influence each other in any way?
When you get angry, what language do you find yourself using? What language do you curse in?
When you feel upset, in what language do you express this?
When you're happy etc
Which language/s do you use: to talk to yourself/to think/to write diaries/to dream/spiritual questions/to pray/to take notes/to argue, for passionate debate
Does this vary at all? Does this change when you change contexts? What have you noticed about this?
Would you say there are feelings you have in one language but not in another? Feelings that are harder to express in one than the other?
Can you tell jokes in both/all your languages? Is your sense of humour the same in your different languages?
Do you ever switch languages when you are thinking or talking to yourself?
If you are stuck or confused, do you ever switch to thinking about this in another language to see what happens?
Do you ever have the experience of suddenly finding yourself thinking or speaking in another language in a situation where you usually speak the other?
Do you ever have the experience of mixing up words from one language to another?
Would you say that there are experiences that you have in one language that you don't have in another?

Experiences and presentation of self
Do you think you present yourself differently in your different languages? Do you think you behave differently in different languages? If so, what is your explanation for this? connected to aspects of the language? issues of culture? Do you behave differently in different cultural contexts?
How would you describe yourself/be described in each language?
Can you give me an example of a story told about yourself in each language.

If you behave/experience yourself differently in different contexts, do others realise this/acknowledge this?

Moving between languages
Are there any words (or concepts) which are untranslatable from one of your languages to the other? What about metaphors or sayings?
If so, what is it like for you that there are untranslatable words between your languages?
Does this have an effect on your relationships in any way?

Relationship to languages
Do you feel 'at home' in one language more than another? for what reasons?
Do you feel you value your languages differently?
Has this changed over time/in different contexts/for what reasons?
Does this link to your view of how and which languages valued in present context?

Advantages/disadvantages of speaking several languages
Do you think being able to use more than one language has been advantageous for you?
Have there been disadvantages?
Would you consider yourself positioned in two/more cultures? If so, has this been advantageous to you? disadvantageous?
Has this changed over time? How connected to how cultures valued in present context?
How would you define your concept of 'home'?
Are there other aspects of being able to use more than one language which you think are important?
Are there other aspects of being positioned in more than one culture which you think are important?

Seeking help/therapy
If you were to consider having therapy, which language would you have it in?

Questions about the interview
Are there any other questions you think I should have asked?
Has this interview raised any new questions/thoughts for you? if so, what?

Appendix 2: Transcription Notations

The transcription notations used were as follows:

(.)	Untimed pause which is noticeable but too short to measure.
(2)	Time pause to nearest second.
word	Italic – emphasis placed on words by speaker.
(overlap)	Overlapping utterance
....	Speaker trails off. If followed by (overlap) then indicates that speaker has been interrupted. At the beginning of a sentence it indicates continuance of statement after (overlap)
(indistinct)	Inaudible. This will refer to one of two words. It will be indicated if longer section of dialogue.
(?)	Preceding word not 100 per cent clear.
(laughs)	Non-verbal information
CB	Researcher's contributions
[. . .]	Section of extract left out

References

Abley, Mark (2002) The Verbs of Boro. *Brick*. 69. Spring. 8–13.

Abley, Mark (2003) *Spoken Here: Travels Among Threatened Languages*. London: William Heinemann.

Abu-Ravia, Salim (1995) Attitudes and Cultural Background and Their Relationship to English in a Multicultural Social Context: The Case of Male and Female Arab Immigrants. *Educational Psychology* 15 (3): 323–36.

Adler, Max K. (1977) *Collective and Individual Bilingualism: a Sociolinguistic Study*. Hamburg: Helmut Buske Verlag.

Akhtar, Nameera and Tomasello, Michael (1998) Intersubjectivity in Early Language Learning and Use. In Stein Bråten (ed.) *Intersubjective Communication and Emotion in Early Ontogeny*. Cambridge and Paris: Cambridge University Press and Editions de la Maison des Sciences de l'Homme.

Alibhai-Brown, Yasmin (1997) The Quest for a Core: Multiple Identities and the Crisis of Self. Paper presented at Understanding Cultural Identity Conference, The Freud Museum/SOAS, London.

Alladina, Safder and Edwards, Viv (eds) (1991a) *Multilingualism in the British Isles 1: The Older Mother Tongues & Europe*. London: Longman.

Alladina, Safder and Edwards, Viv (eds) (1991b) *Multilingualism in the British Isles 2: Africa, The Middle East & Asia*. London: Longman.

Althusser, L. (1971) *Lenin and Philosophy and Other Essays*. London: New Left Review.

Amati-Mehler, Jacqueline, Argentieri, Simona and Canestri, Jorge (1993) *The Babel of the Unconscious: Mother Tongue and Foreign Languages in the Psychoanalytic Dimension*. Madison, Ct: International Universities Press Ltd.

Anderson, Benedict (1983) *Imagined Communities*. London: Verso.

Anderson, Harlene and Goolishian, Harry (1988) Human Systems as Linguistic Systems: Preliminary and Evolving Ideas about Implications for Clinical Theory. *Family Process* 27: 371–93.

Antaki, C., Condor, S. and Levine, M. (1996) Social Identities in Talk: Speakers' Own Orientations. *British Journal of Social Psychology* 35: 473–92.

Anthias, Floya and Yuval-Davis, Nira (1992) *Racialized Boundaries: Race, Nation, Gender, Colour and Class and the Anti-Racist Struggle*. London: Routledge.

Anzaldua, Gloria (1987/1999 2nd edn) *Borderlands. La Frontera. The New Mestiza*. San Francisco: Aunt Lute Books.

Apfelbaum, Erika (1997) The Impact of Culture in the Face of Genocide. Struggling Between a Silenced Home Culture and a Foreign Host Culture. Paper presented. Fifth European Congress of Psychology. Dublin, Ireland, July.

Arnberg, Lenore (1987) *Raising Children Bilingually: the Preschool Years*. Clevedon: Multilingual Matters.

Asad, T. (1986) The Concept of Cultural Translation. In J. Clifford and G.E. Marcus (eds) *Writing Culture: The Poetics and Politics of Ethnography*. Berkeley: University of California Press.

Auer, J.C. Peter (1985) The Pragmatics of Code-Switching: A Sequential Approach. In L. Milroy and P. Muysken (eds) *One Speaker, Two Languages*. Cambridge: Cambridge University Press.

Auer, J.C. Peter (1988/2000) Conversation Analysis, Code-Switching & Transfer. In Li Wei (ed.) *The Bilingualism Reader*. London: Routledge.

Austin, J.L. (1962/1980 2nd edn) *How to Do Things with Words*. Oxford: Oxford University Press.

Baker, P. and Mohieldeen, Y. (2000) The Languages of London's Schoolchildren. In P. Baker and J. Eversley (eds) *Multilingual Capital*. London: Battlebridge Publications.

Bakhtin, Mikhail Mikhailovich (1981) *The Dialogic Imagination: Four Essays*, edited by Michael Holquist. Austin: University of Texas Press.

Bakhtin, Mikhail Mikhailovich (1986) *Speech Genres and Other Late Essays*, trans. V.W. McGee. Austin: University of Texas Press.

Balkan, L. (1970) *Les Effets du Bilinguisme Française-Anglais sur les Aptitudes Intellectuelles*. Bruxelles: Aimav.

Barth, Frederick (1969) *Ethnic Groups and Boundaries*. Boston, MA: Little, Brown.

Bartlett, Dean and Payne, Sheila (1997) Grounded Theory – Its Basis, Rationale and Procedures. In G. McKenzie, J. Powell and R. Usher (eds) *Understanding Social Research Perspectives on Methodology and Practice*. London: Falmer Press.

Bateson, Gregory (1979) *Mind and Nature: a Necessary Unity*. Toronto: Bantam Books.

Bateson, Gregory, Jackson, Don, Haley, Jay and Weakland, John (1956). Toward a Theory of Schizophrenia. *Behavioral Science* 1: 251–64.

Beebe, Beatrice and Lachman, Frank (2002) *Infant Research and Adult Treatment*. London: Analytic Press.

Benjamin, Jessica (1998) *Shadow of the Other: Intersubjectivity and Gender in Psychoanalysis*. London: Routledge.

Benjamin, Walter (1973/1992) *Illuminations*. London: Fontana Press.

Bentovim, Arnon (1997) *Trauma-Organised Systems: Systemic Understanding of Family Violence. Physical and Sexual Abuse*. London: Karnac.

Ben-Zeev, S. (1977) The Influence of Bilingualism on Cognitive Strategy and Cognitive Development. *Child Development* 48: 1009–18.

Berko, Jean and Ely, Richard (2001) Gender Differences in Language Development. In Ann McGillicuddy-De Lisi and Richard De Lisi (eds) *Biology, Society and Behaviour: the Development of Sex Differences in Cognition*. Greenwich, CT: Ablex.

Berman, R.A. and Slobin, D.I. (1994) *Relating Events in Narrative: a Crosslinguistic Developmental Study*. Hillsdale, NJ: Lawrence Erlbaum Associates.

Bhabha, Homi K. (1994) *The Location of Culture*. London: Routledge.

Bhabha, Homi K. (1996) Culture's In-Between. In Stuart Hall and Paul du Gay (eds), *Questions of Cultural Identity*. London: Sage Publications.

Bhavnani, KumKum and Phoenix, Ann (eds) (1994) Shifting Identities Shifting Racisms: an Introduction. In *Shifting Identities Shifting Racisms*. London: Sage.

Bialystok, Ellen (1988) Levels of Bilingualism and Levels of Linguistic Awareness. *Developmental Psychology* 24 (4): 560–7.

Bialystok, Ellen (1991) Metalinguistic Dimensions of Bilingual Language Proficiency. In Ellen Bialystock (ed.) *Language Processing in Bilingual Children*. Cambridge: Cambridge University Press.

Bialystok, Ellen (1997) Effects of Bilingualism and Biliteracy on Children's Emerging Concepts of Print. *Developmental Psychology* 33 (3): 429–40.

Binder, J.R., Frost, J.A., Hammeke, T.A., Cox, R.W., Rao, S.M. and Prieto, T. (1997) Human Brain Language Areas Identified by Functional Magnetic Resonance Imaging. *Journal of Neuroscience* 17 (1): 353–62.

Borland, Katherine (1991) "That's Not What I Said": Interpretive Conflict in Oral Narrative Research. In Sherna Berger Gluck and Daphner Patai (eds) *Women's Words: The Feminist Practice of Oral History*. London: Routledge.

Borštnar, Jana, Močnik Bučar, Mojca, Rus Makovec, Maja, Burck, Charlotte and Daniel, Gwyn (2000) *Co-Constructing a Cross-Cultural Family Therapy Course in Slovenia: Resisting and Replicating Colonising Practices*. Presentation at Family Therapy Training Conference. Tavistock Clinic, London.

Bottomley, G. (1992) *From Another Place: Migration and the Politics of Culture*. Cambridge: Cambridge University Press.

Bourdieu, P. (1991) *Language and Symbolic Power*. Oxford: Polity Press.

Brah, Avtar (1996) *Cartographies of Diaspora: Contesting Identities*. London: Routledge.

Brah, Avtar, Hickman, Mary J., and Mac an Ghaill, Mairtin (eds) (1999) *Thinking Identities: Ethnicity, Racism and Culture*. London: Macmillan Press Ltd.

Braidotti, Rosi (1994) *Nomadic Subjects: Embodiment and Sexual Difference in Contemporary Feminist Theory*. New York: Columbia University Press.

Brodsky, Joseph (1986) *Less Than One: Selected Essays*. London: Penguin.

Bruner, Edward, M. and Gorfain, Phyllis (1991) Dialogic Narration and the Paradoxes of Masada. In Ivan Brady (ed.) *Anthropological Poetics*. Maryland: Rowman & Littlefield Publishers.

Bruner, Jerome (1986) *Actual Minds, Possible Worlds*. Cambridge, MA: Harvard University Press.

Bucholtz, Mary (1995) From Mulatta to Mestiza: Passing, the Linguistic Reshaping of Ethnic Identity. In Kira Hall and Mary Bucholtz (eds) *Gender Articulated: Language and the Constructed Self*. London: Routledge.

Budwig, N. (1998) Language and the Construction of Self: Developmental Reflections. Paper accessed at http://www.massey.ac.nz/~alock/nancy/nancy2.htm

Bull, Malcolm (2001) Hate is the New Love. Review of The Fragile Absolute by Slavoj Zizek. *London Review of Books*, 25 January.

Burck, Charlotte (1997) Language and Narrative: Learning from Bilingualism. In Renos K. Papadopoulos and John Byng-Hall (eds) *Multiple Voices: Narrative in Systemic Family Psychotherapy*. London: Duckworth.

Burck, Charlotte and Daniel, Gwyn (1995a) *Gender and Family Therapy*. London: Karnac.

Burck, Charlotte and Daniel, Gwyn (1995b) Moving On: Gender Beliefs in Post-Divorce and Stepfamily Process. In Charlotte Burck and Bebe Speed (eds) *Gender, Power and Relationships*. London: Routledge.

Burck, Charlotte and Frosh, Stephen (1994) Research Process and Gendered Reflexivity. *Human Systems* 3: 109–22.

Burman, Erica (1994) *Deconstructing Developmental Psychology*. London: Routledge.

Burnham, J. (1993) Systemic Supervision: the Evolution of Reflexivity in the Context of the Supervisory Relationship. *Human Systems* 4: 349–81.

Burton, Pauline (1994) Women and Second Language Use. In Pauline Burton, Ketaki Kushari Dyson and Shirley Ardener (eds) *Bilingual Women*. Oxford: Berg.

Burton, Pauline, Dyson, Ketaki Kushari and Ardener, Shirley (eds) (1994) *Bilingual Women. Anthropological Approaches to Second Language Use.* Oxford: Berg.

Butler, Judith (1990) *Gender Trouble: Feminism and the Subversion of Identity.* London: Routledge.

Butler, Judith (1997) *Excitable Speech: a Politics of the Performative.* New York and London: Routledge.

Byrne, Nollaig O'Reilly and McCarthy, Imelda Colgan (1998) Marginal Illuminations. A Fifth Province Approach to Intracultural Issues in an Irish Context. In Monica McGoldrick (ed.) *Re-visioning Family Therapy: Race, Culture and Gender in Clinical Practice.* New York: Guilford Press.

Carringer, D. (1974) Creative Thinking Abilities of a Mexican Youth: the Relationship of Bilingualism. *Journal of Cross-Cultural Psychology* 5: 492–504.

Cecchin, Gianfranco (1987) Hypothesising, Circularity and Neutrality Revisited: an Invitation to Curiosity. *Family Process* 26: 405–13.

Chamberlain, Mary (1997) *Narratives of Exile and Return.* London and Basingstoke: Macmillan Press Ltd.

Charnaz, Kathy (1995) Grounded Theory. In J. Smith, R. Harré and L. van Langenhove (eds) *Rethinking Methods in Psychology.* London: Sage.

Chary, P. (1986) Aphasia in a Multilingual Society. In J. Vaid (ed.) *Language Processing in Bilinguals: Psycholinguistic and Neuropsychological Perspectives.* Hillsdale, NJ: Lawrence Erlbaum Associates.

Chomsky, Noam (1976) *Reflections on Language.* Glasgow: Fontana.

Clachar, A. (1997) Ethnolinguistic Identity and Spanish Proficiency in a Paradoxical Situation: the Case of Puerto Rican Return Migrants. *Journal of Multilingual and Multicultural Development* 18 (2): 107–24.

Connell, R. (1987) *Gender and Power.* Cambridge: Polity Press.

Constantinidou, Evi (1994) The 'Death' of East Sutherland Gaelic: Death by Women? In Pauline Burton, Ketaki Kushari Dyson and Shirley Ardener (eds) *Bilingual Women.* Oxford: Berg.

Cowley, Peter (2003) Lost and Found – the Language of Exile. *Mots Pluriels* no. 23. http://www.arts.uwa.edu.au/MotsPluriels/MP2303pc.html

Cromdal, Jakob (2000) *Code-Switching for All Practical Purposes.* Tema Barn, Department of Child Studies. Linkoping Universitet, Sweden.

Cross, T. (1977) Mothers' Speech Adjustments: the Contribution of Selected Child Listener Variables. In C. Snow and C. Ferguson (eds) *Talking to Children.* Cambridge: Cambridge University Press.

Cummins, J. (1984) *Bilingualism and Special Education: Issues in Assessment and Pedagogy.* Clevedon: Multilingual Matters.

Daniel, Gwyn and Thompson, Paul (1996) Stepchildren's Memories of Love and Loss: Men and Women's Narratives. In Selma Leydesdorff, Luisa Passerini and Paul Thompson (eds) *Gender and Memory: International Yearbook of Oral History and Life Stories*, 4. Oxford: Oxford University Press.

Davies, Bronwyn and Harré, Rom (1997) Positioning: the Discursive Production of Selves. *Journal for the Theory of Social Behaviour* 20: 43–63.

Deane, Seamus (1998) Secrets, Their Social Functions and Dysfunctions. Presentation. London, Tavistock Clinic, 26 November.

Derrida, Jacques (1978/1997) *Writing and Difference.* London: Routledge.

Derrida, Jacques (1985) *The Ear of the Other.* New York: Schocken Books.

Derrida, Jacques (1998) *Monolingualism of the Other; or, The Prosthesis of Origin*. Stanford, CA: Stanford Press.

DiNicola, Vincenzo F. (1986) Beyond Babel: Family Therapy as Cultural Translation. *International Journal of Family Psychiatry* 7 (2): 179–91.

DiNicola, Vincenzo F. (1997) *A Stranger in the Family: Culture, Families and Therapy*. New York and London: W.W. Norton & Co.

Di Pietro, R. (1977) Code-switching as a Verbal Strategy Among Bilinguals. In F. Eckman (ed.) *Current Themes in Linguistics: Bilingualism, Experimental Linguistics and Language Typologies*. Washington, DC: Hemisphere Publishing.

Donovan, Mary (2001) Towards an Ethical Position in Family Therapy. The Application of Habermas's Thinking. Unpublished MSc Dissertation. Tavistock Clinic and University of East London.

Dorfman, Ariel (1998) *Heading South, Looking North: a Bilingual Journey*. London: Hodder & Stoughton.

Doyle, A., Champagne, M. and Segalowitz, N. (1978) Some Issues on the Assessment of Linguistic Consequences of Early Bilingualism. In M. Paradis (ed.) *Aspects of Bilingualism*. Columbia, SC: Hornbeam Press.

Du Bois, W.E.B. (1903/1989) *The Souls of Black Folk*. New York: Bantam.

Dunn, Judy (ed.) (1995) *Connections Between Emotion and Understanding in Development*. Hove: Lawrence Erlbaum Associates.

Dyson, Ketaki Kushari (1994) Forging a Bilingual Identity: a Writer's Testimony. In P. Burton, Ketaki Kushari Dyson and Shirley Ardener (eds) *Bilingual Women*. Oxford: Berg.

Edwards, Derek (1997) *Discourse and Cognition*. London: Sage.

Edwards, Derek and Middleton, D. (1988) Conversational Remembering and Family Relationships: How Children Learn to Remember. *Journal of Social and Personal Relationships* 5: 3–25.

Edwards, John (1994) *Multilingualism*. London: Routledge.

Erikson, Erik H. (1968) *Identity: Youth and Crisis*. New York: Norton.

Ervin, S. (1964) Language and TAT Content in Bilinguals. *Journal of Abnormal and Social Psychology* 68: 500–7.

Ervin, S. and Osgood, C.T. (1953) Second Language Learning and Bilingualism. *Journal of Personality and Social Psychology* 58: 139–45.

Ervin-Tripp, S. (1968) An Analysis of the Interaction of Language, Topic and Listener. In J. Fishman (ed.) *Readings in the Sociology of Language*. The Hague: Mouton.

Ervin-Tripp, S. (1973) Identification and Bilingualism. In A. Dil (ed.) *Language Acquisition and Communication Choice*. Stanford, CA: Stanford University Press.

Fairclough, Norman (1992). Discourse and Text: Linguistic and Intertextual Analysis within Discourse Analysis. *Discourse and Society* 3: 192–217.

Falicov, Celia Jaes (1995) Training to Think Culturally: A Multidimensional Comparative Perspective. *Family Process* 34: 373–88.

Falicov, Celia Jaes (1998) *Latino Families in Therapy: a Guide to Multicultural Practice*. New York: Guilford Press.

Falicov, Celia Jaes (2002) Migration, Ambiguous Loss and Resilience Through Rituals. Scientific Lecture. Tavistock Clinic, London, 11 February.

Felman, S. and Laub, D. (1992) *Testimony*. New York: Routledge, Chapman & Hall.

Fine, Michelle (1994) Working the Hyphens. Reinventing Self and Other in Qualitative Research. In N.K. Denzin and Y.S. Lincoln (eds) *Handbook of Qualitative Research*. London: Sage.

Fisher, Richard I. (1974) A Study of Non-Intellectual Attributes of Children in First Grade Bilingual – Bicultural Program. *Journal of Educational Research* 67 (7): 323–8.

Fishman, Joshua A. (1967/2000) Bilingualism With and Without Diglossia; Disglossia With and Without Bilingualism. In Li Wei (ed.) *The Bilingualism Reader*. London: Routledge.

Fishman, Joshua A. (1996) What Do You Lose When You Lose Your Language? In G. Cantoni (ed.) *Stabilizing Indigenous Languages*. Flagstaff Centre for Excellence in Education. North Arizona University. NCBE Home Page: http://www.ncbe.gwu.edu

Fitzherbert, Katrin (1997) *True to Both My Selves*. London: Virago.

Forché, Carolyn (2001) Mahmoud Darwish. Exiled in Language. *Brick* 68: 65–6.

Forrester, Michael A. (2001) The Embedding of the Self in Early Interaction. *Infant and Child Development* 10: 189–202.

Foucault, Michel (1980) *Power/Knowledge: Selected Interviews and Other Writings 1972–1977* (edited by C. Gordon). Brighton, Sussex: Harvester Press.

Freeman, Mark (1993) *Rewriting the Self: History, Memory, Narrative*. London: Routledge.

Frosh, Stephen (2001) Things that Can't be Said: Psychoanalysis and the Limits of Language. *International Journal of Critical Psychology* 1: 28–46.

Frosh, Stephen, Phoenix, Ann and Pattman, Rob (2002) *Young Masculinities: Understanding Boys in Contemporary Society*. Basingstoke: Palgrave.

Gallagher, C. (1968) North African Problems and Prospects: Language and Identity. In J. Fishman, C. Ferguson and J. Das Gupta (eds) *Language Problems in Developing Nations*. New York: Wiley.

Gee, J.P. (1991) A Linguistic Approach to Narrative. *Journal of Narrative and Life History* 1: 15–39.

Gee, J.P. (1998) Two Styles of Narrative Construction and Their Linguisitic and Educational Implications. In J. Cheshire and P. Trudgill (eds) *The Sociolinguistics Reader. Volume 2: Gender and Discourse*. London: Arnold.

Geissler, H. (1938) *Zweisprachige Deutscher Kinder in Ausland*. Stuttgart: Kohlhammer.

Genesee, Fred (1989/2000) Early Bilingual Language Development: One Language or Two? In Li Wei (ed.) *The Bilingualism Reader* (2000). London: Routledge.

Genesee, Fred, Tucker, R. and Lambert, William E. (1975) Communication Skills of Bilingual Children. *Child Development* 46: 1010–14.

Gentzler, Edwin (1993) *Contemporary Translation Theories*. London: Routledge.

Gergen, Kenneth J. (1985) The Social Constructionist Movement in Modern Psychology. *American Psychologist* 40: 266–75.

Gergen, Kenneth J. (1994) *Realities and Relationships*. Cambridge, MA: Harvard University Press.

Gilbert, Jack (1994) *The Great Fires: Poems 1982–1992*. New York: Alfred A. Knopf.

Gilroy, Paul (2000) *Between Camps: Nations, Cultures and the Allure of Race*. London: Allen Lane.

Glaser, B.G. and Strauss, A.C. (1967) *The Discovery of Grounded Theory: Strategies for Qualitative Research*. Chicago: Aldine.

Goffman, Erving (1959) *The Presentation of Self in Everyday Life*. New York: Doubleday.

Goffman, Erving (1979) Footing. *Semiotica*. 25 (1/2): 1–29.

Green, Julian (1987) *Le Langage et Son Double*. Paris: Editions du Seuil.

Greenson, Ralph R. (1950) The Mother Tongue and the Mother. *International Journal of Psychoanalysis* 31: 540–52.

Grinberg, Léon and Grinberg, Rebeca (1989) *Psychoanalytic Perspectives on Migration and Exile*. New Haven and London: Yale University Press.

Grosjean, François (1982) *Life with Two Languages*. Cambridge, MA: Harvard University Press.

Gumperz, John (1982) *Discourse Strategies*. Cambridge: Cambridge University Press.

Gumperz, John (1992) Contextualisation Revisited. In P. Auer and A.D. Luzio (eds) *The Contextualization of Language*. Amsterdam: John Benjamins.

Gumperz, John J. and Levinson, Stephen C. (eds) (1996) *Rethinking Linguistic Relativity*. Cambridge: Cambridge University Press.

Haarmann, Harald (1986) *Language in Ethnicity: a View of Basic Ecological Relations*. Berlin, New York and Amsterdam: Mouton de Gruyter.

Hakuta, Kenji (1999) A Critical Period for Second Language Acquisition? A Status Review. Stanford University. Accessible at http://www.stanford.edu/~hakuta/Docs/CriticalPeriod.PDF

Hakuta, Kenji, Bialystok, Ellen and Wiley, Edward (2001) Critical Evidence: A Test of the Critical Period Hypothesis of Second Language Acquisition. Article on Internet. Stanford University. Accessible at: http://www.stanford.edu/~hakuta/Docs/Critical%20Evidence.pdf

Hall, Stuart (1987). Minimal Selves. In *Identity. The Real Me*. ICA Documents No. 6, London: ICA.

Hall, Stuart (1989) New Ethnicities. In Kobena Mercer (ed.) *Black Film, British Cinema*. ICA Documents 7: London: ICA.

Hall, Stuart (1996) Introduction: Who Needs Identity? In Stuart Hall and Paul du Gay (eds) *Questions of Cultural Identity*. London: Sage Publications.

Hall, Stuart (1999) Subjectivity. Scientific Lecture. Tavistock Clinic, London, 14 June.

Halliday, M.A.K. (1975) *Learning How to Mean: Explorations in the Development of Language*. London: Arnold.

Hamers, Josiane F. and Blanc, Michael, H.A. (2000) *Bilinguality and Bilingualism*, 2nd edn. Cambridge: Cambridge University Press.

Harré, Rom (ed.) (1986) *The Social Construction of Emotion*. Oxford: Basil Blackwell.

Haugen, E. (1956) *Bilingualism in the Americas: a Bibliography and Research Guide*. Alabama: University of Alabama Press.

Heelas, Paul (1986) Emotion Talk Across Cultures. In Rom Harré (ed.) *The Social Construction of Emotions*. Oxford: Basil Blackwell.

Heilbrun, C.G. (1988) *Writing a Woman's Life*. New York: Ballantine Books.

Henriques, Julian, Hollway, Wendy, Urwin, Cathy, Venn, Couze and Walkerdine, Valerie (1984) *Changing the Subject: Psychology, Social Regulation and Subjectivity*. London: Methuen.

Henwood, Karen and Pidgeon, Nick (1996) Grounded Theory. In J.T.E. Richardson (ed.) *Handbook of Qualitative Research Methods*. Leicester: BPS.

Hobson, R. Peter (2002) *The Cradle of Thought: Exploring the Origins of Thinking*. London: Macmillan.

Hoffman, Eva (1989) *Lost in Translation: a Life in a New Language*. London: Minerva.

Holmes, J. (1998) Narrative Structure: Some Contrasts Between Maori and Pakeha Story-Telling. *Multilingua. Journal of Cross-Cultural and Interlanguage Communication* 17 (1): 25–57.

hooks, bell (1989) *Talking Back: Thinking Feminist, Thinking Black*. London: Sheba Feminist Publishers.

Horton-Salway, Mary (2001) The Construction of M.E.: The Discursive Action Model. In Margaret Wetherell, Stephanie Taylor and Simeon J. Yates (eds) *Discourse as Data*. London: Sage.

Hughes, G.W. (1981) Neuropsychiatric Aspects of Bilingualism: a Brief Review. *British Journal of Psychiatry* 139: 25–8.

Hymes, D.H. (1972) On Communicative Competence. In J.B. Pride and Janet Holmes (eds) *Sociolinguistics*. Harmondsworth, England: Penguin Books.

Ianco-Worrall, A. (1972) Bilingualism and Cognitive Development. *Child Development* 43: 1390–1400.

Irigaray, L. (1985) *The Sex Which is Not One*. Ithaca, NY: Cornell University Press.

Iyer, Pico (2000) *The Global Soul*. London: Bloomsbury Publishing.

Jackson, Richard. (2001) From Translation to Imitation. Accessible at http://www.utc.edu/~engldept/pm/ontransl.htm

James, William (1890) *The Principles of Psychology*, vol. 1. New York: Dover.

James, A. and Prout, A. (eds) (1990) *Constructing and Reconstructing Childhood*. Brighton: Falmer Press.

Javier, R.A. (1996) In Search of Repressed Memories. In R. Pérez Foster, M. Moskovwitz and R.A. Javier (eds) *Reaching Across Boundaries of Culture and Class: Widening the Scope of Psychotherapy*. Norvale, NJ: Jason Aronson.

Jorgenson, J. (1991) Co-Constructing the Interviewer/Co-Constructing 'Family'. In F. Steier (ed.) *Research and Reflexivity*. London: Sage.

Kanno, Yasuko (2000) Bilingualism and Identity: the Stories of Japanese Returnees. *International Journal of Bilingual Education and Bilingualism* 3 (1): 1–18.

Kaplan, Alice (1994) *French Lessons: a Memoir*. Chicago: University of Chicago Press.

Kim, K.H., Relkin, N.R., Lee, K.M. and Hirsch, J. (1997) Distinct Cortical Areas Associated with Native and Second Languages. *Nature* 388: 171–4.

Kirkman, Maggie (1997) *Plots and Disruptions: Narratives, Infertility and Women's Lives*. Unpublished PhD. La Trobe University, Victoria, Australia.

Kleinman, A. (1988) *The Illness Narratives: Suffering, Healing and the Human Condition*. London: Basic Books.

Kopijn, Yvette J. (1998) The Oral History Interview in a Cross-Cultural Setting. An Analysis of its Linguisitic, Social and Ideological Structure. In Mary Chamberlain and Paul Thompson (eds) *Narrative and Genre*. London: Routledge.

Krause, Inga-Britt (1998) *Therapy Across Culture*. London: Sage Publications.

Krause, Inga-Britt (2002) *Culture and System in Family Therapy*. London: Karnac.

Kress, Gunther (2001) From Saussure to Critical Sociolinguistics: the Turn Towards a Social View of Language. In Margaret Wetherell, Stephanie Taylor and Simeon J. Yates (eds) *Discourse Theory and Practice: A Reader*. London: Sage Publications.

Kristeva, Julie (1969/1986) *The Kristeva Reader*, edited by Toril Moi. Oxford: Blackwell.

Kuhl, Patricia, K. (1998) Language, Culture and Intersubjectivity: The Creation of Shared Perception. In Stein Bråten (ed) *Intersubjective Communication and Emotion in Early Ontogeny*. Cambridge: Cambridge University Press & Paris: Editions de la Maison des Sciences de l'Homme.

LaFromboise, Teresa, Coleman, Hardin L.K., and Gerton, Jennifer (1993) Psychological Impact of Biculturalism: Evidence and Theory. *Psychological Bulletin* 114 (3): 395–412.

Laing, R.D. (1965) *The Divided Self*. London: Pelican.

Lambert, William, E. (1977) The Effects of Bilingualism on the Individual: Cognitive and Socio-Cultural Consequences. In P. Hornby (ed.) *Bilingualism. Psychological, Social and Educational Implications*. New York: Academic Press.

Lamendella, John, T. (1978) General Principles of Neurofunctional Organisation and Their Manifestation in Primary and Nonprimary Language Acquisition. *Language Learning* 27 (1): 155–96.

Lau, Annie (1984) Transcultural Issues in Family Therapy. *Journal of Family Therapy* 6: 91–112.

Lau, Annie (1995) Gender, Power and Relationships: Ethno-cultural and Religious Issues. In Charlotte Burck and Gwyn Daniel (1995) *Gender, Power and Relationships*. London: Routledge.

Lenneberg, E. (1967) *The Biological Foundations of Language*. New York: John Wiley and Sons.

Lincoln, Yvonna S. and Guba, E.G. (1994) Paradigms of Research. In Norman, K. Denzin and Yvonna S. Lincoln (eds) *Handbook of Qualitative Research*. London: Sage.

Linde, Charlotte (1993) *Life Stories: the Creation of Coherence*. Oxford: Oxford University Press.

Lockhart, Greg (1992) Introduction. In *The General Retires and Other Stories* by Nguyen Huy Thiep. Singapore: Oxford University Press.

Loomba, Ania (1998) *Colonialism/Postcolonialism*. London: Routledge.

Lyon, J. (1996) *Becoming Bilingual: Language Acquisition in a Bilingual Community*. Clevedon: Multilingual Matters.

Maalouf, Amin (2000) *On Identity*. London: The Harvill Press.

Maffi, Luisa (ed.) (2000) *On Biocultural Diversity: Linking Language, Knowledge and the Environment*. Washington, DC: Smithsonian Institution Press.

Mama, Amina (1995) *Beyond the Masks: Race, Gender and Subjectivity*. London: Routledge.

Maschler, Yael (1994) Metalanguaging and Discourse Markers in Bilingual Conversation. *Language in Society* 23: 325–66.

Maybin, Janet (1998) Children's Voices: Talk, Knowledge and Identity. In J. Cheshire and P. Trudgill (eds) *The Sociolinguistics Reader. Volume 2: Gender and Discourse*. London: Arnold.

Maybin, Janet (1999) Framing and Evaluation in Ten- to Twelve-Year-Old School Children's Use of Repeated, Appropriated, and Reported Speech in Relation to Their Induction into Educational Procedures and Practices. *Text* 19 (4): 459–84.

Maybin, Janet (2001a) Language, Struggle and Voice: Bakhtin/Volosinov Writings. In Margaret Wetherell, Stephanie Taylor and Simeon J. Yates (eds) *Discourse Theory and Practice*. London: Open University and Sage.

Maybin, Janet (2001b) Voices, Morals and Identity in Ten-to-Twelve-Year-Olds. In I.M. Blayer and M. Sanchez (eds) *Storytelling: Interdisciplinary and Intercultural Perspectives*. New York: Peter Long.

McKay, Sandra Lee and Wong, Sau-Ling Cynthia (1996) Multiple Discourse, Multiple Identities: Investment and Agency in Second-Language Learning Among Chinese Adolescent Immigrant Students. *Harvard Educational Review* 66 (3): 577–608.

McLaughlin, B. (1978) *Second Language Acquisition in Childhood*. Hillsdale, NJ: Lawrence Erlbaum Associates.

Mead, George Herbert (1913) The Social Self. *Journal of Philosophy, Psychology and Scientific Methods* 10: 374–80.

Miller, Jennifer, M. (2000) Language Use, Identity and Social Interaction: Migrant Students in Australia. *Research on Language and Social Interaction* 33 (1): 69–100.

Mills, Jean (2001) Being Bilingual: Perspectives of Third Generation Asian Children on Language, Culture and Identity. *International Journal of Bilingual Education and Bilingualism* 4 (6): 383–402.

Mistry, Jayanthi (1997) The Development of Remembering in Cultural Context. In Nelson Cowan (ed.) *The Development of Memory in Childhood*. Hove: Psychology Press.

Mkilifi, M. (1978) Triglossia and Swahili-English Bilingualism in Tanzania. In J. Fishman (ed.) *Advances in the Study of Societal Multilingualism*. The Hague: Mouton.

Modood, T. (1992) *Not Easy Being British: Colour, Culture and Citizenship*. Stoke on Trent: Trentham Books.

Morris, Brian (1994) *Anthropology of the Self: the Individual in Cultural Perspective*. London: Pluto Press.

Morris, J.S., Scott, S.K., Dolan, R.J. (1999) Saying it With Feeling: Neural Responses to Emotional Vocalizations. *Neuropsychologica* 37 (10): 1155–1163.

Mukherjee, Bharati (1999) Imagining Homelands. In André Aciman (ed) *Letters of Transit. Reflections on Exile, Identity, Language and Loss*. New York: The New York Public Library.

Norton, Bonny (2000) *Identity and Language Learning: Gender, Ethnicity and Educational Change*. London: Pearson Education Ltd.

Nuffield Languages Inquiry (2000) *Languages: The Next Generation. The Final Report and Recommendations of the Nuffield Languages Inquiry*. The Nuffield Foundation. http://www.nuffieldfoundation.org/languages/inquiry/

Ochs, E. (1996) Linguistic Resources for Socializing Humanity. In J.J. Gumperz and S.C. Levinson (eds) *Rethinking Linguistic Relativity*. Cambridge: Cambridge University Press.

Papadopoulos, Renos and Hildebrand, Judy (1997) Is Home Where the Heart Is? Narratives of Oppositional Discourse. In Renos Papdopoulos and John Byng-Hall (eds) *Multiple Voices: Narratives in Systemic Family Psychotherapy*. London: Duckworth.

Paradis, M. (1980) Contributions of Neurolinguistics to the Theory of Bilingualism. In *Applications of Linguistic Theory in the Human Sciences*. Department of Linguistics, Michigan State University.

Paradis, M. (1977) Bilingualism and Aphasia. In H. Whitaker and H. Whitaker (eds) *Studies in Neurolinguistics*, vol. 3. New York: Academic Press.

Pavlenko, Aneta (2002) Bilingualism and Emotions. *Multilingua* 21: 45–78.

Peal, E. and Lambert, W.E. (1962) Relation of Bilingualism to Intelligence. *Psychological Monographs* 76: 1–23.

Pease-Alvarez, Lucinda (1993) Native Language Maintenance and Shift in Mexican-Descent Children. University of California, Santa Cruz.

Pérez Foster, RoseMarie (1996) The Bilingual Self. Duet in Two Voices. *Psychoanalytic Dialogues* 6 (1): 99–121.

Pérez Foster, RoseMarie (1998) *The Power of Language in the Clinical Process. Assessing and Treating the Bilingual Person.* Northvale, NJ: Jason Aronson Inc.

de Peuter, Jennifer (1998) The Dialogics of Narrative Identity. In Michael M. Bell and Michael Gardiner (eds) *Bakhtin and the Human Sciences.* London: Sage.

Phillips, Adam (2000) *Promises. Promises.* London: Faber & Faber Ltd.

Phoenix, Ann (1998) (Re)Constructing Gendered and Ethnicised Identities: Are We All Marginal Now? Inaugural Lecture, Universiteit voor Humanistiek Utrecht.

Phoenix, Ann and Owen, Charlie (1996) From Miscegenation to Hybridity: Mixed Relationships and Mixed-Parentage in Profile. In B. Bernstein and Julia Brannen (eds) *Children, Research and Policy.* London: Taylor & Francis Ltd.

Phoenix, Ann and Woollett, Anne (1991) Motherhood: Social Construction, Politics and Psychology. In Ann Phoenix, Anne Woollett and Eva Lloyd (eds) *Motherhood. Meaning, Practices and Ideology.* London: Sage.

Pidgeon, Nick (1996) Grounded Theory: Theoretical Background. In J.T.E. Richardson (ed.) *Handbook of Qualitative Research Methods.* Leicester: BPS.

Pinker, Stephen (1994) *The Language Instinct: the New Science of Language and Mind.* London: Allen Lane.

Polonoff, D. (1987). Self-deception. *Social Research* 54 (1): 45–53.

Poplack, S. (1980) Sometimes I'll Start a Sentence in English y Terminó en Español: Towards a Typology of Code-switching. *Linguistics* 18: 581–616.

Potter, Jonathan and Wetherell, Margaret (1987) *Discourse and Social Psychology: Beyond Attitudes and Behaviour.* London: Sage.

Pouratian, N., Bookheimer, S.Y., O'Farrell, A.M., Sicotte, N.L., Cannestra, A.F., Becker, D. and Toga, A.W. (2000) Optical Imaging of Bilingual Cortical Representations – Case Report. *Journal of Neurosurgery* 93 (4): 676–81.

Radhakrishnan,, R. (2000) Adjudicating Hybridity, Co-ordinating Betweenness. *Jouvert. A Journal of Postcolonial Studies* 5 (1). Available online at: http://social.class.ncsu.edu/jouvert/v5i1/radha.htm

Rampton, Ben (1995) *Crossing: Language and Ethnicity Among Adolescents.* London and New York: Longman.

Raval, Hitesh (1996) A Systemic Perspective on Working with Interpreters. *Journal of Child Psychology and Psychiatry* 1: 29–43.

Rennie, David, L., Phillips, Jeffrey, R. & Quartaro, Georgia K. (1988) Grounded Theory: A Promising Approach to Conceptualisation in Psychology? *Canadian Psychology/Psychologie Canadienne* 29 (2): 139–50.

Ricoeur, Paul (1984) *Time and Narrative,* vol. 2. Chicago: University of Chicago Press.

Ricoeur, Paul (1985) *Time and Narrative,* vol. 2. Chicago: University of Chicago Press.

Riessman, Catherine K. (1993) *Narrative Analysis.* London: Sage.

Riessman, Catherine, K. (2001) Analysis of Personal Narratives. In J.F. Gurbium and J.A. Holstein (eds) *Handbook of Interviewing.* London: Sage.

Rindstedt, Camilla (2000) Growing up in a Bilingual Quichua Community: Play, Language and Socialising Practices. Working Papers on Childhood and the Study of Children. Linköping: Linköping University Press.

Rindstedt, Camilla and Aronsson, Karin (2001) Growing Up Monolingual in a Bilingual Community: The Quichua Revitalization Paradox. Linköping University, Sweden.

Rodriguez, Richard (1982) *Hunger of Memory*. New York: Bantam Books.

Romaine, Suzanne (1989) *Bilingualism*. Oxford: Basil Blackwell.

Romaine, Suzanne (1995) *Bilingualism*, 2nd edition. Oxford: Blackwell.

Ronjat, J. (1913) *Le Developpement du Langage Observé Chez un Enfant Bilingue*. Paris: Champion.

Rorty, Richard (1989) *Contingency, Irony and Solidarity*. Cambridge: Cambridge University Press.

Rose, Jacqueline (1996) *States of Fantasy*. Oxford: Clarendon Press.

Rose, Jacqueline (1997) Understanding Cultural Identity. Paper presented at Understanding Cultural Identity Conference, The Freud Museum/SOAS, London.

Rose, Jacqueline (2001) Response to Edward Said. Freud and the Non-European. The Freud Museum Lecture, London, 6 December.

Said, Edward W. (1993) *Culture and Imperialism*. London: Vintage.

Said, Edward W. (1998) Between Worlds. *London Review of Books* 20 (9): 3–7.

Said, Edward W. (1999) *Out of Place: A Memoir*. London: Granta Books.

Said, Edward W. (2000) *Reflections on Exile and Other Literary and Cultural Essays*. London: Granta.

Said, Edward W. (2001) Freud and the Non-European The Freud Museum Lecture, London, 6 December.

Sante, Luc (1997) Lingua Franca. *Granta* 59. Autumn.

Sante, Luc (1998) *The Factory of Facts*. London: Granta Books.

Saunders, G. (1982) *Bilingual Children: Guidance for the Family*. Clevedon: Multilingual Matters Ltd.

Scott, S. (1973) *The Relation of Divergent Thinking to Bilingualism: Cause or Effect*. Unpublished Manuscript. Department of Psychology, McGill University. Montreal, Canada.

Sebba, M. and Wootton, A. (1998) We, They and Identity. Sequential versus Identity-related Explanation in Code-Switching. In P. Auer (ed.) *Code-Switching in Conversation: Language, Interaction and Identity*. London: Routledge.

Seliger, H. (1989) Deterioration and Creativity in Childhood Bilingualism. In K. Hytelstan and L.K. Obler (eds) *Bilingualism Across the Lifespan: Aspects of Acquisition, Maturity and Loss*. Cambridge: Cambridge University Press.

Shotter, John (1989) Social Accountability and the Social Construction of 'You'. In John Shotter and Kenneth J. Gergen (eds) *Texts of Identity*. London: Sage.

Shotter, John (1993) *Conversational Realities: Constructing Life through Language*. London: Sage.

Shotter, John and Billig, Michael (1998) A Bakhtinian Psychology: From Out of the Heads of Individuals and into the Dialogues Between Them. In Michael Mayerfield Bell and Michael Gardiner (eds) *Bakhtin and the Human Sciences*. London: Sage.

Silverman, Max and Yuval-Davis, Nira (1999) Jews, Arabs and the Theorisation of Racism in Britain and France. In Avtar Brah, Mary J. Hickman and Mairtin Mac

An Ghaill (eds) *Thinking Identities: Ethnicity, Racism and Culture*. London: Macmillan Press Ltd.

Simon, S. (1996) Some Border Incidents. *Brick* 55: 22–4.

Skutnabb-Kangas, T. and Toukomaa, P. (1976) *Teaching Migrant Children's Mother Tongue and Learning the Language of the Host Country in the Context of the Socio-Cultural Situation of the Migrant Family*. Helsinki: Finnish National Commission for UNESCO.

Slavin, Robert E. and Cheung, Alan (2003) *Effective Reading Programs for English Language Learners: a Best-Evidence Synthesis*. CRESPAR Report No. 66. December. www.csos.jhu.edu/crespar/techReports/Report66.pdf

Slobin, D.I. (1996) From "Thought and Language" to "Thinking for Speaking". In J.J. Gumperz and S.C. Levinson (eds) (1996) *Rethinking Linguistic Relativity*. Cambridge: Cambridge University Press.

Smith, Gerrilyn (2005) Children's Narratives of Traumatic Experiences. In Emilia Dowling and Arlene Vetere (eds). *Narrative Therapies with Children and Their Families: A Practitioner's Guide to Concepts and Approaches*. Brunner/Routledge.

Smith, Howard L. (1999) Bilingualism and Bilingual Education: the Child's Perspective. *International Journal of Bilingual Education and Bilingualism*. 2 (4): 268–81.

Smolicz, J. (1979) *Culture and Education in a Plural Society*. Canberra: Curriculum Development Centre.

Squire, Corinne (2000) Situated Selves, the Coming-Out Genre and Equivalent Citizenship in Narratives of HIV. In Prue Chamberlayne, Joanna Bornat and Tom Wengraf (eds) *The Turn to Biographical Methods in Social Science*. London: Routledge.

Stam, Robert (1998) Hybridity and the Aesthetics of Garbage: the Case of Brazilian Cinema. *E.I.A.L.* 9 (1) June. Available online at http://www.tau.ac.il/eial/IX_1/stam.html

Stavans, Ilan (2002) *On Borrowed Words: a Memoir of Language*. New York: Penguin.

Stead, Peter (1997) Conference Presentation, Cultural Identity. Freud Museum and SOAS, 6 December.

Steier, Frederick (1991) *Research and Reflexivity*. London: Sage.

Steiner, George (1998a) *After Babel: Aspects of Language and Translation*, 3rd edn. Oxford: Oxford University Press.

Steiner, George (1998b) *Errata: an Examined Life*. London: Phoenix.

Stern, Daniel (1985) *The Interpersonal World of the Infant*. New York: Basic Books.

Stern, Sergio, Doolan, Moira, Staples, Emma, Szmukler, George, L. and Eisler, Ivan (1999) Disruption and Reconstruction: Narrative Insights into the Experience of Family Members Caring for a Relative Diagnosed with Serious Mental Illness. *Family Process* 38: 353–69.

Stroud, Christopher (1998) Perspectives on Cultural Variability of Discourse and Some Implications for Code-Switching. In Peter Auer (ed.) *Code-Switching in Conversation: Language, Interaction and Identity*. London and New York: Routledge.

Suárez-Orozco, Carola and Suárez-Orozco, Marcelo M. (2001) *Children of Immigration*. London: Harvard University Press.

Swain, M. and Cummins, J. (1979) Bilingualism, Cognitive Functioning and Education. *Language Teaching and Linguistics: Abstracts* 12: 4–18.

Taylor, Stephanie (2001) Locating and Conducting Discourse Analytic Research. In Margaret Wetherell, Stephanie Taylor and Simeon J. Yates (eds) *Discourse as Data: a Guide for Analysis*. London: Sage and Open University.

TES (2003) English is Second Tongue for One Tenth of Pupils. 4 July.

Tesone, Juan-Eduardo (1996) Multi-Lingualism, Word-Presentations, Thing-Presentations and Psychic Reality. *International Journal of Psycho-Analysis* 77: 871–81.

Thomas, Lennox (1995) Psychotherapy in the Context of Race and Culture: An Intercultural Therapeutic Approach. In Suman Fernando (ed.) *Mental Health in a Multi-ethnic Society: a Multi-disciplinary Handbook*. London: Routledge.

Thomas, Lennox (2001) Proficiency and Psychotherapy in the Language of the Colonizer. Burgh House Lecture. London, 6 October.

Tizard, B. and Phoenix, A. (1993) *Black, White or Mixed Race*. London: Routledge.

Tomm, Karl (1987) Interventive Interviewing: Part II. Reflexive Questioning as a Means to Enable Self-healing. *Family Process* 26: 167–83.

Tomm, Karl (1988) Interventive Interviewing: Part III. Intending to Ask Lineal, Circular, Strategic and Reflexive Questions. *Family Process* 27: 1–15.

Trevarthen, Colin (1977) Descriptive Analyses of Infant Communicative Behaviour. In H. Schaffer (ed.) *Studies in Mother–Infant Interaction*. London: Academic Press.

Tsonis, A.A. (1992) *Chaos: From Theory to Applications*. New York: Plenum Press.

Tual, A. (1986) Speech and Silence: Women in Iran. In L. Dube, E. Leacock and S. Gardener (eds) *Visibility and Power: Essays on Women in Society and Development* Delhi: Oxford University Press.

Turner, J.E. (1991) Migrants and Their Therapists: a Trans-Context Approach. *Family Process* 30: 407–19.

Uguris, Tijen (2000) Gender, Ethnicity and 'the Community'. Locations with Multiple Identities. In Suki Ali, Kelly Coate and Wangui wa Goro (eds) *Global Feminist Politics: Identities in a Changing World*. London: Routledge.

Ussher, Jane (1996) Researching Child Sexual Abuse. Presentation at Research Forum. Tavistock Clinic, London.

Venuti, Lawrence (1995) Translation and the Formation of Cultural Identity. In *Cultural Functions of Translation*, vol. 1 no. 3. Aston University, Department of Languages and European Studies.

Vološinov, V.N. (1986) *Marxism and the Philosophy of Language*, trans L. Matejka and I.R. Titunik. Cambridge, MA: Harvard University Press.

Wachtel, Eleanor (2000) A Conversation with Edwidge Danticat. *Brick* 65/66. Fall. 106–19.

Walcott, D. (1963) Codicil. in *The Gulf* p32–33.

Weedon, C. (1997) *Feminist Practice and Poststructuralist Theory*, 2nd edn. London: Blackwell.

Wei, Li (2002) 'What Do You Want Me to Say?' On the Conversational Analysis Approach to Bilingual Interaction. *Language in Society* 31 (2): 159–80.

Wei, Li (2000) Dimensions of Bilingualism. In Li Wei (ed.) *The Bilingualism Reader*. London: Routledge.

Weinreich, U. (1953/1970) *Languages in Contact*. The Hague: Mouton.

Wetherell, Margaret (1998) Positioning and Interpretative Repertoires: Conversation Analysis and Post-Structuralism in Dialogue. *Discourse and Society* 9 (3): 387–412.

Wetherell, M. (2001) Debates in Discourse Research. In M. Wetherell, S. Taylor and S.J. Yates (eds) *Discourse Theory and Practice*. London: Open University and Sage.

Widdicombe, Sue (1998a) 'But You Don't Class Yourself': The Interactional Management of Category Membership and Non-membership. In Charles Antaki and Sue Widdicombe (eds) *Identities in Talk*. London: Sage.

Widdicombe, Sue (1998b) Identity as an Analyst's and a Participant's Resource. In Charles Antaki and Sue Widdicombe (eds) *Identities in Talk*. London: Sage.

Wierzbicka, A. (1997) The Double Life of a Bilingual. a Cross-cultural Perspective. In M.H. Bond (ed.) *Working at the Interface of Cultures: Eighteen Lives in Social Science*. London: Routledge.

Wilkinson, Sue and Kitzinger, Celia (1996) Theorising Representing the Other. In Sue Wilkinson and Celia Kitzinger (eds) *Representing the Other: a Feminism and Psychology Reader*. London: Sage.

Winnicott, D.W. (1960) Ego Distortion in Terms of True and False Self. In *The Maturational Processes and the Facilitating Environment*. (1965) London: Hogarth Press and Institute of PsychoAnalysis.

Wittgenstein, L. (1953) *Philosophical Investigations*. Oxford: Blackwell.

Wittgenstein, L. (1961) *Tractatus Logico Philosophicus*. London: Routledge & Kegan Paul.

Yamamoto, M. (1995) Bilingualism in International Families. *Journal of Multilingual and Multicultural Development* 16 (1–2): 63–85.

Zeldin, Theodore (1996) Translation and Civilisation. In J. Taylor, E. McMorrant and G. Leclercq (eds) *Translation. Here & There. Now & Then*. Exeter: Elm Bank Publishing.

Zentella, Ana Celia (1997) *Growing Up Bilingual*. Oxford: Blackwell.

Zournazi, Mary (1999) *Foreign Dialogues*. Australia: Pluto Press.

de Zulueta, Felicity (1984) The Implications of Bilingualism in the Study and Treatment of Psychiatric Disorders: a Review. *Psychological Medicine* 14: 541–57.

de Zulueta, Felicity (1990) Bilingualism and Family Therapy. *Journal of Family Therapy* 12: 255–65.

Index

accent 16, 22, 23, 70, 103, 106,
   160, 178
advantages of bilingualism/
   multilingualism 8, 15, 108, 150,
   156, 168, 170, 184–7, 188, 190,
   192–3
   creativity 15, 27, 111, 130, 170,
      185, 188, 192, 193, 195
   flexibility of thinking 16, 32, 170,
      181
   generate alternative
      perspectives 111, 113, 120, 192
   radical change 168, 185, 195
agency 48, 81, 83
alliances in family 7, 150–3, 180, 190
ambiguity 29, 90, 95, 120, 167, 179,
   180, 186, 192
ambiguous loss 21, 187
appropriated speech 140, 146
assimilation, pressure of 1, 10,
   19, 25, 133
authenticity 52, 83, 91, 93,
   95, 174, 177

Bakhtin, M.M. 81, 177–8
   centrifugal of language 184
   dialogic 27, 44, 97, 110,
      130, 156, 182
   heteroglossia 44, 82, 112, 142
   hybridization 44, 108–21, 185,
      186, 193
   hybridity 27, 44, 108, 109, 181,
      185, 192, 193
   monologic 5, 82, 130, 156
   social of language 82
belonging 20, 70, 71, 91, 94, 99, 103,
   106, 149, 150, 156, 179, 181, 183
'beyond language' 13, 64
Bhabha, H.
   mimicry 47
   third space 4, 63, 71, 73
bicultural competence 25, 127, 189

biculturalism 2, 25–6
bilingual education 14
bilingualism, definitions of 9, 16

childhoods in several languages 3, 4,
   34, 46–75, 171–2
   research on effect of
      bilingualism 15–16
   research on sustaining children's
      languages 13–15
children's greater fluency than
   parents 7, 122–7
children's language acquisition
   10–12, 21
children's storytelling 25
Chomsky, N. 10, 18
class 20, 23, 28, 55, 78, 126
code switching 28, 29, 30, 111,
   114, 120, 139–42, 192
   as parent 139–42
   for meta-languaging 29, 140, 180
   internal code-switching 111
coherence
   demands for 24, 25, 42, 86,
      87, 165, 176
coherence systems 8, 182
colonization and colonialism 6, 10,
   46–54, 73, 101–2, 174, 185, 187
constructions of speakers 76–91, 107,
   171
contextual influences 10, 15, 18–19,
   48, 66, 73, 74, 91, 101–5,
   109, 136, 161, 179, 181,
   181–2, 190, 192
contingency 6, 7, 70, 89, 91,
   114, 177, 184
conversation analysis 28
critical linguistics 18
cross-language relationship 105–8,
   127–30, 159, 181, 192
culture 11, 23, 178, 182
   contested 23

de-authorizing   19
Derrida, J.   26, 85, 188
dialogic   27, 44, 97, 110, 130,
    156, 182
diaspora identity and space   64,
    176, 183
diglossic and triglossic   54, 55, 73,
    175
discourse
    dominant discourse   144, 145,
        155, 181, 189
    discourse analysis   43, 44
    discursive practices   11, 24, 25, 27,
        43, 83
    discursive psychology   34, 35
    discursive resources   8, 29, 32, 65,
        75, 79, 91, 100, 120, 169, 182,
        189, 190, 192
    discursive 'work'   4, 172, 173–6
    interpretative repertoire   86, 133,
        134, 144, 184
    'language as work'   95, 133, 134,
        144, 157
disjuncture   4, 5, 69, 72, 74, 77, 80,
    88, 172, 181, 185
dominant language   14, 55, 93,
    127, 130, 140, 144, 149, 151,
    153, 155, 170, 187
dominant language speaker   14, 65,
    102, 154, 172, 178
Dorfman, A.   97, 108–9
double-voicing   29, 110
doubleness   5, 8, 56, 59, 69, 70, 74,
    85–91, 100, 102, 109, 141, 173–6,
    186
    different languaged worlds   56, 57,
        58, 60, 65, 74
doxic   80, 191

embodiment   93
emotion
    construction and expression of   17,
        35, 51, 72, 82, 89, 92, 106,
        114–15, 116, 171, 186
    expressiveness   92, 95, 100, 130, 132
entering a new language   99–100
    as enabling change   76–9, 171, 172
    coming to own a language   84–5,
        91, 93, 110, 178

effect of inarticulacy   79
    see also performance
ethnicity   2, 22–3, 178

family relationships   2, 7, 122–57,
    179–81, 187–90
    alliances in family   7, 150–3, 180,
        190
    exclusion and inclusion   150–2, 190
fathering and language   7, 134–9
    'father tongue'   139
first language   6, 16–18, 87, 92–4, 99,
    100, 123, 131–7, 142, 157, 172,
    179, 188
    as educational   135, 139
    for cultural continuity   135, 136, 180
    for emotional expressiveness   51, 92
    for fathering   134–9
    for intimacy   51, 71, 92, 128, 132,
        136, 139, 152, 157, 160, 179
    for mothering   131–3, 137–9
    for play   93, 111, 132, 186
    private language   93
    secret language   49, 159
fluency   29, 67, 68, 72, 74, 79, 80, 84,
    85, 94, 95, 102, 103, 107, 122–7,
    129–30, 144, 156, 157
    loss of fluency   94, 95, 172
'footing'   29
Foucault, M.   43
'frozen' identity   5, 87, 88, 91, 100

gender   2, 20, 21, 31, 33, 68, 72, 83,
    118, 131–9, 154, 155, 157, 179
grammatical differences of
    languages   12, 97
grounded theory approach   41, 42

heteroglossia   44, 82, 112, 142
hierarchy of languages   19, 46, 73
Hoffman, E.   68, 89, 113, 175
'home', constructions of   20, 64, 70,
    72, 91, 94, 104, 137, 138, 160, 183
homelessness   72
humour   6, 93, 106–7, 130, 188
hybridization   44, 108–21, 185, 186,
    193
hybridity   27, 44, 108, 109, 181, 185,
    192, 193

identification 116, 120, 154
identity 21, 27–8, 29, 31, 32, 44, 60,
    72, 81, 83, 86, 87, 90, 99, 103,
    119, 139, 148, 157, 169, 185
  claim of identity 7, 24, 28, 33, 44,
      72, 74, 91, 102, 103, 106, 114,
      116–20, 148–56, 172, 178, 180,
      187, 188, 193
  contestation of identity 103
  cultural identity 22–3, 27, 98, 139,
      154, 178
  doubled identity *see* doubleness
  'frozen' identity 5, 87, 88, 91, 100
  identity project 22, 79
  making identities salient 29, 116,
      117, 118, 180, 186
  national identity 27
  racialized identity 2, 22, 64, 102,
      187 *see* racialization processes
  split identity 65, 190
ideological dilemma 83
'imagined communities' 172, 180
imitation 10, 81
inarticulacy 51, 66–8, 79–80, 95,
    188, 189
'in-between' 26, 141, 188
inclusion and exclusion 150–2, 190
individualism 184
insufficiencies of language 68,
    130, 184
interactional development of
    language 10
internal language 111, 177, 183
interpretative repertoire 86, 133,
    134, 144, 184

language
  constructions of language 91–9,
      100, 131–2, 135, 137–9
  grammatical differences of
      languages 12, 25, 97
  internal language 111, 177, 183
  language ability as 'natural' 170
  language as constitutive 115, 119,
      154, 177, 187
  language as 'culture soaked' 23
  language as marker of
      difference 56–61, 58, 65, 74,
          152, 157, 178

'language as work' 95, 133, 134,
    144, 157
  owning a language 84–5, 91, 93,
      110, 178
  private language 151
  'purity' of language 133, 134
  reclaiming language 25
  see also first language; second
      language
language acquisition
  children's language
      acquisition 10–12, 21
  critical period for language
      acquisition 16
  necessity in language
      acquisition 16, 67, 73,
          122, 170
  sensitive period for second language
      acquisition 16
  see also entering a new language
language choice
  as protective 142, 143, 144,
      167, 186, 191
  as relational 11, 135, 138
  for children's educational
      success 142, 148, 179
  for cultural continuity 135,
      136, 180
  loyalty issues 123, 180, 187
  see also for identity claims
  to invoke cultural
      expectations 118, 180
'language deaths' 20
lifecycle stage 87, 96
limits and insufficiencies of
    language 26, 130, 184
loss 66, 67, 68, 72, 74, 157, 180
  of biodiversity 1
  of language 1, 8, 14, 15, 19, 28, 68,
      89, 145, 148, 157, 167, 170, 172,
      180, 181, 187, 188, 190, 193

marital/partner relationships
    7, 127–30, 148–9, 156
meanings of language speaking 30,
    34, 46, 55, 68–71, 69, 85, 93, 95,
    98, 99, 121, 170, 178–9, 187–92
  symbolic meaning of language
      19, 27

memory   17, 34, 71, 171
meta-languaging   29, 140, 180
metaphor   77, 81, 95
migration   2, 19–21, 56–73,
    76–100, 187
minoritized languages   30, 56–65, 74,
    101, 139, 152, 155, 170, 171, 178,
    188, 189
miscommunications   6, 105–8,
    121, 192
  mismatch of assumptions
    107–8, 130
monolingual
  Englishness as monolingual   8, 155
  monolingual norms   10, 32,
    133, 134
  monolingualism   9, 64, 155, 170
monologic   5, 82, 130, 156
'mother tongue'   3, 7, 11, 14,
    132, 133, 135, 137, 138,
    157, 179, 188
mothering and language   7, 20,
    131–3, 137–9
  women as guardians of culture and
    language   20, 179
multiple subjectivity   2, 21–2, 33, 53,
    54, 61, 62, 63, 71–5, 90, 100, 113,
    120, 121, 156, 169, 174, 176
multiplicity   7, 16, 51–4, 71, 73, 90,
    169, 171–2, 185, 186, 189, 193
  contradictions   27, 44, 181,
    189, 193

narrative
  canonical narratives   24, 25, 34, 42,
    72, 171, 173, 182, 184
  evaluative aspect of narrative   43,
    165–6
  narrative analysis   42, 43
  narrative of self   21, 79, 88, 94, 172,
    182, 193
  narrative theory   23–4, 25, 34, 42
'native speaker'   11, 16, 85, 106
'natural', construction of   11, 84,
    94, 131, 133, 134, 137, 138,
    139, 170, 177
  language ability as 'natural'   170
necessity in language acquisition   16,
    67, 73, 122, 170

negativity about bilingualism   80,
    145, 161, 162, 168, 170
  deficit model in research   9, 15
neurolinguistic research   17, 171
  brain imaging techniques   17

'othering'   47, 50, 75, 95, 102,
    164, 178
outsider   65, 69, 70, 71, 74, 112,
    117, 143, 175, 179

parental authority   127
parenting
  constructions of   7, 20, 137–9,
    143, 156–7, 179, 188
  'one person–one language'   13
  parenting in a first language   7,
    131–7, 142, 150, 157
  parenting in a second language   7,
    142–8, 157
performance   5, 44, 47, 48, 52, 56,
    60, 67, 78, 80–5, 91, 99, 100, 114,
    116, 140, 174, 177–9, 180, 189
  reiterative performance as
    constitutive   177, 178
place, constructions of   104, 183
polarization   64, 74, 109, 117, 143,
    182, 189
political struggle   55, 74
positioning   23, 26–7, 33, 43, 44,
    53, 67, 71, 73, 79, 85, 97, 98,
    112, 123, 129–30, 156, 165,
    169, 174, 182
power relationships   2, 3, 18, 23,
    30, 33, 54, 55, 74, 99, 109, 149,
    164–5, 170, 172, 185, 189
power in family relationships
    122–30, 180
professionals   145, 190–3
prosodic elements of language   6, 92,
    105–6, 108, 121, 178
psychosis   17, 171

racialization processes   6, 50, 54,
    61, 65, 74, 79, 101–5, 121,
    152, 178–9, 183, 187
racism   19, 20, 47, 48, 79, 103,
    104, 142, 187, 188
refugee   66–73

relationship to language   68, 88,
   92, 95, 100, 109, 183
relativity   12, 113, 187
religion   135
representing the other   36, 164–5
research in bilingualism   2, 9–31
   language competence   9, 18, 32
   language use   32
research study (explorations of life in
   several languages)
   analytic approach   41–5
   data as performative and
      referential   35
   epistemological framework   34,
      158–9, 161–4, 166
   ethical accountability   35, 158,
      164, 165–6
   interview   34, 35–6, 161–4, 194–6
   use of circular and reflexive
      questions   35, 161–2
   participants   36–7, 38–40, 163
   rationale   32–3, 158
   research questions   3, 33–4
   sampling   3, 37
   research relationship   36, 162,
      164–5
   transcription   37, 41, 197
researcher
   hypotheses   159–61
   personal contexts   159–61, 166–8
   self-reflexivity   8, 41, 158–9, 166
resilience   170
resistance through language
   19, 26, 48
rhetorical strategies   83, 114, 116,
   117, 118, 139–42, 149, 180

Said, E.   101–2, 110, 186, 193
Sante, L.   88, 90, 177
second/subsequent language   6,
   16–18, 95, 96, 99, 100, 142–8,
   179, 188, 191
   difficulties with humour   6, 93,
      106–7, 130, 188
   distance created by   95, 100, 146,
      167, 187, 191
   enabling talk about trauma   191
   for intimacy   128
   for parenting   142–8

freedom from constraints   77–9,
   95, 128
honing communication   80,
   130, 192
metaphors for   95
self
   constructions of   21, 24, 57, 89, 91,
      99, 100, 119, 171, 173–6, 188
   'core' self   5, 86, 87
   see also doubleness
   essentialist self   174
   hypothetical self   70, 89, 175
   'inner' and 'outer' self   5, 90, 174
   self-consciousness   173–4
   self-presentation   112
   'true' and 'false' self   174
self-reflexivity   7, 53, 112, 115, 142,
   146, 147, 158–9, 169, 180, 182,
   186, 190
   relational reflexivity   186
semilinguals   10
shame   51, 73, 170
sibling relationships   15
signifier   22, 26, 27, 31, 98, 106, 148,
   155
silence   25, 190
singularity   86, 108, 113, 120,
   156, 172, 176, 181, 185,
   186, 189, 193
   ideal of monolingual subject   64
social constructionism   3, 13, 34,
   41, 158
social-historical conditions   13
sociolinguistics   30
socio-political context   18, 98, 121,
   138, 155, 159–60
speakers' accounts   3, 30, 32, 41
status of language   5, 50, 51, 54, 95,
   99, 127, 149, 155, 170
stereotypes   5, 59, 79, 81, 82, 97, 99,
   103, 181
subject positions   44, 62, 89
subjectivity   21, 33, 98, 187
   postmodern conceptualization of
      subjectivity   91, 174
sustaining minoritized languages   2,
   8, 13, 15, 156, 170
suture between subjectivity and
   culture   5, 178

theory of mind   12, 181
'thinking for speaking'   25, 115
third space   4, 63, 71, 73, 182
transculturalism   25, 64
transforming context   62–5,
      71–3, 182
translation   18, 26, 89, 98, 115, 123,
      161, 181, 188, 191
traumatic experience   4, 66–73, 191
trope   68, 175–6
troubled and untroubled subject
      position   44, 50, 62, 120

universal grammar   10

validation of multiplicity   63, 65, 72,
      73, 74, 91, 109, 181, 192
values, different in different
      languages   17, 171, 179
voice   29, 68, 77, 110

warranting   149, 170, 180
whiteness   49, 61, 65, 103,
      160, 179
Whorf hypothesis   12, 97